Edited by Leung Ping-kwan and Andrea Riemenschnitter
Translated by students from the Institute of East Asian Studies, University of Zurich,
Leung Ping-kwan (Chinese) and Helen Wallimann (English)
with illustrations by Julia Steiner
and an essay on Swiss Alpine films by Natalie Böhler

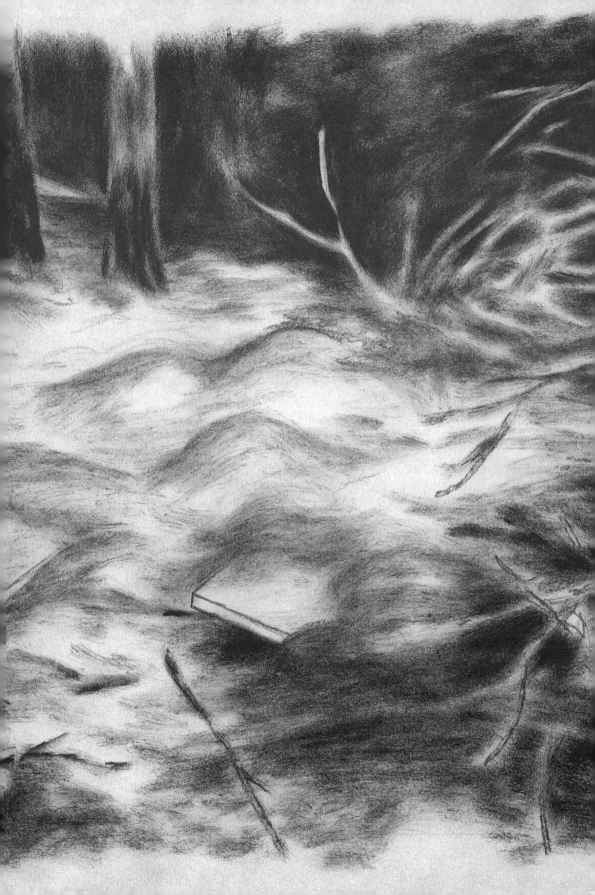

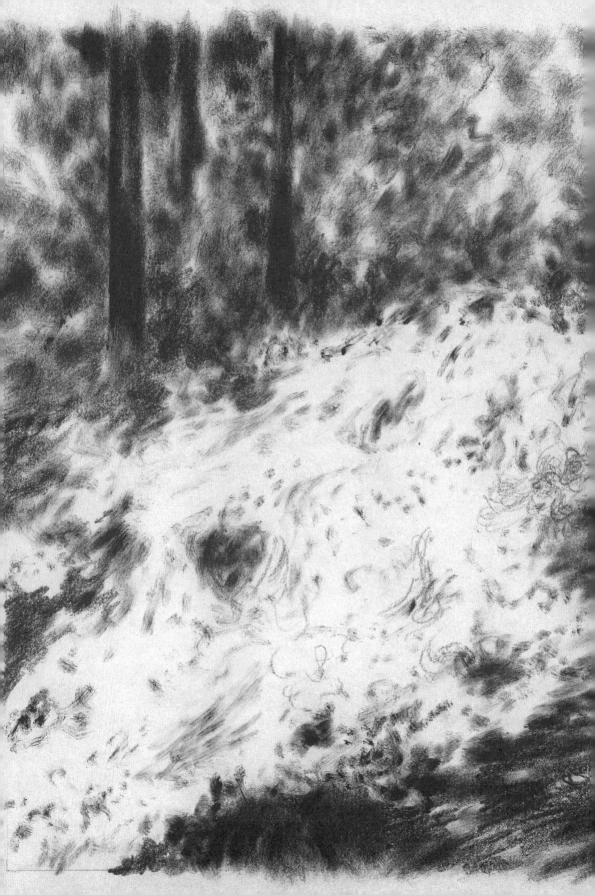

瑞士
阿爾卑斯山的傳說

梁秉鈞、洪安瑞 編

Legends
from
the
Swiss Alps

Leung Ping-kwan
Andrea Riemenschnitter, ed.

mccmcreations

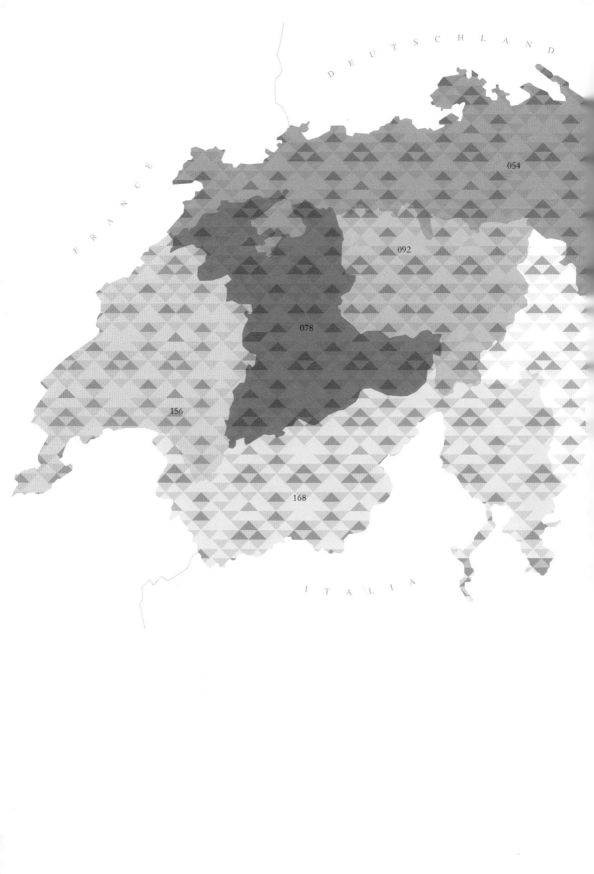

Contents 目錄

ÖSTERREICH

198

Urban Culture and Nature

— Legends from the Alps for Metropolitan Sleepwalkers

Leung Ping-kwan, Andrea Riemenschnitter, May 2009

Legends, like nightmares, often take place in sublime settings. "Boy", the nameless deaf-mute protagonist of the 1985/6 international award-winning alpine movie *Soul Sister* by Fredi M. Murer, lives in almost total isolation. Together with his parents and elder sister, he dwells in a remote mountain farm, with no contact to the outside world except through occasional reading lessons given him by his sister and the local gossip about demonic creatures haunting humans as reflected in his mother's religious behaviour. In adolescence, Boy invests his surplus energy in the traditional way, that is, by piling up a wall of rocks on a mountain slope in the middle of nowhere. As the narrative unfolds, the camera time and again slowly roams a bizarre panorama of grotesquely meandering, superfluous walls shaping this otherwise untamed Alpine environment. They have been erected by generations of lonesome yet agitated male adolescents who were haunted by their sexual desire and in urgent need of a means to exhaust their virile energy. During a never-ending winter season, the sister shows the first signs of pregnancy – she's carrying her brother's child – and both parents get killed in a way reminiscent of a Greek tragedy. The parents' frozen corpses remain exposed under a window in front of the farm as two additional, now visible, ghosts from the past. The brother and sister live on in their deeply troubled mutual affection, thus contributing their own layer of haunted oral history to the region.

This cinematic narrative contains neither explicit social criticism nor any solution to the people's problems. Yet, as tourism and industry and the accompanying technology invade the Alps we, the spectators, are aware that this strange world of solitary mountain dwellers is rapidly vanishing, leaving behind little more than a few legends and traces in the recently urbanized environment. But feelings of nostalgia and loss, or optimism as to a better future for the mountain dwellers, are rendered equally unsuitable by the film's narrative.

In this respect, the mystery thriller *Marmorera* (Markus Fischer, 2007), whose narrative revisits the sinister realm of collective guilt and its distinctly Swiss Alp-referenced regional symbolic markers, adds a further dimension of self-reflexive modernity to the landscape. Fifty years after the flooding of a whole mountain village for the construction of a reservoir, a young female corpse is found floating on the site. The woman returns to life and is taken to a psychiatric clinic in Zurich.

Her strange behaviour spills over onto her psychiatrist and, as a consequence, a modern fairy tale of nature's revenge for ruthless human exploitation unfolds.

Bollywood films present a totally different picture of the Swiss mountainscape – a glamorous, globalized, consumer-friendly picture showing absolutely nothing of the process of Alpine urbanization. Rather, the visual references to the Alps made for Indian eyes focus on the sublime spectacle of solitary, snowy peaks as a majestic foil to the imminent domestication of its urbanite protagonists' passions. Bollywood thus continues a tradition of utopian metropolitan fairy tales which provide a therapeutic dreamscape for exhausted, overcivilized citizens, the successors of Clara, the sickly German girl from Frankfurt who is cured by a rustic Swiss mountain maiden in the globally successful, transnational Alpine narrative *Heidi* by the Swiss woman writer Johanna Spyri (1880).

Since the late 20th century, the concept of alpine ecotourism has taken shape and will gain momentum as climate change, with its melting glaciers and green slopes even in winter-time, progresses. Braunwald, a region with notoriously insecure snow conditions situated in the canton of Glarus, has exploited the suggestive potential of a local product, the modern fairy tale about *Zwäärg Baartli* (literally: Dwarf Short-Beard) by Eleonore (Lorly) Jenny (1900-1982), in order to secure the region's development. A fairy-tale path with several picturesque and easy-to-reach Baartli stages in an area completely closed to motorized traffic attracts numerous families with small children who are looking for relaxing yet adventurous holidays. The magic of a faraway world of dwarfs and talking animals can hold sway in a place where the various voices of the mountain fauna can still be heard, undisturbed by the noise of traffic or the pervasive musical entertainment in trendy mountain resorts. The tale of Baartli itself is a nostalgic response to the cultural shock of modernity, as is the moral imperative embedded within the tale, namely, that of a respect for alien worlds – in this case, the worlds of the animals, trees, flowers, stones and human mountain dwellers. Even though our imagination can more or less capture these worlds poetically in order to deal with them in everyday life, it cannot truly understand and respect them without a certain degree of anthropomorphization.

On an intellectually more sophisticated level, a tiny mountain village in the

Engadin valley, Sils Maria, has developed into an aesthetically and spiritually charged resort ever since Nietzsche's occupation of a modest room in a Sils Marian mountain chalet (now being transformed into a museum)[1] for his summer retreats in 1881 and from 1883-1888, when he was in search of creative inspiration and reconvalescence. So far, the village has successfully resisted the most destructive forms of touristic exploitation by relying almost exclusively on the otherworldly beauty of the lake and its surrounding landscape on the one hand, and Nietzsche's aura in the museum on the other. Both phenomena have never ceased to attract artists, scholars, and informed travellers in great numbers. Treading in Nietzsche's footsteps, writers, intellectuals and artists from all over the world have not only roamed the site, but have also left their poetic marks. Nietzsche himself had opened the literary round with the lines:

> *Here I sat waiting, waiting – yet for Nothingness*
> *Beyond good and evil, sometimes enjoying*
> *The light, sometimes the shadow, all only game*
> *All lake, all noon, all time without end*
> *[...]*

Gottfried Benn responded with more sinister thoughts:

> *There was no snow, but light*
> *glowing down from high up*
> *there was no death, but everyone deemed himself near death –*
> *it was so white, no pleading*
> *penetrated the opal anymore,*
> *a monstrous suffering*
> *hovered over this valley.*

The Chinese poet Yang Lian (born in Basel in 1955) countered with his own gloomy visions:

> *The Non Personal Snow, Sils Maria2*
>
> *the snowy ground is covered with blind men   they can't see*
> *the poem that died in the hotel*
> *and   the valleys that breed the fearsome sunlight*

below the same precipices they lose their shadows
become thin black needles on the garden sundial
wash their feet in laughter

take pains to carve patterned vessels from a dead bird
drink deep at picnic time of the scarlet stream
noon   the scarlet stream exuded by blind eyes

they can't see   the tourists in the poem
lying naked in hotel beds
no need to fall   to get to the depths of an avalanche²

And finally, the lines which Zhang Qinghua elegantly offered to the Nietzsche House guest book after a lake tour on July 19, 2006, under brighter skies:

Nurtured in dazzling sunlight
Your wild thoughts
Emit lightning flashes
From jagged white peaks
Which form scars
On the hearts of the gods

And does one know who is being addressed here – the lake, the philosopher, the poet, the *genius loci*?

For the last couple of thousand years, the Alps have traditionally fulfilled a dual function as a cultural barrier and a transit region. A natural obstacle for both enemies and travellers and, at the same time, a rather unattractive destination for immigrants, the Alps have nevertheless encouraged locals to create trade routes and secure the traffic between neighbouring communities. The great linguistic diversity of this narrow region not only attests to its geographical distinctiveness; it also shows that traditions are better maintained in isolated areas. The permanent threat of the forces of nature to the existence of these communities has arguably nourished within them a particular affinity to the belief in supernatural phenomena, which were employed as explanations for all sorts of uncanny, irrational and contingent experiences. This religious consciousness was persistently interspersed with atavistic local cults and myths (as is reflected in the above-mentioned film by Fredi M. Murer as well as in many local legends). Together with the sublime landscape (which has in the meantime also been promoted by a lively marketing industry) it has, since Goethe and romantic painters like Caspar David Friedrich[3], increasingly fascinated urban tourists weary of civilization. Breaking out of the stress of their metropolitan lives, they seek refuge in the exotic otherness of this supposedly untamed world of the mountains – to overcome, or at least momentarily forget, among other things, their personal existential crises – by means of high-tech mountaineering tours on foot or on bikes, skis, helicopters, etc. and during short weekend visits comfortably spent in Switzerland's famous grand-view five-star peak hotels. Early on, humour got hold of this aspect of recycled sublime wilderness. The Romantic poet Heinrich Heine (1797-1856) once mocked the mechanical emotionality of mawkish tourists watching a sunset:

> For about a quarter of an hour everybody stood in grave silence, and watched the beautiful fireball sinking slowly in the west; the faces were bathed in the light of the setting sun; hands folded unawares; it was as if we, a silent congregation, were standing in the nave of an immense cathe-dral, and the priest now raised the Body of the Lord, and Palestrina's eternal hymn poured down from the organ. While standing lost in meditation, I heard someone next to me calling out: 'How beautiful nature generally is!' These words came out of the sentimental chest of my roommate, the young merchant. They brought me back to my workaday mood, and I was now able to tell the ladies many courteous things about the sunset, and to lead them to their room quietly, as if nothing had happened.

During the 17th century, eccentric Chinese literati of the late Ming Dynasty, such as Yuan Hongdao, Zhang Dai and Chen Jiru, similarly mocked the ambitious-ness of their past and contemporary fellow men of letters, whose conventional mountain and landscape idylls are an omnipresent feature of China's long literary history.

However, what past landscape nostalgia critics from both cultural traditions failed to realize, or rather couldn't possibly imagine, was the large-scale damage that would one day be inflicted on nature by the great masses of "mountain lovers", today's hikers and trippers. The Alpine regions had of course long ceased to be a wilderness, and had mutated into a fragile cultural landscape long before the tourist industry began its large-scale colonization, particularly through mass winter sports. Driven as it is by economic greed, the ruthless exploitation of nature cannot be counteracted by metaphysical threats of devils and demons any more, and environmental damage is, sooner or later, likely to render the whole mountain region unfit for any kind of human use. Following the logic of traditional cultural practice, what the threatened ecosystem of the Alps now needs is not only better institutional protection, more balance; it also needs modern tales appealing to the responsibility of each individual – convincing narratives, which can alert the public to the existential importance of landscape protection and the danger of the region's imminent destruction. This time, however, the situation is not the same as it was a hundred years ago: a landscape, a natural albeit tamed world, is now being so violently reshaped by the onslaught of man-made, technologically provoked disasters that its function as a protector of the climate and a provider of natural resources, as well as its cultural value as a place of sublime beauty for the regeneration of exhausted urbanites are rapidly vanishing.

Nevertheless, Switzerland can proudly present Alpine attractions like the Jungfrau UNESCO World Natural Heritage area in the heart of the Bernese Oberland to the global metropolitan summer tourists who year by year gather together on the "Top of Europe" in huge flocks like migratory birds. Among them, Chinese travelers arrive in increasing numbers to enjoy the most spectacular scenic sites of the Swiss mountains. However, they certainly perceive them differently, with a background consisting of their own cultural imaginary of mountainscapes. Ever since the earliest collection of poems, *the Book of Songs*, was put together during the early 5th century B.C., landscape poetry has flourished in China. Some poets described the joy of doing things in accordance with the pulse of nature, others borrowed the symbolic dimension of natural phenomena in order to express the whole emotional spectrum of the human world. Beginning with the *Book of Mountains and Seas* (that contains materials dating back as far as the third millenium B.C.), there has been no shortage of creative imagination in response to nature and landscapes. Among the traditional literary genres, poetry about immortals and *zhiguai* (literally: "recording the abnormal") stories also frequently deal with a world in which spirits and demons roam among mountains, valleys and waterways, a world which has always been used by humankind to reflect its ways of thinking and feeling. With the Qing Dynasty author Pu Songling's (1640-1715) *Strange Stories from Liaozhai Studio*, the *zhiguai* genre reached the acme of perfection. In these stories, we frequently find all sorts of brave and beautiful human maidens, who are the sometimes good sometimes evil metamorphoses of flowers, birds, foxes, and snakes, and who have the power either to weaken and destroy men, or lovingly and loyally to rescue some innocent scholar from an imminent disaster.

When, in 1949, China embraced socialism, campaigns against superstition and a ban on ghost stories were side-effects of the propagation of critical realism as the only permissible school of thought in the arts. With the Cultural Revolution (1966-1976), absolutely everything that was considered as belonging to the "Four Olds" – including landscape writing, traditional drama, and novels – became taboo. In post-1949 Hong Kong, on the contrary, traditional literature and drama were preserved, and the ancient supernatural fantasy figures derived from *zhiguai* stories survived and were even transformed into a distinctly modern phenomenon in the framework of commercialized movie productions. The frequency of the appearance of Pu Songling's *Liaozhai* stories on screen is exemplary. Some of these films are by outstanding directors like King Hu, who translated the original story "The Woman Warrior" *(Xianü)* into the feature film *A Touch of Zen*; or Tsui Hark and Ching Siu-tung, who made the cinematic trilogy *A Chinese Ghost Story* from the *Liaozhai* story "Little Qian". These are just the best-known examples of modern film using awe-inspiring mountainous landscapes combined with the *zhiguai* literary genre to portray stories of heroism, chivalry and romance.

Hong Kong originally possessed all the charm and beauty of the southern Chinese countryside. However, due to the density of the population and the exiguity of its territory, Hong Kong's modernization has given rise to severe environmental problems. Only some protected areas – like the Mai Po sanctuary for migratory birds, situated in the northwestern part of the New Territories, and Wetland Park – could be preserved. Since the Hong Kong hand-over, communications with

China's southern region, especially with the cities of Guangzhou and Shenzhen have developed fast. The 5.5 km dual three-lane carriageway, the Western Corridor Shenzhen Bridge Highway, constructed to facilitate commercial and industrial transport between Hong Kong and the Mainland, and the explosion of both real estate development and coastal land reclamation have severely disturbed the whole region's ecological balance. However, compared to Mainland China in Hong Kong's north, this is no more than a case of "a little witch facing the big sorceress". Since the end of the Cultural Revolution, China with her vast territory and gigantic population has gradually opened to the world. Since the 1990s, she has accelerated her industrial development, building hydro-electric power plants, exploiting mines, expropriating farmers, and tolerating the environmental pollution caused by the waste from chemical plants ... This has produced a number of problems: not only have residential areas become polluted on account of their over-rapid development, but there have also been numerous cases of acute poisoning or long-term damage to human health due to polluted foodstuffs. Nowadays, it would be difficult for China's authors to return to writing idyllic pastoral poems. They prefer to write documentary essays on the worsening situation in the countryside.

Hong Kong's both privileged and marginal situation in between two cultures and embraced by the natural barriers of mountains and sea naturally led to a hybrid landscape imaginary. After 1949, the British colony continued to preserve the traditional thought systems of Confucianism, Daoism, and Buddhism. Likewise, considerable parts of folklore were maintained, including the practice of spirit invocation and divination; *fengshui* superstition, too, was not abolished. Many popular legends live on, such as the legend of Lovers' Rock on Hong Kong Island, where youngsters can seek help to find the appropriate mate, or the myth of a Stone Toad, which has been climbing the Peak since Hong Kong was founded. The moment it reaches the summit, Hong Kong is doomed to perish. But Hong Kong has preserved more of Chinese tradition than just old legends and superstitions. After the earliest branch of New Confucian philosophy was established during the 1950s, scholars like William Yeh and Lin Niantong discussed landscape poetry and the aesthetics of cinema in accordance with traditional Confucian aesthetic thought. The author Leung Ping-kwan experimented with materials from the

Liaozhai stories and the traditional topos of the lotus leaf, using them to form two cycles of modern poetry. He also breathed new life into traditional *zhiguai* fiction by narrating urban hikers' encounters with mountain sprites and ghosts, thus representing a Hong Kong citizen's reflections and moods concerning contemporary China. And so he welcomed the opportunity to join the workshop devoted to a cross-cultural, interdisciplinary exploration of Alpine legends that was carried out by Swiss students and teachers of Chinese Studies in summer 2004, and derived considerable personal inspiration from the experiment.

In the light of the postmodern tension between urbanization on the one hand and the quest for natural space on the other, we, during our cross-cultural encounter, focused our approach on the different, culturally impregnated forms of alienation in artistic representations of the super-natural. The young Swiss artist Julia Steiner appeared to us to be the ideal partner for such an endeavour. In her pictures, we can immediately sense modernity's impossible desire for the simultaneous existence of urban sophistication and primordial authenticity. At the same time, we get the haunted feeling of the return with a vengeance of some atavistic spectres – such as the demons of destruction in the Alps – to our postmodern collective imaginaries. The particular appeal of Julia Steiner's drawings was aptly described by Madeleine Schuppli, director of the Thun Art Museum, in her speech at the awarding of the Aeschlimann Corti Grant Award in 2007:

> In mood, Julia Steiner's pictures oscillate between paradise and the apocalypse. The gouache "Frühstück auf dem Rock (Breakfast on the Skirt)" has fairytale traits and we are reminded of book illustrations. "Fossil", on the other hand, is characterized by some dark fantastical energy, like that to be found in fantasy films or illustrations of fantasy tales. Julia Steiner's work also contains formal references to the art of French Impressionists like Edgar Degas or Odilon Redon. At the same time the pictures are firmly rooted in today's photographic imagery. This can be seen in the artist's use of framing, her play with sharp and blurred contours or with frozen motion. The artist chooses from a wide repertoire, and thus creates her own individual, singular language. Agitated forms correspond to the turbulent content. Various motifs overlap each other. The artist herself speaks of "story scraps" that resist classification, or of "chopped thoughts". Thus her pictures are

*composed out of the condensation of fragments derived from dreams and
real life, from memories and expectations, from conscious experience and
the subconscious. All these facets are combined with great artistic power.*

Our seminar in the mountains consisted of alternating units of hikes, lectures,
readings and film screenings, during which we and our students explored the
significance of these differences in perception. The event was conceived as an
integral experience of intercultural dialogue, to be experienced through both
linguistic and sensorial channels. The translations of the selected Swiss Alpine
legends presented in this publication were submitted by the participants of the
excursion, all of them students of the Institute of East Asian Studies, University of
Zurich, except for our "virtual guest", Dr. Clemens Treter from Munich, who is one
among Leung Ping-kwan's many friends from the world's departments of modern
Chinese studies and was unfortunately prevented from joining us in person. Leung
Ping-kwan and his associates in Hong Kong later helped us eliminate the stylistic
and grammatical flaws through a thorough revision of all the translations. Helen
Wallimann rendered the legends into an English which successfully captures the
tone of the original. She also thoroughly revised the English of the other parts of
the manuscript. What we now make available to our Chinese- and English-reading
audience is the result of a lively intercultural exchange which can only very rarely
take place in such a form.

[1] http://www.nietzschehaus.ch
[2] Yang Lian, "The Non-personal Snow Sils Maria 2", in: *Notes of a Blissful Ghost*, tr. By Brian Holton,
    Hong Kong: Renditions Paperbacks 2002: 58.
[3] http://www.smart-art.at/alpen/sitemap-text/berg-im-bild-bildbeschreibungen.htm

Picturing Swissness

— The Alps in Swiss Films

Natalie Böhler

The Alps are probably the most awe-inspiring natural feature of Switzerland. Therefore it is hardly surprising that they play an important part in many Swiss films. Their sheer magnificence makes them a fascinating setting for filmmakers and audiences alike. And there's hardly a more suitable medium than film for showing ice glistening in the sun, the dizzying view from a mountain peak, or mountain goats nibbling on Alpine flowers.

What's more, the Alpine region plays a significant part in the imagery of Switzerland – for the tourist industry of course, but also in the collective self-image of the Swiss population. Thus, as a departure point for filmic tales, the Alps offer countless opportunities. The imaginary spaces they represent have changed repeatedly in Swiss history and are, today, manifold and complex.

One constant in the field of aesthetically appropriated alpine imaginary distinctions, is the SBB, the state-run railway system. It is a Swiss national icon which owes much of its popularity to the fact that it whisks its passengers from city centres to the mountains in a very short time and with frequent connections. This is especially attractive for an urbanized population that longs to reconnect with nature and its own physicality and counts hiking among its favourite leisure activities. This smooth transition between normally diametrically opposed symbolic spaces – the one of urban sophistication and that of a landscape that is both archaic and sublime – has provided inspiration for many a cinematographic rendition of the Swiss Alpine mountainscape.

The yearning for the natural beauty of the mountains is mirrored in the work of Erich Langjahr: *Sennen-Ballade (Alpine Ballad)*, 1996; *Hirtenreise ins dritte Jahrtausend (Shepherds' Journey into the Third Millenium)*, 2002; *Das Erbe der Bergler (Alpine Saga)*, 2006. His documentaries show the mountains as a pastoral idyll, a bucolic sphere inhabited by farmers and herdsmen who live in harmony with their animals and with nature. The films show ancient work traditions like the *Wildheuete*, the mowing of wild Alpine grass on incredibly steep slopes high up above the farmhouses. We see an unspoilt world of purity, simplicity and innocence, of hard work and well-earned rest, free of materialism and technology, where nature inspires religious feelings and humans live by its laws, in respect and harmony.

Hinterrhein (Lisa Röösli, 2005) portrays a small village in Graubünden, which many of its inhabitants have been forced to leave for the city, in search of jobs. An elderly man, who left Hinterrhein decades ago, speaks of the way the village has continued to reappear in his dreams every single night since his departure. It's the mountains surrounding Hinterrhein, he says, that are and will always be his only true home.

This haunting memory is characteristic of Swiss people's relationship to the Alps. One of its main traits is the nostalgic longing for home. This is understandable, as many of the people from Alpine regions have had to leave their villages, usually as young adults, for schools and jobs in the urbanized parts of Switzerland. A prototype is Heidi, the title character of Johanna Spyri's famous novel, feeling homesick in Frankfurt. Remarkably, though, this nostalgia is also often experienced by Swiss who don't come from mountain villages, but have grown up in cities or suburbs. For them the Alps are an imaginary, collective home: unspoiled, unambiguous, a realm of authenticity and freedom, a link to one's true nature and soul as well as to one's past – in Swiss thinking, the mountains are often linked with childhood experiences, such as school outings and family holidays.

There are, however, other films whose characters would strongly disagree with these nostalgic feelings. The Alps can also be perceived as a place of long winters, stifling cold, loneliness and depression. Little villages and farms become isolated spots shrouded in fog, far away from the rest of the world. In *Tout un hiver sans feu* (*A Long Winter Without Fire*. Greg Zglinski, 2006), the snow and fog turn the images blindingly white until the entire screen seems to go blank – resembling the state of depression the characters live through. This is the other, darker side of the autonomous mountain world: it cuts its inhabitants off from human contact and civilization, sometimes trapping them inside their own inner worlds. Especially during the dark cold winter months, the mountains can turn into a hostile environment. Charles Ferdinand Ramuz (1878-1947), a Swiss writer from Lausanne whose stories inspired many filmic renditions, was fascinated by this aspect. In his novels, he explored the impact of the surroundings on their inhabitants, concentrating on dark powers and their metaphysical edge. For example, in *Si le soleil ne revenait pas* (*If the Sun Didn't Rise Again*), a prophet announces that the sun will never shine on the village again, causing a collective crisis of faith. *La grande peur dans la montagne (Terror on the Mountain)* portrays a mountain community getting more and more caught up in superstitions, leading to a mass tragedy. *Derborence (When the Mountain Fell)* describes how a landslide wiped out the village of the same name and many of its inhabitants. The survivors subsequently find themselves exposed to piercing questions concerning the meanings of Good, Evil and God's will.

In between those two extremes of the Alps as a kind of primeval paradise on the one hand, and as hostile and dangerous wilderness on the other there lies a tension that is a source of great artistic creativity. The Alps provide a field of energy and mysticism that has generated a wealth of folk myths and local legends, many of which are featured in this book. The mythic heritage of the region makes it a source of inspiration for stories that stay closely in touch with the original myths, as in *Jenatsch* (Daniel Schmid, 1987). While doing research on the historical character of Jürg Jenatsch, a politician in seventeenth-century Graubünden, a modern-day journalist becomes increasingly obsessed with his subject matter. His confusion grows as the boundaries between the past and the present, between Jenatsch's life and his own, become fluid and finally dissolve.

In Swiss film history, the Alps were often used as a signifier of human ambition, providing riveting images of nature being conquered by man. Mountaineer films typically show groups of men bravely scaling peaks, overcoming great obstacles and courageously enduring the harsh climate and physical strain. The end of the adventure usually features the view from the top, and celebrates male comradeship. Postwar Swiss films often feature soldier stories. Here, the Alps are cast in the role of natural boundaries ensuring Switzerland's safety. The massive boulders serve as a fortress, guarding the country from intruders – especially German forces – and have formed the Swiss myth of the national réduit, the Alpine military citadel of resistance. The bunkers built into the Gotthard, the massive mountain in the centre of Switzerland, are modern-day national legends.

From the point of view of immigrants, also, the Alps can be seen as a fortress – keeping them out of the country. *Reise der Hoffnung (Journey of Hope)* (Xavier Koller, 1990) tells the story of a poor Turkish family which dreams of starting a new life in Switzerland. They illegally make their way as clandestine immigrants via Italy to the Swiss border, where a truck picks them up and drops them at the Splügen Pass. From here on, the family continues on foot through the winter night. The cold and the exhaustion are too hard for the young son: by morning, he has frozen to death in his father's arms. Using the fierce cold as a metaphor, the filmmaker criticizes the human coldness shown by the government's policy towards immigrants.

A different kind of immigration topic that we could describe as early modern Alpine cosmopolitanism was established with Thomas Mann's novel *Der Zauberberg* (*The Magic Mountain*, 1924). The subject matter treated in this famous German author's novel, the Swiss mountains as a transcendental, salvational realm for consumptive European aristocrats and members of the grande bourgeoisie as well as their sometimes less well-to-do descendants, has been more or less ironically reflected in various movies. *Snow White* (Samir, 2005) is an attempt to update the classic fairytale. The main character, Niko, is not as innocent as her fairytale model. She is a young woman from a rich family living a superficial, meaningless and decadent life in Zurich that soon leads her astray: she develops a cocaine habit that grows more and more serious until she is taken to a sanatorium in the snowy mountains. The mountain snow symbolizes purity and redemption, and is set in contrast to the soullessness and materialism of city life and to the vice of the drug, which appears just as purely white as snow. Salvation is not granted, though: Niko dies on a snowy slope.

Das Fräulein (Andrea Staka, 2006) shows us scenes from the everyday life of three very different women. All three of them are immigrants from the Balkan countries, now living in Zurich and bonding over the struggle with their past. During a mountain outing, two of the women take a chair lift to the top. However, the lift suddenly stops, leaving the women suspended in the middle of nowhere. For Swiss citizens used to mountain outings, this experience is no big deal, as stops are frequent and usually brief, thus not causing any concern. The foreign women, however, begin to feel slightly uncomfortable, glancing down at the ground and trying to make conversation to take their minds off the situation. At Swiss screenings, the awkwardness of this scene usually provokes giggles – owing to the very Swiss experience of the harmlessness of being stuck on a chair lift. The humour is slightly ironic, but nevertheless tender – it doesn't mock its characters, but for a short moment enjoys the transnational perspective the filmmaker has on the story, being a Swiss with Croatian roots.

It seems that contemporary filmmakers are no longer simply aestheticizing or idealizing the Alps – nor are they turning their backs on them. The scenery is probably just too inspiring, and too deeply inscribed in the Swiss identity. Postmodern scepticism sometimes shows up: in his film essay *Hans im Glück* (*Lucky Jack*, 2004), the filmmaker Peter Liechti walks from Zurich to St. Gallen, his home town, in an attempt to stop smoking. Ravaged by withdrawal symptoms, he is far too busy dealing with his own demons to appreciate the beauty of his surroundings, muttering about the "stupid mountains", only to film them all the more beautifully.

The Matterhorn is the mountain of mountains and the prime icon of Swissness. Even though it has been made famous by calendars and chocolate wrappers, it remains a striking sight, all the more so because of its endless reproductions. Actually seeing the Matterhorn, it's hard to believe that this is now, finally, the real thing. In *Lenz* (Thomas Imbach, 2006), images of the Matterhorn constantly reappear. The mountain mirrors the protagonist's inner world and constantly changes its appearance, depending on the weather and the time of day. Zermatt, by contrast, displays the tourist industry in all its ugliness, and supplies a hostile environment for the protagonist's sensitive inner world: human civilization is seen as a menace for the struggling artist's genius that reveals itself only in the solitude of nature. It thus comes as no surprise that so many Swiss works of art feature nature – not merely as a natural surrounding, but as the spirit that has brought them forth.

Moreover, these films illustrate the truism that there is no guarantee for urban nostalgia to restore, or produce, natural beauty. Like the cornucopia of more or less sinister Alpine legends from the past they underscore the fact that the spirit of the Alps can be feared, attacked, religiously invoked, or secretly inscribed into rational images by human beings, but it cannot be domesticated, however much we might wish to take benefit from its primordial power.

城市文化與大自然

——都市夢遊者的阿爾卑斯傳說

梁秉鈞、洪安瑞

傳說，跟噩夢一般，通常在空靈肅穆的環境下誕生。費地梅利1985年獲獎的電影《靈魂姊姊》，描述一個與世隔絕的聾啞「男孩」。他跟父母和姊姊一起住在僻遠的山莊裏，跟外界的唯一接觸，是來自姊姊偶然教授的課本，以及虔誠的母親所深信的鄉野鬼怪傳聞。少男的精力以傳統方式發洩，就是在杳無人煙的山坡上砌石牆。故事鋪展下去，電影鏡頭於一道道石牆之間來回游動。一道道陰森怪異、在荒野山間蜿蜒不絕的石牆，由一代代孤獨而躁動的少年豎立起來，以發洩他們充滿慾念的精力。在一個漫長的冬季，姊姊懷孕了——她懷了弟弟的孩子；父母也像希臘悲劇的角色一般被殺害了，他們雪封的屍體，像過去兩個可見的鬼魂，豎立在農莊窗前。姊弟兩人帶著彼此之間深深的愛，心懷困擾繼續地生活下去，為當地的鬼靈傳聞，添加了自己的故事。

電影沒有明顯對社會控訴，或對人的困境提出解決方法。然而，當旅遊和工業隨著科技侵入阿爾卑斯山，我們作為旁觀者，察覺到孤寂的山居者那奇特的世界正急速消失，只在剛城市化的背景中留下幾則傳說、一點軌跡。電影沒有懷舊，沒有表現失落，對山居者的前景亦沒半點樂觀的感覺。

電影《馬木利那》（馬卡斯非沙2007年導演）卻有另一層自省的現代觀。它是一齣充滿集體罪疚意識以及瑞士阿爾卑斯山地域象徵的懸疑電影。整條山村因建築水庫而被淹沒，五十年後，一個女子的屍體被人發現了。誰料，女子復活過來，給帶到蘇黎世一間診所去。她奇異的行為影響了她的心理醫生。於是，源於人類對大自然的破壞，一個關於大自然對人類進行大報復的現代童話產生了。

寶萊塢電影中刻劃的瑞士山脈，卻是一幅完全相異的圖畫；它們對全球消費者極其友善，但對阿爾卑斯山都市化的過程卻全無提及。相反，電影中所描述的阿爾卑斯山是一片孤寂冰封的空靈景象，用以對抗都市主角馴化了的感情。寶萊塢於是延續了自己烏托邦式的城市童話傳統，為疲乏而過分文明的都市居民（如瑞士女作家約翰娜詩皮里於1880年寫的超國界名著《海蒂》的主角克拉拉），提供一個治療性的夢境。

自二十世紀後期，阿爾卑斯生態旅遊的概念逐漸成形；隨著氣溫轉變，冰河融化，冬日綠林等等現象日趨明顯，這概念更越來越受到重視。一個坐落在格拉魯斯州布勞恩瓦爾德原本雪封的危險地區，借用了伊蓮娜珍妮（1900-1982）寫的一個關於侏儒巴迪（短鬍子侏儒）的現代童話故事，有了相當穩定的發展。一條童話徑，沿途設有幾個美麗而容易到達的巴迪景點，加上禁止行車的措施，就吸引了不少家庭帶著小孩前來度假。這樣一個魔幻而遙遠的侏儒國度，充滿會說話的動物，又不受汽車及滑雪勝地種種噪音騷擾，是有相當吸引力的。巴迪童話本身，是對現代生活帶來的文化衝擊作出的一種懷舊式反響，亦是童話的中心思想，一種對異類生物世界——對動物、花朵、石塊等等的世界——的尊重。雖然人類可以借想像力在某一程度上捕捉這世界，以便在日常生活中與它們共處，然而沒有擬人化的大自然象徵，人類是不可能徹底瞭解它們的。

在一個較複雜的知性層面上，自從尼采於1881年夏天，在恩嘎丁山谷裏西爾絲瑪利亞小村落一所高山旅舍（現在變成尼采博物館）的小房間居住過，再在1883至1888年重臨休養，以尋覓靈感後，那裏便發展成一個人們尋求精神慰藉的優美休憩所[1]。直至現在，這小小的村落藉著它的湖泊和周遭景色所構成的一種世外的美，以及博物館中尼采的光環，成功抗拒了旅遊業最大的破壞。這兩種現象不息止地吸引著無數藝術家、學者和慕名的旅客。步著尼采的足跡，全世界的作家、知識分子和藝術家，不光遍遊山野，還留下他們的足印。尼采藉以下的句子，開始了文學的圓舞曲：

> 這裏我坐著等待，等待——卻只有虛無
> 在善惡以外，時而欣賞
> 光，時而陰影，全只是遊戲
> 全是湖泊，全是正午，全是沒有盡頭的時間
> ……

戈特弗里德貝恩以稍嚴肅的句子回應：

> 這裏沒有雪，只有光
> 從上方照下

沒有死亡，但每人都相信自己接近死亡——
它這麼白，再沒有哀求
進入乳白的石裏，
碩大的苦痛
在這山谷的上空盤旋。

中國詩人楊煉（1955年生於巴塞爾）以灰暗的觀感反駁：

無人稱的雪之二　西爾斯　馬利亞[2]

雪地上布滿了盲人　他們看不見
一首死人在旅館裏的詩
和　繁殖著可怕陽光的山谷
他們在同一座懸崖下失去了影子
變成花園日規上黑瘦的針
用笑聲洗腳
用一隻死鳥精心製作雕花的器皿
野餐時痛飲鮮紅的溪流
正午　盲人盲目分泌的溪
他們看不見　一首詩裏的遊客
都裸體躺在旅館的床上
無須陷落　就抵達一場雪崩的深度

最後，張清華於2006年7月19日觀湖後，在明亮的星光下於嘉賓冊上寫道：

陽光下生長的
是你瘋狂的思想
雪山上閃耀的
是眾神心上的傷痕

可知道他說的是誰——是湖泊，是哲學家，是詩人，是天才的瘋子？

過去幾千年，阿爾卑斯山脈在傳統上具有文化屏障和邊境區域的雙重功能。對敵人和旅客而言，它是一道天然障礙，對移民亦毫無吸引力；但它促使村民建立經商通道，亦成為鄰近地區溝通的橋樑。在這狹窄的地域中，多種語言同時存在，顯示了它在地理上的獨特性，亦同時証明傳統在隔絕的地區保存得更好。大自然的力量對村民來說是一種永恆的威脅，他們虔心相信有一種超然的秩序，可以解釋一切偶發的事件，再經他們的想像重組和分析，就成為超自然的現象了。這種宗教意識，穿插著當地的迷信與神話，（見於前述費地梅利的電影和無數阿爾卑斯山脈的傳説），加上超凡的景色，再經市場工業重複製造，自哥德和浪漫派畫家卡士柏費烈德治[3]開始，令無數厭倦文明的旅客著迷。他們衝出緊張的都市生活，在異鄉未被馴化的山巒間尋求庇護，意圖征服，或至少暫時忘卻個人的存在危機。這種再造的空靈感很早便受到嘲弄。浪漫詩人海涅亦曾嘲笑濫情遊客在觀看日落時的機械化感情：

　　　　大約十五分鐘之久，人們沉默肅穆地站著，凝視著那美麗的火球緩慢地在西方沉沒；他們的臉孔沐浴在落日的餘暉之中，訝異地抱著手；彷彿我們這群沉默的信徒，正站在偌大的教堂內，而神父剛高舉主的身體，柏勒天那的聖詩從風琴裏緩緩流出。正陷入沉思之際，我聽見身旁的人嚷起來：「大自然真美麗啊！」説這話的是我的室友，他是個多愁善感的年青商人。它們把我帶回日常的情緒中，我現在可以對女士説很多關於日落的得體話了，然後悄悄領她們回房間，彷彿什麼都沒有發生過。

　　十七世紀晚明時期的中國，狂放文人如袁宏道、張岱、陳繼儒等對古今附庸風雅者，也作過類似的嘲諷：「談山林之樂者，未必真得山林之趣；厭名利之談者，未必盡忘名利之情。」這些文人的田園山水詩文，正是中國悠長的文學史中常見的文類。

　　這兩種來自不同文化傳統的論者，同樣對人們表面化地看待自然風景有所批評，但他們無法理解或想像的是，數量龐大的現代攀山者及短程旅客，已對大自然做成極其巨大的傷害。阿爾卑斯山區當然早已不是曠野。旅遊工業開始前，它變成了一片脆弱的文化風景，主要是各種冬季運動大規模殖民了瑞士山脈。由於人類過分的貪婪，大自然受到的傷害再不可能以妖魔鬼怪等形而上的抗爭抵消，而對環境的毀壞，亦令整個山區無法適合人類生活。根據傳統的文化慣例，受威脅的阿爾卑斯生態環境，現在需要更多的保護和平衡，需要藉現代童話提示我們這是每個人的責任，需要有說服力的論點提高人們的警覺，注視整個地區行將毀滅的危機。然而，這次的處境跟一百年前是不一樣的：一片風景，或一個自然世界雖被馴化了，但人為及科技帶來的災難，卻暴力地扭曲了它的面貌，它的各種功能亦快速消失，再無法有效地保護氣溫，提供資源，或為疲乏的都市人保留一片幽美的文化空間，讓他們復原。

當然，瑞士仍是能夠在伯爾尼茲山中央，向國際都市的遊客，展示像少女峰這樣的聯合國教文組織世界自然遺產項目的阿爾卑斯景點，讓他們年復一年像候鳥南飛般聚集在「歐洲的頂峰」。亦有越來越多中國遊客前來欣賞瑞士群山迷人的景致。然而，他們的文化視野不同，對山景自有不同的觀點。自西元前五世紀中國第一本詩集《詩經》給輯成以來，山水詩便成為主要的詩文類別。詩人有些描寫隨大自然脈搏起伏作息的愉悅；有些借自然現象的象徵意義，表達整個人類世界的感情幅度。自《山海經》（不少段落可上溯自西元前三世紀）開始，中國文學作品對山水風景便不乏創意的想像回響。在傳統的文類中，有關仙靈的詩文及「誌怪」（記錄怪異之意）的故事亦多述及幽靈妖魔，及周圍山谷河川的世界，作者亦多藉此表達自己對事物的觀點與感情。清代作家蒲松齡寫的《聊齋誌異》是「誌怪」文體的巔峰之作。故事中各個勇敢美麗的姑娘，蛻變自花朵鳥雀、狐狸蛇蟲，時而善良，時而邪惡，皆具有超凡的力量，或引誘及控制男性，或忠誠又憐愛地搭救大難臨頭的無辜書生。

中國自1949年奉行共產主義以來，批判寫實主義便成為主要的文藝表達方式，反迷信及禁鬼神的諸種運動亦隨之而生。在文化大革命的狂飆中，凡屬「四舊」的文類，包括山水詩、帝王將相的傳統戲劇、才子佳人的言情小說等等，皆成禁忌。反之，傳統的文學及戲劇卻在香港流傳，而來自「誌怪」故事的遠古超自然幻想性人物鳥獸，亦可繼續存在，甚至轉化成商業電影中的特殊現象，蒲松齡的聊齋故事不斷給搬上銀幕便是很好的例子。這些電影往往由優秀的導演拍攝，胡金銓便把聊齋故事《俠女》拍成同名電影，徐克及程小東則把聊齋故事「小倩」拍成《倩女幽魂》三部曲。這雖只是幾個著名的例子，但已説明現代電影善於利用奇麗山景，加上「誌怪」的文學手法，來表達英勇浪漫的故事。

香港原本具有中國南方郊野種種的美和魅力，只是人口密集，土地稀少，而且現代化帶來了嚴重的生態問題，就剩下幾個地區——如坐落新界西北部的米埔自然保護區及濕地公園——相對受到保護。回歸以後，香港跟中國南部城市如廣州及深圳的交通日益頻繁，為便利香港跟中國工商業交流而興建的西部通道深圳灣公路大橋（長5.5公里，三線行車），加上地產業及沿海填土區的急速發展，已嚴重影響整個地區的生態平衡。然而，這跟大陸相比，還只是小巫見大巫。中國地廣人多，文化大革命後逐漸向世界開放，1990年開始工商業迅速發展，興建水電廠，開發煤礦，徵收農地，亦容忍化工廠排污，種種因素引起的環境問題，不只住宅區受到污染，不少農物牲口亦遭殃，人吃了，便引致食物中毒，甚而對健康做成永久傷害。今天，中國作家難以回到過去，再無法書寫優美的田園詩了，他們只有選擇記錄日漸惡化的種種農村狀況。

香港處於兩種文化中間，佔有利亦邊緣的位置。圍繞的群山和海洋形成了天然屏障，亦成就了香港拼集的山水觀。1949年後，英屬殖民地的香港保留了儒道佛等傳統思想架構，大部分民間風俗，包括招魂和占卜等都給保留下來，風水迷信亦未被禁絕。坊間傳說如情人石（青年男女向情人石祈求姻緣）及石蟾蜍（據說，蟾蜍在香港開埠初期便開始往太平山上爬，當牠爬到山頂，香港便會消失）等神話亦繼續流傳。除古老傳說及風俗迷信外，香港亦保留了其他傳統。例如1950年代新儒家學者在香港講學及著書，六七十年代的學者葉維廉及林年同嘗試在儒道的美學範疇內討論山水詩及電影美學。本文作者之一的梁秉鈞曾借聊齋故事及傳統蓮葉題材，實驗寫成兩組迥異的現代詩。他亦重寫神話，及把新生命注入傳統的「誌怪」小說，敍述都市旅客與山林妖怪鬼魅的相遇，從而表達一個香港人對現代中國的種種反思和感情。梁秉鈞有幸參與2004年夏天由蘇黎世大學中文系洪安瑞老師和同學合辦，跨文化、跨學系的阿爾卑斯神話研究工作坊，從中獲得不少創作靈感。

大自然都市化與重拾大自然空間的過程中，存在著種種矛盾，因此我們這次跨文化交流，集中研究超/自然的藝術論述裏，各種由不同文化影響的孤絕感。年輕的瑞士藝術家茱莉亞史泰拿，對我們來說是這計畫理想的合作夥伴。在她的作品中，我們意識到現代主義那種對都市的複雜而原始的可信同時並存的渴求，那種強烈但無法達成的慾望。與此同時，我們亦不安地感覺到遠古的幽靈——例如破壞阿爾卑斯山的鬼魅——正強烈地在我們後現代的集體想像中再度出現。圖恩藝術博物館館長馬德蓮舒柏里，於2007年艾殊裏曼卡提資助金頒授禮中致詞時，對茱莉亞史泰拿這種特別的風格有很詳盡的説明：

> 就情緒而言，茱莉亞史泰拿的作品擺盪於天堂與天譴之間。樹膠水彩畫「裙子上的早餐」充滿童話色彩，令人想起書本的插畫；「化石」卻瀰漫著黑暗的想像力，像幻想電影或幻想小説的插圖。茱莉亞史泰拿的作品，形式上帶有法國印象派畫家如艾格狄加和奧地倫列東的影子，與此同時，她的作品卻又深深植根於現今的攝影意象。這在她對框邊的運用、對明晰及朦朧輪廓之把玩，及對動作凝鏡的處理上，都可以清楚看到。她取材廣泛，因此創造了自己個人的獨特語言。雜亂不安的形式呼應了煩躁激盪的內容。不同的主題彼此重疊。她談及自己抗拒分類的「故事段落」或「思想碎屑」，因此她的作品是由夢與現實、記憶與期望、自覺的經驗與潛在的意識的各個片段凝固組合，再借一股強大的藝術力量結集成形。

我們山上的研討會包括攀山、演講及電影播放，目的在探討不同觀點的重要性，希望藉語言和感官的管道，提供文化對話的全面經驗。本書所選的阿爾卑斯傳説，翻譯者都是參與旅行的蘇黎世大學東亞研究所學生，以及雖未前來，卻仍積極參與的慕尼黑「虛擬客人」卡拉文泰特博士。他是現代中國文學學者，亦是梁秉鈞的朋友。梁秉鈞和他的同事幫助我們仔細校訂中文譯稿，修改文體和文法上的錯誤。海倫瓦莉曼把傳説翻譯成英文，並小心修訂文稿其他部分。我們這本書可以和中、英讀者會面，全是這次深入而難得的文化交流帶來的成果。

注释：

[1] http://www.nietzschehaus.ch

[2] 楊煉，「無人稱的雪之二 西爾斯　馬利亞」《快樂的鬼魂筆記》，白賴恩何頓翻譯，香港：譯文叢書2002：58。

[3] http://www.smart-art.at/alpen/sitemap-text/berg-im-bild-bildbeschreibungen.htm

瑞士影像

——瑞士電影中的阿爾卑斯山

妮坦莉波勒

　　阿爾卑斯山相信是瑞士最令人驚歎讚賞的自然景象，因此，它在瑞士電影中扮演如此重要的角色，是不足為奇的。阿爾卑斯山宏偉壯觀的氣勢，成為電影中扣人心弦的背景。沒有其他媒介比電影更能表達太陽下冰雪閃耀的山峰，不論是峰頂上眩目迷人的風光，或是懸崖上細嚼野花的山羊。

　　另外，阿爾卑斯地區對瑞士的形象亦非常重要——當然不單只在旅遊業的範圍，亦在瑞士人心中的集體自我形象方面；因此，阿爾卑斯山給電影故事的背景提供了無限素材，所代表的想像空間，在瑞士歷史上經過多重變化，現在變得多面而複雜了。

　　阿爾卑斯山的影像中，一個美學上非常突出的例子是國家鐵路系統。它是瑞士形象之一，主要是可以在很短的時間內把乘客從市中心載到山上，接駁點亦多。這對都市一族來説是極具吸引力的，他們渴望與大自然重新聯繫，亦把登山視作心愛的休閒活動之一。這兩個通常對立的象徵空間順利銜接——一個是現代進步的都市空間，另一個是古老空靈的山林景象——給予人不少靈感，拍攝出瑞士阿爾卑斯山脈的種種面貌。

　　這種對山野自然美景的渴望，正從艾力蘭捷的作品反映出來：《阿爾卑斯浪漫組曲》，1996；《進入第三千禧的牧童之旅》，2002；《阿爾卑斯行記》，2006。他的紀錄片把阿爾卑斯山脈拍成一闋優美的田園頌曲，是一片農夫及牧人跟動物及大自然和諧共處的田園美景。影片拍攝了種種古老的工作傳統，例如在農舍背後極其險峻的山脊上修剪阿爾卑斯野草。我們看到一個未經污染的世界，簡單、純潔無邪，人們作息有序，不受物質主義和科技污染，大自然啓迪了他們的宗教情懷，他們帶著尊敬和諧的心謹守自然的法度。

　　《萊因河》（麗莎盧斯列，2005）描述格勞賓登一條小村莊很多村民被迫離家到城市找工作。一個離鄉數十年的老人訴説自他離開後，村子的種種景象總是每個晚上，毫不間斷地在他的夢中。他説，環繞萊因河的山脈才是他永遠真正的家。

　　這種魂牽夢縈的記憶，是瑞士人與阿爾卑斯山關係的特色。其中一個共通點是對回家的渴望。這是可以理解的，因為許多阿爾卑斯地區的居民，自少年開始便要離開鄉村到瑞士城市讀書或工作。其中一個典型的例子，便是約翰娜詩皮里的名著《海蒂》裏的主角，她身處法蘭克福，卻心懷瑞士家鄉。很奇怪，這種懷鄉的感覺，就算不是在山村出生，而是在城市或近郊長大的瑞士人，亦往往感受得到。對他們來說，阿爾卑斯山脈是集體想像中的家鄉：未經污染、澄明純樸，是一個誠懇自由的地方，聯繫著一個人的真正本質和靈魂，還有他的過去——在瑞士人的思維裏，瑞士山脈往往跟童年記憶，如學校遠足和家庭假期相關。

然而，亦有些電影角色不甚認同這種懷鄉感。在許多人心中，阿爾卑斯山脈是一個冬季漫長、寒風凜烈、充滿孤寂與抑鬱的地方。小小的村落與農舍都被濃霧籠罩，遠遠孤立於世界之外。在《沒有火的冬季》（格力瑟凌斯基，2006）裏，雪與霧把所有影像變成眩目的白色，直至整個畫面彷彿變成空無一物——就如電影人物心中揮之不去的憂鬱。這是自主的山中世界黑暗的一面：它隔絕了山中居民與他人及文明的接觸，把他們囚於自己的內心世界裏；尤其在黑暗的冬季，群山變成了一個充滿敵意的地方。一位來自洛桑的瑞士作家查理士拉默斯（1878-1947）被山巒這一面深深吸引。他很多故事都被改編成電影，而他常常在小說裏探討環境對人的影響，尤其注意各種黑暗力量，及它形而上的特質。例如，《若太陽永不升起》裏的一位先知宣告太陽將永遠不再在這村子升起，便引發了一場集體的信仰危機。《山中的恐懼》描述一條山村裏的居民越來越迷信，結果引致集體悲劇。《當山塌下》訴說一場山崩如何摧毀整條村子和大部分村民，倖存者最終必須面對善、惡及上帝意旨等等尖銳的問題。

阿爾卑斯山一方面是一個原始樂園，另一方面卻是一處危險荒野，這兩個極端中間存在著一種張力，構成了偉大的藝術創作泉源。阿爾卑斯山脈提供了無限能量與神秘感，啟發了無數神話和民間傳說，其中很多都收集在這本書裏。阿爾卑斯的神話傳統，成為眾多故事的靈感來源，許多亦緊貼原本的神話故事，如《占納殊》（丹尼爾史密，1987）。一名生活於現代的記者，著手研究十七世紀格勞賓登一位政客楊格占納殊。他對這位歷史人物越來越著迷，當存在於過去及現在，於占納殊及自己一生的界線變得模糊而終於消失時，他亦越來越迷亂了。

瑞士電影中的阿爾卑斯山脈，通常用來象徵人類的野心，給人類征服大自然的過程提供了懾人的影像。登山電影往往拍攝一支登山隊伍勇敢地攀山越嶺，排除萬難，英勇地忍受惡劣的天氣與身體的損耗。影片的結尾，大都是拍攝從山峰鳥瞰大地，歌頌隊員的兄弟情。戰後不少瑞士電影述說士兵的故事，影片中阿爾卑斯山是天然邊界，聳立的巨大岩石就是堡壘，守護國家免受外敵——尤其是德軍——入侵，確保瑞士的安全。阿爾卑斯山是瑞士神話中的國家防衛站、軍事抗戰教堂。在瑞士中部高聳的聖哥達山建設的燃料庫，則是現代的國家傳奇。

從移民的觀點看，阿爾卑斯山同樣是一座堡壘，阻礙他們進入瑞士。《希望之旅》描述一個貧窮的土耳其家庭夢想到瑞士開始新生活。他們非法地從義大利入境到達瑞士邊界，再乘坐一輛貨車到史柏盧根峽道，接著在冬夜徒步攀行。最小的兒子受不住冰寒和勞累，早晨時終在父親的臂彎內凍斃了。導演以嚴寒作為隱喻，批評瑞士政府冷酷無情的移民政策。

另外一種可以稱作「早期阿爾卑斯現代國際主義」的移民題材，在湯馬斯曼的小說《魔山》（1924）內可見端倪。這本德國名著中，瑞士山脈對患癆疾的歐洲貴族，及布爾喬亞階層和他們不甚長進的後代來說，是一個超越世俗、救贖性的領域。但在後來的不少電影中，這題材卻或多或少成為諷刺的對象。《白雪公主》（沙摩，2005）是童話故事的現代版。主角妮珂可不像童話的公主那麼純潔，她是生於富裕家庭的一名年青女子，過著浮淺、頹廢，無甚意義的生活，終於誤入歧途。她染上可卡因毒癮，情況越來越嚴重，最後要到雪山一所療養院裏接受治療。山上的雪象徵純潔與救贖，用以對比沒有靈魂而充滿物質主義的城市生活，以及毒品之邪惡。諷刺的是，可卡因亦是潔白如雪的。最終，救贖沒有出現，妮珂在雪封的斜坡上死去。

《三女性》（安德莉史特卡，2006）描述三個截然不同的女子的日常生活。她們是巴爾幹國家的移民，移居蘇黎世後，都希望擺脫過去，因而結成好友。一次，她們登山旅遊。乘升降椅到山頂去時，升降椅突然停了，她們滯留半空，四周杳無人煙。這幾個從外地來的女子感到不安，不時望向地面，又努力閒聊，好分散注意。電影在瑞士放映時，這尷尬的情景引起不少笑聲，因為對習慣登山的瑞士居民來說，升降椅故障是常見的，不是大問題，且時間不長，根本不用擔心。這幽默有點諷刺性，卻是溫和的，亦沒有嘲弄電影角色，只展示導演這種跨國界的觸覺——

她是祖籍克羅地亞的瑞士人。

電影工作者好像不再單純美化或理想化阿爾卑斯山，但也不是要徹底否定它。只是，瑞士風景可能太富啓發性，而瑞士身份的烙印亦太深刻了，後現代的懷疑論有時還會出現。紀錄片《幸運的傑克》裏，導演彼德黎次特為了戒煙，從蘇黎世走到故鄉聖加侖。途中，煙癮難熬，他得竭力抵抗誘惑，因而無法欣賞周圍的美景。只是，他一邊大罵「蠢山」，一邊卻把山拍得美麗異常。

山中之山馬特宏峰，是瑞士本質的代表。令馬特宏峰聞名遐邇的，固然是日曆及巧克力包裝紙上無數複製的影像，但它仍是獨特而美麗的，有時看著它，實在很難相信它真的屹立在眼前。《蘭斯》裏，馬特宏峰的影像不斷重現，還依著天氣或一天不同的時分，不斷改變外貌，以反映主角的內心世界。《沙密》一片則完全相反，它展示了旅遊業最醜惡的一面，給主角敏感的內心世界製造了一個充滿敵意的環境：這掙扎中的藝術家只有在孤寂的大自然中，才可以展露他的天分；人類文明對他來説是一個威脅。很多瑞士藝術作品以大自然為題材，這是不足為奇的，因為，大自然不單是四周的環境，亦是啓發創作的精神。

這些影片還展示一個不言而喻的道理：都市人的鄉土情懷並不保證可以恢復或製造大自然的美景。像過去阿爾卑斯傳説中的羊角盃，或其他比較負面的故事，它們強調了一項事實：阿爾卑斯山的精靈可以給人類畏懼、攻擊、召喚，或秘密地刻畫成理性的影像，卻不可以被馴化，儘管，我們多麼希望從它的原始力量中取得利益。

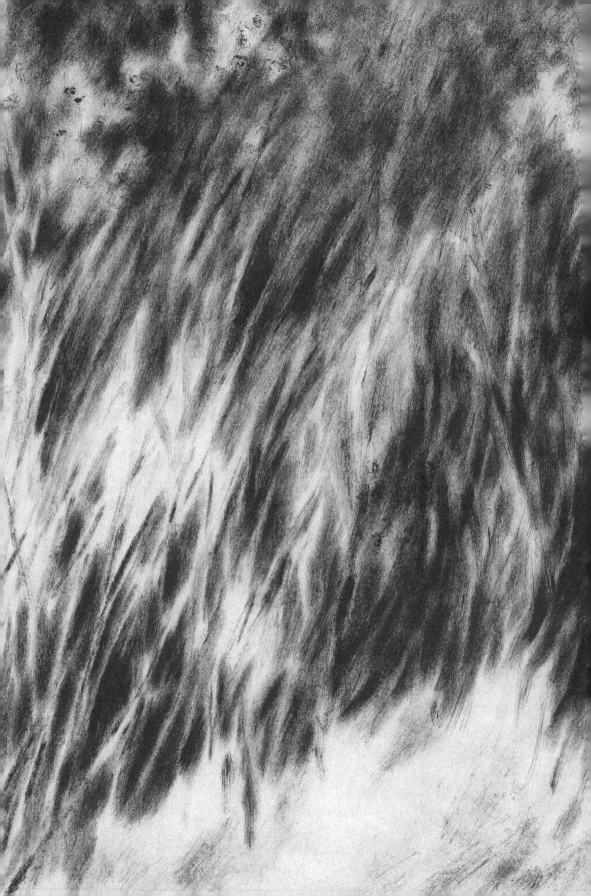

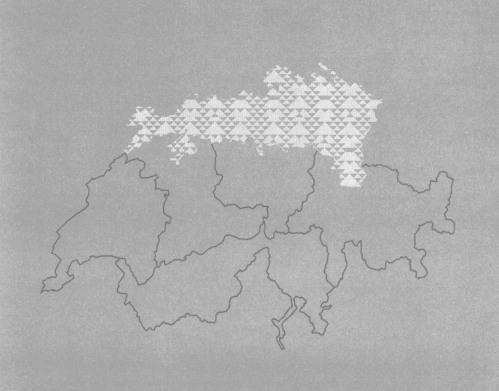

水國之門　The Gateway to
The Underwater Kingdom

蘇黎世州位於克羅登和布拉治之間有一個
池塘，居民稱之為「黃金之門」。池塘不
深，但某些地方卻有深不見底的洞，金黃
色的細沙不時從洞中緩緩地流出來。

　　一天，一個牧羊的男孩在池塘濱躺下
休息。突然，他看見水面泛起漣漪，池底
一個洞流出金黃色的細沙，接著水面分開
了，一個異常綺麗的少女出現，男孩驚訝
萬分。少女微笑地遞給男孩一枚純金指環
時，但當男孩要接過指環，少女就靈巧地
把手縮回去。男孩腳步不穩，向前趺到水
裏，少女便擁抱著他，拉他到水中深不可
測的地方去。

　　不遠處一名農夫聽見男孩驚恐的叫
喊，立刻跑過來看個究竟。他來到池塘，

Between Kloten and Bülach in the canton of Zurich, there is a pond known as the Golden Gateway. It is not very deep, but it does have a number of deep holes that are said to be unfathomable, and which emit a steady trickle of tiny golden grains of fine sand.

One day, a shepherd boy was having a rest on the edge of the pond, when suddenly the water started rippling and a stream of golden sand floated to the surface. Then, before his astonished eyes, the waves parted and a beautiful maiden appeared. Smiling sweetly, she held out a golden ring towards him. As he reached out to grab it, she drew back her hand, thereby making him lose his balance and fall into the water. Immediately, she clasped him in her arms and dragged him down into the fathomless depths.

A farmhand, who had heard the boy's anguished cries, rushed to the scene. He looked down into the water, but although it was shallow and absolutely clear, he could discern nothing. He was about to turn back, when all at once the boy shot out like a dart from one of the deep holes. He was already unconscious when the farmhand pulled him out of the water.

After he had recovered his senses, the boy told the man what had happened. The maiden had taken him deeper and deeper down through the water until, suddenly, they were on firm ground and surrounded by beautiful countryside. In front of them stood a magnificent city with a golden gate. While he stood there transfixed, a young girl stepped out through the gateway. The maiden left hold of him and rushed toward her with open arms. But no sooner had she released him than he was projected up to the surface of the pond at such a speed that he fainted. And that was all he remembered.

Since then, the pond has been known as the Golden Gateway.

就只看到淺淺的池水清澈透明，其他什麼也不見。農夫準備回去的時候，男孩從一個泉洞飛鏢似的給射出來。農夫把男孩拉到安全的池濱上時，男孩已經沒了知覺。

男孩蘇醒過來，告訴農夫發生的一切。原來，那少女把他帶到水中無法量度的深處去。當他們穩站在地上，周圍是夢一般美麗的田園風景，前面矗立著一道金黃色的門，門後遠遠通往一座華麗的城市。男孩站著發呆的時候，從門內走來一名年輕的女孩。少女要張手擁抱女孩，便把男孩放開。少女放開手的瞬間，湍急的水流把男孩沖上岸，令他昏厥過去。他記得的，就只有這些。

從此以後，那池塘便被稱為「黃金之門」。

The Mountain Maiden
from the Canton of Aargau

某個禮拜日,一位非常漂亮,但無人認識的女孩在阿爾高州頁仁丁恩下村的舞會中,邀請一個害羞的男孩跳舞。男孩快樂地同意了,兩人在舞場上享受著美麗的音樂和舞蹈,愉快地度過了一天。暮色降臨,女孩要回家了,她請男孩陪她回去,他當然開心地答應了。女孩沒有和別人一樣去頁仁丁恩上村,卻帶了男孩去稱為「小北山羊」的一片小小而荒涼的原野。他們走到原野後面一座小山丘。

「我屬於那座山,」女孩對男孩說:「我受了詛咒,要住在這座小山丘裏。豐富的財寶在那裏等著勇敢的人闖進去哩。你只要跟著我走進去,跟守衛著寶藏的兩條憤怒的火龍搏鬥,便可以得到一切。」

她再說:「若你今天不敢闖進去,那就等耶穌受難節那天日出的時候來,我會坐在小山丘右邊一堆黃花九輪草上。我不可以先跟你說話,但可以回答你的問話。你得輕鬆地邊說話邊採一些花兒。我會幫助你,告訴你接下來該怎麼辦。」

One Sunday, an exceptionally beautiful girl no one had ever seen before appeared at the village dance in Lower Ehrendingen in the canton of Aargau, and asked a shy young lad to dance with her. He accepted with delight, and they spent the rest of the day together, enjoying the music and dancing the lively rounds. Then, as twilight set in, the girl said it was time for her to go home and asked the boy to accompany her. Of course he was happy to accept. However, instead of making for Upper Ehrendingen, she led her dancing partner to Steinböckli, a small, bare heath with a hillock.

"This is where I belong," said the fair maiden, "condemned by an evil spell to dwell inside this hill. There are great treasures waiting there for anyone bold enough to venture inside. He need only follow me into the hillock, and brave the grim guardians of the treasure trove, two fiery dragons."

Then she added, "If you don't dare come today, try on Good Friday at daybreak. I'll be sitting on some cowslips on the right-hand side of the hillock. I'm not allowed to address you, but I can answer you. All you need do is be bold enough to start up some light-hearted conversation with me. At the same time, you should pick some of the flowers. Then I'll help you, and I'll tell you what else you have to do."

As she said this, doors like those of a great castle swung open in the side of the hillock. The boy caught a glimpse of a golden cave guarded by the two fire-breathing dragons, who reared up at the sight of the stranger. The fair maiden walked into the hill, but the lad was too shy to follow. The secret entry closed behind her, and the door disappeared from view.

Sadly, the young man returned home. He told no one of his adventure. But day and night he never stopped dreaming of the extraordinary maiden inside the hill.

At last Good Friday came. Punctually, at the first light of dawn, he arrived at the appointed spot. There, bathed in the rays of the rising sun, lay a little heap of cowslips. And on top of them sat the maiden, a bunch of keys by her side. She gazed intently at her erstwhile dancing partner. But her gaze so confused the shy youth that his courage failed him. He was tongue-tied. All he could do was pick up one single cowslip before fleeing back to his village.

On the way home, he noticed that the flower had been transformed into a golden coin. With regret, he realised what good fortune and wealth he had forfeited due to his shyness.

Subsequently, several of his friends to whom he had told the story sought their luck – but not one of them ever found the entrance to the little hill, or the girl from the dragons' cave with her golden flowers.

這時，小山丘一邊的門像城門似的打開了。男孩看見一個金黃色的洞穴，兩條會噴火的龍守衛著，牠們看見陌生人便直立起來。那漂亮的女孩走進小山丘裏，但男孩太害羞了，不敢跟著她。那秘密入口便在女孩背後關上，門也消失了。

男孩非常難過地回家了，他沒有和別人說起他的遭遇，只是終日思念著山中那個不尋常的女孩。

耶穌受難節終於來了。第一線晨光初現，男孩依約走到小山丘那兒。女孩果然坐在一小堆黃花九輪草上，她帶著鑰匙串，急切地瞧著男孩。女孩的目光使男孩緊張起來，他的勇氣消失了，就連跟女孩說一句話也不敢。他只拿了一支黃花九輪草便逃走了。

路上，男孩發覺手裏的花變了金幣。他知道自己因害羞而失去了幸福和財富，因此懊惱不已。

男孩的幾個朋友聽過了這個故事後，都想碰碰自己的運氣，但是他們既沒找到小山丘的入口，又沒看到龍穴旁坐在黃花九輪草上的女孩。

The Solothurn
Thunder Brothers

索洛圖恩之雷鳴兄弟

一天，在索洛圖恩州肝山縣一條叫斜爾雜的村子裏，有些年輕人正在玩地滾球。突然來了三個長了長鬍子的陌生人，他們是三兄弟。他們建議來個小比賽：「每投擲一次，算一升葡萄酒吧！」

斜爾雜的年輕人同意了，可是很快就後悔起來。三位陌生人做過熱身運動後，就越長越大。不久，他們變得高大又強壯，像超自然的巨人似的，居民都嚇得目瞪口呆。一球一球，他們投得那麼狠，連谷裏的人都以為聽到雷響了。

巨人技巧熟練，球被投得很遠，越過地滾球場的盡頭，往汝拉山脈上滾。有的回來了，有的越過山和針葉林，到了後面的山谷。滾球在貝特拉和格倫興市之間的山牆岩石上留下了長而筆直的痕跡，現在仍然能看到。

當然，斜爾雜人得花錢買他們那場敗仗的酒。當葡萄酒全部喝過，沒什麼可打賭的時候，三位長鬍子的巨人踏著蹣跚的步伐，愉快地離開了。他們是從何處來？又往何處去？可無人知道呢。

One day, the young lads from Selzach, a village in the district of Leberberg in the canton of Solothurn, were enjoying themselves playing skittles when, unexpectedly, three bearded strangers, brothers all, turned up and suggested playing a match. "After each game the winners shall get a measure of wine," they said.

The Selzach lads consented. But before long they were to regret their decision. For, as soon as the three strangers had warmed up, they started growing bigger and bigger. Soon, to the astonished eyes of the young lads, they appeared as tall and strong as enormous supernatural giants. And then they started bowling ball after ball with such violence that people in the valley mistook the sound for rolls of thunder.

The huge giants hurled the balls with such consummate skill that they overshot the pitch and flew up towards the Jura mountain range. There some of them bounced back from the cliffs, but others were projected right over the mountain tops from where they rolled down through the pine forest to the valley on the other side. The long straight paths the balls carved into the mountainside between Bettlach and Grenchen can still be seen clearly and distinctly to this day.

Of course the Selzach lads had to pay for the match they had so hopelessly lost. But after they had drunk all there was to drink and there was no wine left to be bowled for, the three bearded giants amiably took their leave and shambled off. No one knows whence they came, no one knows whither they went.

Justice for Lowly Creatures

為低等動物討公道

As everyone knows, the great conqueror of the Western World, the Emperor Charlemagne, liked staying in Zurich. It was there he had the great Minster built. And there he lived, right beside the Minster, in a house known as 'The Hole'.

The Emperor wished with all his heart for justice to reign throughout the world. To this end, on the very spot where, during the Roman conquest, the town saints had been decapitated for their Christian faith, he had a tall pillar erected from which he hung a bell that could be heard far and wide. Criers were sent out to all the surrounding lands to announce that whoever wanted to demand his rights could sound the bell. He could come at any time: even if the Emperor was at his imperial midday meal he would leave the table to give ear to the claimant's suit.

And so it happened that one day, at midday, the bell rang out. However, the servant who rushed out

大家都知道，西方世界的征服者沙樂美國王很喜歡在蘇黎世停留。他還在那裏蓋了一座大教堂。他住在那座教堂旁一個叫「洞孔」的房子裏。

國王心裏最大的願望是全世界都得到公義，因此，他在古羅馬人因宗教理由而把聖人砍頭的地方，立了一根很高的圓柱，還在上面掛了一個聲徹雲霄的鐘。國王派人到各地宣告：誰有申訴，都可以隨時敲響圓柱上的鐘，連國王吃午飯的時候也不例外，他會立刻離開桌子來聽人們的訴求。

一天中午，鐘給敲響了。國王的隨從跑出來看個究竟，但是見不到敲鐘的人，他失望地回去了。不一會兒，鐘又響起來了。隨從再跑出來，但仍徒勞無功。

第三次鐘響時，隨從終於看到什麼生物向國王求助了。那是一條蛇，牠蜷著圓柱往上爬，敲響掛在圓柱上的鐘。

智慧的國王沙樂美聽了隨從的報告，立刻擱下午餐站起來說：「沒有智慧的動物也有牠們的權利。」

Legends from the German-speaking Plateau and Basel-Land 德語區平原的傳說

那條蛇在國王跟前鞠躬，然後爬行到水旁牠藏蛋的地方。蛋上邊坐著一隻有毒的蟾蜍，蛇顯然無法維護自己的權利。國王立刻下令拿掉蟾蜍，把牠活生生的燒死，以作懲罰。

第二天，蛇來到國王的宮殿，爬行到沙樂美國王的桌子，向他鞠躬，然後在他水杯裏放了一塊十分貴重、閃閃發亮的寶石。

對沙樂美國王來説，這禮物證明了他在蘇黎世建教堂是個好主意。這亦證明，就連有毒的蛇蟲也是上帝創造的神聖奇跡。

to find the ringer could not see anyone anywhere. So he went back inside, disappointed. But as soon as he had got in, the justice bell sounded again. Again the servant rushed out in vain.

It was not until the third ringing that the man noticed what creature it was that wanted to appeal to the Lord of the Western World for help. It was a snake that had wound itself around the pillar and hung itself onto the bell rope, thereby causing the bell to ring.

Hearing what had happened, wise Emperor Charlemagne immediately got up from his meal saying, "Even dumb animals have their rights."

The snake bowed down before the Emperor and then led the way to a place near the water where she had hidden her eggs. A big fat venomous toad was sitting on them. Clearly the serpent was powerless to defend her rights. The Emperor immediately ordered the toad to be removed and condemned it to be burnt alive for its crime.

The day after the Emperor had rescued her eggs, the snake appeared in the imperial hall, crept onto the table in front of Charlemagne, and, bowing down before him, dropped an exceedingly precious, shining gem into his goblet.

For Charlemagne, this gift confirmed that he had been right to build his church in Zurich. He also took it as proof that even the world of poisonous serpents is a part of divine creation and full of sacred miracles.

沙樂美國王和神奇寶石

Charlemagne and
the Magic Gem

The Emperor Charlemagne now considered this gem – the snake's reward for his sense of justice – as his most precious jewel. Out of the fondness of his heart he gave it to his wife. Soon, the clever woman discovered that it possessed extraordinary magical powers.

Previously, Charlemagne had often exchanged amorous glances with other women. But now he was consumed with passionate love for his empress alone. She had to be at his side at all times. She, too, loved him passionately, and when she was on the point of death she found it quite unbearable to think that her husband might soon forget her. So she hid the gem under her tongue, thus taking it with her into her coffin.

The magic snake power of the gem proved itself beyond all expectations: the Emperor continued to feel the same passion for his deceased beloved as though she were still a living woman! He had wise doctors from the Orient embalm the corpse to

沙樂美國王把那塊寶石──蛇為答謝他公正而送給他的禮物──看成是最珍貴的寶物，因此把它送給他心愛的妻子。這個聰明的女人很快就發現那塊寶石的魔力。

以前，國王還不時和別的女人眉來眼去，不過現在卻火熱地只愛王后一個。不管什麼時候，國王都要她陪伴左右，她也狂熱地愛著他。王后去世之前，她很害怕丈夫會忘記她，因此她把那塊魔石放在自己的舌頭下，準備帶進棺材裏。

結果，寶石的蛇魔力繼續保持：國王對他逝去妻子的愛，跟她還活著的時候一樣火熱。國王讓東方有智慧的醫生給王后的屍體注入香油，免得腐爛，從此無論去哪兒，他都一直帶著妻子的屍體。

這個情況維持了十八年。一天，一個聰明的騎士覺得國王對一個已去世的女人還愛得如此火熱，很是奇怪，於是仔細研究王后的屍體，最後找到了那神秘的寶石，他相信這便是國王如此依戀王后的原因。騎士一把那塊魔石放進自己的口袋後，國王對亡妻的愛便熄滅了，還下令馬上把屍體埋葬。

不過，國王突然愛上了那個聰明的騎士。不管騎士有什麼願望，願望有多奢侈，國王都為他一一實現，又送他數不清的禮物和榮譽。

一開始，騎士很享受這麼多的恩惠，但很快他便發現，王宮裏的人懷疑他和國王的關係，開始散播難聽的謠言。他覺得寶石雖然帶來好運，但也成為他很大的負擔，於是一次和國王騎馬的時候，騎士把那塊寶石扔到沼澤裏。他想，這樣就不會有人得到它了。

從那刻開始，國王對騎士完全失去興趣，卻非常喜歡那塊藏有寶石的沼澤地，於是，他在那裏興建了一座很漂亮的城市，更愛屋及烏，對搬來這城市居住的人民特別好，他們有什麼要求，國王都會答應。國王給這個城市起了一個名字「亞琛」。人們把這個城市看成是蘇黎世的女兒市。

preserve it from decay. Then he took it with him on all his exploits and adventures.

This lasted for eighteen years. Then, one day, it occurred to a shrewd knight that there was something not quite normal about this incredible love. He examined the dead body carefully and, sure enough, he found the mysterious gem. He concluded that it must be the cause of the Emperor's abnormal attachment. And indeed, as soon as the bold man put the magic gem into his pocket, the Emperor's affection for his deceased wife faded away. He ordered the corpse to be buried.

But now it was the shrewd knight who became the object of Charlemagne's loving affection. The Emperor hastened to fulfil his minion's every wish, no matter how extravagant it might be, and bestowed upon him honours and gifts without number.

For a while, the knight greatly enjoyed the boon. But soon he noticed that the courtiers were starting to spread nasty rumours about him and his royal friend. So he felt his good fortune to be burdensome, and one day, as he was riding out with the Emperor not far from the city of Cologne, he cast the gem into a marsh to ensure that no one would ever possess it again.

Immediately, Charlemagne lost all interest in the knight and devoted all his passion to the plot of damp earth where the snake's gift now lay. He found no peace until he had had a fine city built on the spot and endowed its inhabitants with favours of every kind.

And that is why this city – he named it Aix-la-Chapelle – is considered to be a daughter of the city of Zurich.

瑞士乳酪的秘密 | The Swiss Cheese Mystery

Once upon a time there was a king who desperately wanted to have the famous Swiss cheese produced in his kingdom. To that purpose he invited a number of Swiss dairymen to his country. But in spite of all their efforts they were unable to produce cheese of the required quality.

So they advised the disappointed king to send for some Swiss cows – which he did at considerable expense. Now he had Swiss dairymen and Swiss cows. But what they produced still did not taste like Swiss cheese.

After so many failed attempts, the doughty dairymen spoke again to the king saying: "We need your Royal Majesty to send for some Swiss mountains."

But, in spite of his immense wealth, the king did not have the means to do this. Perhaps also he lacked the faith which, as is generally known, can move mountains.

And so he had to make do without the cheese production he had so fervently desired for his kingdom. For you see, to make Swiss cheese you need more than Swiss cows and the skill of experienced dairymen: you also need the lofty Alps with their fragrant, aromatic mountain herbs.

許久以前，有一個國王因為想在自己的帝國裏製造瑞士乳酪，所以請了一些瑞士奶農到他的國家來。奶農雖然盡了很大的努力，但是仍做不出好的瑞士乳酪來。

國王很失望，奶農建議失望的國王運來瑞士的奶牛。雖然買這種牛並不便宜，國王卻同意了。儘管國王有瑞士奶農和瑞士牛了，但真正瑞士乳酪還是做不成。

失敗了好幾回，英勇的奶農再對國王說：「我們想請國王陛下把瑞士的山運過來。」

國王雖然很富有，但卻沒有把山運過來的方法。也許是他缺乏信心，誰都知道，只有信心可以移山。

結果，他希望在自己的帝國裏製造瑞士乳酪的夢想落空了。原來，製造瑞士乳酪不僅需要瑞士的奶農和奶牛，還需要阿爾卑斯山芬芳的香草。

World Change in Basel-Land

巴塞爾鄉村州的巨變

在巴塞爾鄉村州的利斯塔爾附近，一個農民埋葬一具死於瘟疫的動物屍體時，卻發現了一件令人驚歎的東西。他在泥土裏面找到了一塊很巨大的岩石。他想把它挖出來，但盡了力卻沒成功。

最奇怪的是，石頭裏有個鐵製的環，很堅固、結實，又完整無缺。他知道這麼特別的東西不可能是自然形成的，只有智慧的動物能夠創造。只是，他實在難以相信有人有這樣的本領。

這個農民就讓村子裏英明的鐵匠來看看這個奇特的東西。鐵匠仔細研究了一會，便想起了一個古老的傳說：很久以前，萊茵谷地區住過些巨人，男人女人都有。他們在知識和力氣方面都比現代人強。還有，現在的農田以前是個很大的湖——有些人還認為是個大海——一直伸展到山腳那裏。鐵匠想，巨人很可能用那

Once upon a time, near Liestal in Basel-Land, there was a farmer who made a remarkable discovery: while burying one of his animals that had died of a pestilential disease, he happened upon a massive piece of rock that was so big that he couldn't dig it out, however hard he tried.

The strangest thing about it was that there was a strong, solid, absolutely untarnished iron ring set deeply into the stone. The object was clearly the product of a rational creature; but it was quite inconceivable that anything like that could have been produced by human hand.

The farmer showed the sensational heathen object to the local blacksmith. After examining it carefully, the learned man said that it put him in mind of an old legend that related how, in times of yore, giant men and women had lived in the wider regions of the Rhine. These men and women had far surpassed present folk both in knowledge and in physical strength. Besides this, he said, what is now farmland used to be covered by great lakes – some even say a deep sea – right up to the foot of the mountains. Probably, he suggested, the strong ring had been used by the giants to tie up their boats, so that they wouldn't get swept away in storms or overturned by sea monsters.

The farmer, a clever man, was delighted with this information, which, as it seemed to him, just went to prove what great changes had come over our country in all those years. But he also thought: "If I leave the rock uncovered I'll be overrun by inquisitive people, and my fields will be trampled down by the noisy rabble – without my getting a penny in compensation. And there are bound to be treasure-seekers and people of the black arts come to examine these prehistoric relics in search of signs which might justify their shady dealings ..." So he covered up the ring with earth.

And thus his direct descendants are the only people in the world who might still know where the prehistoric giant blacksmiths' marvellous ring is to be found.

個大鐵環繫著他們的船，免得船被暴風雨捲走，或者被湖裏面的怪物弄沉。

農民是個聰明人，他聽了鐵匠的話後，感到很高興。他覺得這故事彷彿證明過去這麼多年，自己的國家確經歷了很明顯的變化。不過他突然想：「如果我把這塊岩石留在地上，很多好奇的人會來這裏看個究竟，踐踏我的田地；他們既嘈吵又粗魯，絕對不會賠償我的啊！天黑以後，還會有尋寶的人來研究這些史前遺物，巫師也會來，找尋什麼徵兆來解釋自己的作為……」於是，他將鐵環重新埋起來。

只有他直接的後代，才知道巨人鐵匠的神奇鐵環埋在哪裏。

艾因西德倫徽章上的烏鴉 / The Ravens in the Einsiedeln Coat of Arms

虔誠的聖麥拉德是一個來自興瑙島的僧人，他在艾茨爾山上蓋了一個小教堂。他當了僧人許久了，便決定作隱士，在荒野建築了個茅舍，自給自足地生活，還得到了周圍老百姓的施捨。他避免任何親密的人際關係，只和兩隻烏鴉在一起生活，愛護牠們，給牠們吃的等等。

他這樣生活了好多年，直至有一天兩個殘暴的兇手闖入他狹小的房子，殘酷無情地殺死他。

之後兩個壞人到了蘇黎世。不過不論他們到哪裏，和尚的兩隻烏鴉都呱呱地追過來，想給牠們的朋友報仇。兩個惡棍因為牠們尾隨不捨，良心越來越不安，其他人也開始對他們有了懷疑。終於，在一個旅店裏，這兩個殺人犯得到了應得的懲罰：他們承認了所犯的殘暴罪行而被判處死刑。

旅店因為這個事故而得到了「烏鴉」這個名稱。目前在麥拉德的小屋那兒，現在是艾因西德倫的寺院。因為兩隻烏鴉那麼忠誠，寺院的徽章上有他們的畫像。

Holy Saint Meinrad, who had for a long time been a monk in Reichenau, had a chapel built on the slopes of Mount Etzel. Later, he decided to become a hermit, and he built his hermitage in the wasteland nearby. There he lived by the work of his hands and alms from the neighbouring folk. He avoided all human converse, communing only with two ravens whom he lovingly fed.

Thus he lived for many a long year, until the day two cruel felons brutally murdered him in his tiny cell.

After their crime, the two evildoers betook themselves to Zurich. But everywhere they went they were tirelessly pursued by the threatening cawing of the two furious ravens crying out for vengeance for their human companion. These singular followers increasingly unsettled the two villains, stirring their conscience and arousing other people's suspicions. Finally, in an inn, the two murderers met their deserved fate: they admitted their heinous crime and were condemned to death.

Following this memorable event, the inn was named 'The Raven'. Einsiedeln Monastery now stands on the spot where Meinrad was murdered. And to commemorate the ravens' loyalty, the abbot had the two birds engraved in the monastery's coat of arms.

失去的運氣 Good Fortune Lost

It has often been said that the reason the gnomes left our neighbourhood was because of man's deceit and his ever-increasing avarice. That is why gnomes are seldom to be seen nowadays. However, there are also stories that show that it was people's curiosity that disturbed them, and also the vain arrogance of the farmers who wanted them to conform to their way of life.

A man from Thurgovia, whose cattle had always been well protected and cared for during the dark nights by a gnome, managed one evening to spy on his tiny helper. He was surprised to see that his little friend from the mountain cave, who was such an expert with cattle, was miserably dressed in rags like a wretched beggar.

"You poor fool," thought the farmer, short-sightedly putting down the shabbiness of the gnome's attire to his poverty or simple-mindedness. "Your clothing is no good, but now I'll reward you for your work."

He took out his best jerkin and had a little coat tailored out of the material. He then laid it at the entrance to the gnome's cave. Then he hid, because he was keen to see how the little fellow would react in the light of such a generous gift.

But the moment the gnome saw the blue coat, he waxed extremely angry. "Vain farmer," he exclaimed, "if you but knew how little I care for your commiseration! Now you can do your work on your own, you've forfeited my help for ever."

Thereupon, he slipped back into his cave and was never seen again.

很多人都説山精靈在我們周圍消失,是因為人們越來越不誠實和貪婪。但也有其他説法:人類的好奇心令山精靈不安。還有,驕傲虛榮的農民總想把他們的生活方式和想法,強加於山精靈身上。

圖爾高州有一個山精靈常常夜裏出沒,幫助一個農民照顧他的牲畜。一天晚上,農民偷看山精靈幹活,驚訝地發現他這個穴居深山,精於飼養牛隻的小友,原來穿的衣服是那麼的破爛,就像很窮的乞丐一樣。農民想:「你這個可憐的傻子,穿的衣服是那麼的破爛,現在我要回報你了。」農民的目光實在短淺,他以為山精靈是因為貧窮或者愚笨,才穿這麼破舊的衣服。

農民把他最好的上衣,改成山精靈合穿的衣服。縫製完了以後,他把這件漂亮的衣服放在山精靈的洞穴前面,然後躲起來,看看小傢伙對他慷慨的禮物有什麼反應。

山精靈一看到那件藍色的衣服,便大為震怒。「你這虛榮的農夫,」他喊道,「我並不需要你的同情!你現在辦自己的事兒好了,我不會再幫忙!」

把話説完以後,山精靈便返回洞穴,從此消失,再也沒有出現了。

Three Merry Days and then to the Devil

三個素不相識的小夥子在旅途中恰巧相遇，他們以為自己所遭遇到的棘手事情特別多，因此對命運都有怨言。三人囊空如洗，連背包中僅有的破爛襯衣都不敢拿到河裏去洗，恐怕整件衣服會在水中散掉。

當他們悶悶不樂，在積塵的路上行走時，其中一名小夥子說：「瞧我，自幼命途坎坷，恨不能可以吃喝玩樂痛痛快快地過一天，事後縱使要效忠魔鬼，我也甘心呢！」

第二個說：「我的遭遇比你的可還差，一輩子就知道黑麥麵包和乳酪的味道，富貴人家天天吃的菜，我壓根兒未曾見過。我很贊同你的看法，那怕就為了短短一段逍遙的日子，出賣這一生也願意！」

年紀最小的第三個說：「直到今天，我可以數算的光是惡劣日子。新近有了份好差事，工錢還不少，卻只恨生病，又白白把它丟失了。可我沒放棄將有好轉的盼頭，就為了美食豪飲，我是不會出賣自己不朽的靈魂的！」

第一個小夥子沒有動搖，他堅定地說：「痛快三天然後效忠魔鬼！」第二個贊成，他們的眼睛閃閃發光。

One day, quite by chance, three journeymen who had never seen each other before met on the road. Each was dissatisfied with his fate, which had been crueller to him than to other people, or so he thought. Not a penny did they have in their pockets, and all they had in their satchels were tattered shirts they didn't dare wash in the stream for fear they might come apart in the water.

As they walked joylessly along the dusty highway, one of them said: "Ever since childhood I've known nothing but hardship. If only I could enjoy myself just once in my life and have enough to eat and to drink, why, I wouldn't mind going to the Devil for it!"

The second one said: "My life has been even harder than yours. I've never eaten anything but rye bread and cheese, and I've never ever even tasted the kind of fine food that gets served at the tables of the rich. So I'm of the same mind. I'd give the rest of my life to be really carefree, even for a very short time."

The third, who was also the youngest, said: "I've had a lot of bad luck too. Recently I was offered a good job with good wages, but then I fell ill and lost it. But I still live in hope of better days, and I wouldn't want to sacrifice my immortal soul just for food and booze."

"Three days and to the Devil!" cried the first, and the second chimed in, and their eyes glistened.

At that moment they saw a finely dressed gentleman coming along the road. They hadn't noticed him before, although the road was dead straight with no paths leading into it.

The strange gentleman was wearing an elegant black suit and a little green hat with a raven's feather in it. He stopped and, with a mocking smile on his lips, said: "What's the matter with you? Your eyes are popping out of your heads like owls that have had nothing to eat for a week. You want three merry days? You can have them. You'll laugh yourselves silly. And when the three days are over, you still won't belong to the Devil yet. All you'll have to do is answer three riddles that are as easy as pie. Nothing else! And if you answer correctly, you'll be free. Well, isn't that a deal?"

The two elder journeymen agreed immediately, and the third fellow also gave his hand to it, albeit reluctantly. The gentleman in black bowed low and disappeared.

Only then did they notice the mark of a cloven hoof in the dust on the highway.

As evening approached the three companions arrived at a village where a jolly feast was in full swing. They sat down at the inn next to the merry lads and lasses and started enjoying themselves. Ordering only of the very best, they treated everyone to joints of meat and fiery wines. And their guests, seeing that the money in their pockets never ran out, concluded that they were wealthy gentlemen. The carousing, the revelry and the dancing lasted all night. Never before had the village known such wild festivity.

The next morning, as the first rays of sunlight

忽而，不知從哪兒來了一位衣著高貴的紳士。筆直的路上可沒有支路啊！

陌生先生戴著綠色小帽，跟他黑色雅致的上衣搭配得宜，帽子上插著一支烏鴉羽毛。他含著嘲諷的微笑對三名小夥子說：「你們怎麼樣了？瞪著眼睛就像一星期沒吃東西的貓頭鷹。你們想玩耍三天！成，我會讓你們笑破肚皮。三天過後，你們仍不用立刻效忠魔鬼，只需要回答三道易如反掌的問題，如能答上，便自由了。來，我們擊掌搞定好了！」

年紀稍大的兩個小夥子立即答應了，第三個似乎老不願意，但結果還是伸出手表示同意。那黑衣先生深鞠躬一下，便消失了。

他們這才發現馬路塵土上的羊蹄印。

傍晚時分，三名小夥子來到了一個村莊，那裏恰巧舉辦盛宴。他們就陪同其他青年男女在旅舍玩個痛快。三人點菜挑酒，要的都是最好的，並招待其他人，只因他們的錢包裏永不缺錢，人家都以為他們是貴家子弟呢。大伙兒吃喝玩樂了一個通宵，如此放縱的盛宴，這村子裏還未曾有過。

第二天早晨，當第一線太陽光穿過窗葉照進來的時候，最年輕的小夥子偷偷地鑽出去了。他問心有愧，想起魔鬼的三道問題，怕有個惡劣的結局，於是遠離村莊，越野而行，到了太陽當空，依著一棵大梨樹躺下來。當他瞧著枝葉和藍天，琢磨魔鬼會提出什麼問題的時候，明晰地聽到從上方傳來的聲音：「就這一次，我會幫助你，不會有下次了。拿你所配的刀子，在樹幹周圍挖地，把泥土覆蓋在自己的頭上吧。即將有上千隻烏鴉飛過來，落在樹枝上。你可仔細聽聽牠們嘮叨的內容。」

那小夥子跳起來了。剛才是做夢嗎？他不知道。他拿出刀子，翻起樹身周圍的草地，把一塊一塊的泥土挖出來後，蓋在自己的頭上。工作一完畢，果真有一群烏鴉飛過來，嘰嘰喳喳地落在樹枝上。這些身披羽毛的魔鬼，把梨樹變成一片黑色。

小夥子一聲不響，細心傾聽。他清清楚楚聽到兩隻在自己頭上的大烏鴉談話：「你這食屍鬼，真沒用，從來沒有捉住個靈魂，我可就一下子得到三個！」

「什麼？你是我們這群中最笨的，哪能一下子得到三個呢？我不相信。」另外那個叫起來。

pierced the shutters, the youngest of the three companions crept away. Suddenly his conscience had assailed him, and he thought with horror of the three riddles the Devil would ask them and of the terrible end that awaited them. He wandered off until the inn was out of sight. On and on he went across the fields, and when the sun had reached its zenith he flung himself down under a great pear tree. As he was staring up through the branches into the blue sky imagining what the Devil would ask, he distinctly heard a little voice above his head say: "For this once I'll help you, but never again. Take your knife, cut out some of the turf at the root of the tree and cover your head with it. A thousand ravens will come flying, and they will settle in the branches. Listen carefully to what they say."

The fellow leapt up. Had he been dreaming in his sleep? He didn't know. He pulled out his knife and cut out patches of turf from the ground around the tree and covered his head with them. He'd hardly finished, when a flock of ravens came flying up and settled chattering and screeching in the branches of the tree, which was soon all black with the feathered devils.

The lad lay there, quiet as a mouse, listening. He distinctly heard two of the blackguards in conversation right above his head.

"You lousy old scavenger, you've never caught a single soul! As for me, I'm getting three at once."

"What? You're the most stupid of us all and you say you've caught three souls. I don't believe it," shrieked the other.

"Well, just you listen to me," croaked his companion. "I hold three journeymen in my clutches. At the moment they're over in the village dancing, eating and boozing to their heart's content. Another two days and they'll be mine!"

"Tell that to your mother! You can't fool me, carrion crow."

"Well, they're mine, as sure as I'm sitting here. They'll have to answer three riddles: what did I give them as a musician, what as a lamp, and what as a blanket? Ha, ha, they'll never guess. But I'll tell you: the musician's the innkeeper's cat; the lamp's the besom broom I stole from the cook; and the blanket is the cowhide I took from the innkeeper. There's no way they'll ever guess."

The croaking and squabbling in the tree grew louder and louder and harsher and harsher. Then, suddenly and all at once, the flock flew up with a great clamour and disappeared.

The journeyman got up from beneath the tree, carefully replaced the clods of turf, folded his knife, and made up his mind to leave his dissolute companions as soon as he had freed them from the Devil's claws. Slowly he wended his way back to the inn, going over and over the three riddles in his mind in order to memorise them.

That night, by the time he reached the inn, the music had died down, and silence had fallen. There, on the stone bench in front of the house, sat his two companions, staring bleakly into the distance, their dishevelled hair hanging down over their faces.

第一隻大烏鴉答覆説：「你聽著吧！我抓住三個小夥子，他們目下還在村子裏狂飲歡宴，跳舞不住，過兩天便都是我的了。」

「找你媽説去吧，你騙不到我的，食屍鬼！」

「我保證他們即將是我的。他們得回答我三個謎語：我會給他們一個怎樣的音樂師，一盞怎樣的燈，一張怎樣的毯子。哈，哈，他們永遠也猜不到，但我告訴你：音樂師是旅舍老闆的貓，燈是掃帚做的，我從廚師那兒偷來的，毯子是旅舍老闆那兒捎來的牛皮。他們不可能猜到哩。」

樹上粗暴的嘈嘈嘈嘈聲越來越大，突然，一整群烏鴉震天價響地一下子飛走了。

樹下的小夥子立刻站起來，他將一塊塊草地放回原地，拼成原狀，收拾了刀子，決定把那兩個放蕩的朋友從魔鬼爪裏拯救出來後，就要離開他們。他徐步朝來路折返，還反復背誦那三道難題，以便牢記。

傍晚時分，他回到了旅舍。音樂已停，喧鬧已畢，那兩個小夥子披頭散髮，坐在房前的石凳上絕望地發呆。魔鬼所應允的快樂日子，三天才過了一天，他們早對這種生活方式感到厭煩了。年輕小夥子不想把他們從沉思中喚醒，於是沒把夢說出來，只管待到第二天、第三天都過去了。老闆常問他們還想吃什麼喝什麼，但是他們已經吃膩了，沒理睬他。

第四天的早上，三人從臥榻起來，收拾行裝，繼續上路，但還未踏出村子，魔鬼就在他們跟前出現了。他臉上含著得意的微笑，摸摸下巴，問了那三道問題。

年長的兩個小夥子當然答不出什麼來，昨夜的狂歡還叫他們頭疼不已。他們嚇得臉孔發青，環顧四周，希望找到人搭救他們。

這時，那年輕小夥子挺身而出，說：「由我來回答吧。」

「瞧你的！」魔鬼獰笑了，「那麼，

Although only the first of the three merry days promised by the Devil had gone by, they already felt wearied. The youth did not rouse his fellow journeymen from their dull brooding. Without telling anyone of his dream, he waited patiently until the second and the third day had passed. During this time, the landlord often asked the three men what else they would like to eat and drink, but they felt surfeited and gave him short shrift.

The fourth day arrived. The three men got up, packed their satchels, and were soon back on the road. But they'd hardly left the village when the Devil appeared in front of them, a satisfied smirk on his face. Stroking his chin, he asked his three questions.

The two elder fellows had no idea what to answer. Their heads were still aching from their carousal. Their faces pale with a deathly fear, they looked around to see if there was no one who could help them out of their horrible predicament.

Then the youngest fellow stepped forward and said: "I will answer your questions."

"Well, what about that!" said the Devil, grimacing and laughing maliciously. "We'll soon see. Well then, what did I give you as a musician?"

"If you had left the innkeeper his cat," answered the lad, "the mice wouldn't have eaten the bacon."

"Hmm, hmm," muttered the Devil, and a shadow fell across his face. "Well, here's the second question: What did I give you as a lamp?"

"If you had left the cook her besom broom, she'd have swept up the cinders better, and the floorboards wouldn't have been scorched."

"Not bad, not bad!" admitted the Devil. "But now here's the third question," he added, standing there with his legs apart, scowling angrily. "What did I give you as a blanket?"

The lad replied without hesitating: "If you hadn't stolen the cowhide from the innkeeper, his wife wouldn't have to go around barefoot!"

All this time, the two elder journeymen had been listening, breathless with amazement. They were completely astounded. But the Devil ran off in a rage, leaving behind him such a stench that the three companions almost fainted.

咱們瞧著吧。我給你們一個怎麼樣的音樂師？」

小夥子回答說：「你要是沒拿走老闆那隻貓，老鼠就不會把燻肉吃掉了！」

魔鬼的臉上掠過了一層陰影，咕噥道：「哼，哼，第二個問題咱來看：我給你們一盞怎麼樣的燈？」

「你如果沒拿走廚師的掃帚，她便會好好兒地打掃煤灰，地板就不可能燒焦了！」

魔鬼說：「觀察得不錯，可就要解答第三個問題了。」魔鬼叉開雙腿，發怒地說：「我給你們一張怎麼樣的毯子？」

小夥子毫不遲疑地說：「你沒偷老闆的牛皮的話，老闆娘就不會赤著腳走路了！」

那兩個年長的小夥子聽著，目瞪口呆，驚訝不已。魔鬼氣沖沖地跑掉，只留下了一股惡臭，差一點使三個小夥子暈倒呢。

Cherryboy

當紳士和百姓還相信巫師和巫術時,蘇黎
世有一個道行很高的巫師。他常坐在一個
木盆裏,飛過山林湖泊去騷擾人民。他能
偷什麼就偷什麼,但是偶爾也把偷來的東
西分給窮人。收穫櫻桃時,他總是第一個
攀上樹去偷櫻桃的,所以被叫做「櫻桃男
孩」。警員和官員都想緝拿他歸案,但總
抓不著他。有一次,他還在蘇黎世街上邊
走邊高聲唱歌,故意挑釁:

> 蘇黎世人可能甚狡猾
> 他們的教堂塔尖也許很高
> 雖然他們有目光敏銳的眼睛
> 卻奈何不了櫻桃男孩鬼靈精

終於,他還是被抓個正著,給困在籠
子裏,很快便會被絞死。處決之前,他可
以許最後一個願望。

「給我一綑藤,」他説。收到藤之
後,他假裝編織;然後把藤球往上扔,順
著藤往上爬,最後消失了。

過了一段時間,警員又抓住他。

In the days when the gentry and the common folk all still believed in witches and witchery, there lived in Zurich a talented young master of witchcraft. He would travel across mountains and lakes in a tub, spreading terror throughout the land. He'd steal whatever came his way, but sometimes he redistributed it among poor people. During the cherry harvest, he'd be the first to climb up the trees to steal cherries, and that's how he got the name of Cherryboy. The sheriff and the bailiff were always hot on his trail, but somehow they never managed to arrest him. Once he even haunted the streets of Zurich singing at the top of his voice:

> *Zurich burghers may be sly*
> *And their church spires may be high*
> *But even their gimlet-sharp eyes*
> *Cannot find where Cherryboy lies.*

But then they did find him. They arrested him and put him into a cage. Sentence was soon passed: he was to be hanged. But before the execution, he was allowed one last wish.

"Give me a ball of twine," he said. They gave him one and – upon my word – he pretended to start knitting. But then, no, he threw the ball up into the sky, climbed up the rope and disappeared from view.

Some time after that, they caught him again.

"No last wish this time!" said the Zurich aldermen. "We'll knock off his block at once. That way the scoundrel won't be able to make fun of us again! Ha, we'll teach him!" And they led him to the scaffold and blindfolded him. The executioner raised his axe ... but then he stopped in mid-air. He had suddenly noticed that Cherryboy had three heads on his neck. Utterly confused, he asked the mayor, "Which of the three heads do you want me to cut off?"

The mayor had no idea what to answer. But then a shout came up from a bystander in the waiting crowd.

"Throw an apple into the air. Cut it apart with your sword as it falls. Then you'll see which head to cut off."

The executioner did as he was told. He threw up the apple and, as it fell, he sliced it exactly through the middle. Therefore he cut off Cherryboy's middle head. And that was the end of rogue Cherryboy.

「這次沒有最後願望了!」蘇黎世的議員說,「馬上砍他的頭,這無賴子便不能再捉弄我們了!哈,合該教訓教訓他!」他們把犯人帶到刑場,把他的眼睛蒙起來。劊子手舉起斧頭準備行刑……卻在半空停下來。他突然發現櫻桃男孩有三個頭,便萬分迷惘地問市長:「三頭之中,我割掉哪一個?」

市長也不知道。觀看處決的觀眾中有人喊道:「把一個蘋果往上扔,蘋果跌下來時你用劍把它切開,這樣你就知道該把哪一個頭割掉。」

劊子手就這樣做。蘋果正好在中間分開,劊子手就把櫻桃男孩中間的頭割掉。無賴的櫻桃男孩就這樣死了。

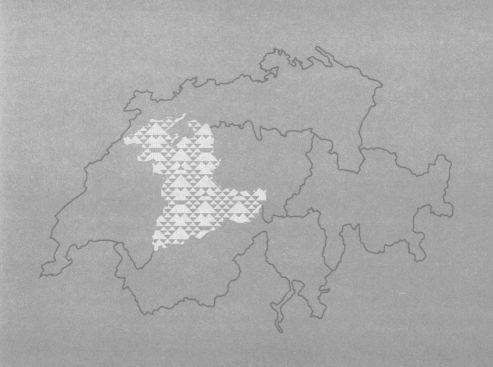

伯爾尼州的傳說

Legends from
the Canton of Bern

Medical Skill in the Emmental

愛蒙塔爾之醫術

十八世紀，來自朗鬧村的米歐利秀琶毫無疑問是頂呱呱的驗尿大師。東西南北各方的高貴人士都來到他在愛蒙塔爾的家中求診，詩人歌德也覺得他了不起。

一天，一個雇農帶了他患病的主人的尿液來，可是他尷尬得一個詞也説不出主人發生了什麼事。米歐利仔細地注視著尿液。

「你的主人，」米歐利開始説：「登上了梯子，然後摔下六級，把左腿折斷了……可是，你是不是在路上潑瀉了一點尿液？」他突然嚴屬地問雇農。雇農好糊塗地點了點頭。「這我早就料到了！」醫師沉思地説，「現在清楚了：他摔下七級！」

In the 18th century, the foremost expert on urine was undisputedly Micheli Schüppach. Fine ladies and gentlemen from all over the world would come to consult him at his home in Lengnau in the Emmental. Even the great poet Goethe was impressed.

One day, a farm labourer brought him urine from his sick master. The lad was too shy, however, to describe the farmer's condition. The doctor examined the urine carefully.

"Your master," began Micheli, "climbed up a ladder, then fell down six rungs and broke his left leg … But are you sure you didn't spill some of his water on the way?" he suddenly asked sternly. The labourer, quite confused, nodded. "That's what I thought," said the doctor pensively. "Now things are clear: he fell down seven rungs."

The Strong Man from Trub

來自吐魯比的力士

Young Millbacher from Trub in the Emmental had drunk of his mother's milk for many more years than was wont. That is why he grew stronger than all his fellows and very soon became the greatest wrestler in the region.

Year after year, at the herdsmen's Annual Wrestling Festival in Bern, he was crowned 'King of Wrestlers'. Only once was he defeated: by one Heineli Roth, a fellow from one of the ancient Swiss cantons on the Lake of Lucerne. But everyone knew Roth had cheated – while shaking hands before the contest, the sly fellow had surreptitiously slipped two solid silver thalers into Millbacher's palm.

The invincible fighter's renown spread far and wide. "Let the Devil come," he boasted arrogantly. "I'll show him my mettle!"

Very soon his urge, or rather, the overwhelming

年輕的米伯查來自愛蒙塔爾的吐魯比,他喝母乳的時間比別人長了好多年,所以他比全部其他小夥子強壯得多,很快便成為這一帶最優秀的摔跤手。

在伯爾尼牧人周年摔跤節中,他給封為「摔跤手之王」已好幾年。他只被打敗了一次:栽在一個來自琉森湖附近古瑞士聯邦的鄉下人小海因裏羅夫的手上。 但是誰都知道羅夫作弊 - 摔跤手握手打招呼時,那狡猾的羅夫把兩塊銀幣塞在米伯查的手裏⋯⋯

米伯查是誰都不能戰勝的摔跤手,他的榮譽傳播得越來越遠。「如果魔鬼也來，我就要給他點顏色看看！」米伯查大放厥詞。

　　不久，米伯查想考驗每個人的力氣，他這種衝動，這種無法壓抑的慾望，很快就使他變成全國畏懼的人物。每一個路上偶然遇到他的人，都馬上給他抓住，狠狠地摔到地上。不久，人們迫不得已雇用特別的「警告者」。不管米伯查要到什麼地方去，這個「警告者」就在他的前邊跑，警告人們遠遠地避開他。

　　這樣過了許久，一位很難看的小個子出現了，他聽到了「警告者」膽怯的警告，只帶笑毫無懼色地向好戰的巨人繼續走去。不出所料，米伯查立刻抓住那小個子，粗暴地把他摔到地上；但是這小個子像閃電一樣快地跳起來，一把抓住強大的吐魯比人的領子，像拖著一個麵粉口袋一樣，拉著他向前走，越過郊野，穿過高山峽谷，跨過地面上的種種障礙，直到米伯查滿身瘀傷，一輩子變成殘廢。

　　米伯查永不可以再在摔跤節中奪取桂冠了。他和周圍的人一樣，都沒有懷疑戰勝他的小個子的真正身份。

and insatiable craving he felt to prove his excessive strength made him the terror of the land. Anyone unfortunate enough to cross his path would be instantly grabbed by the belt and thrown onto his back in the dust. It became necessary to employ a special 'warner' who would run in front of Millbacher whenever he went out, and warn everyone to get out of the way.

Things had gone on like this for quite long enough when, one day, there came an ugly little man who merely smiled at the guard's timorous warning and walked fearlessly on towards the aggressive giant. As was to be expected, Millbacher instantly seized the little fellow in a wrestling hold and threw him roughly to the ground. But in a flash the little man had jumped back onto his feet. Grabbing the powerful man from Trub by the collar, he dragged him cross-country, through hill and dale, over sticks and stones, as if he were but a dusty flour bag, until he was so battered and bruised that he was to remain a poor cripple for the rest of his life.

Never again would he win beautiful laurel wreaths at the wrestling competitions. And that is why, like everyone else in the neighbourhood, he had not the slightest doubt concerning the true identity of the nondescript little man who had defeated him.

The Freemen from Iseltwald

艾素華的自由戰士

One day, a very long time ago, an emperor of the Holy Roman Empire of the German Nation called on his allies in the Bernese Oberland to fulfil their pledge and supply him with militiamen for a new campaign. Whereupon the stalwart mountain men informed him: "We shall send His Imperial Majesty three soldiers from the village of Iseltwald on Lake Brienz."

To the Emperor, this answer smacked of treachery and insubordination. But the mountain men soon managed to reassure him. "Our three men are worth more than a whole army of ordinary folk. Please condescend to take a look at them. Then you will see."

The Emperor soon saw that they were right. The three men from Iseltwald were mighty giants, clothed in the skins of the wild mountain beasts: the bear and the wolf. For weapons they had felled three beech trees with trunks as thick as a man's thighs; they had stripped them of their twigs and branches and now carried them on their shoulders like light javelins. And when the Emperor's armies marched into battle, the colossal giants stood out like moving towers among the mass of the foot-soldiers.

The Emperor soon noticed that if he had had more of those mountain men they would have obstructed one another during the battle, and victory would have been delayed. Indeed, the three men from Iseltwald

古時候，一位德意志族羅馬帝國國王要求跟他結盟的伯爾尼茲山人遵守諾言，在他出征的時候給他提供戰士。忠實的山區居民答應了，「我們送給陛下三個來自布裏恩茲湖艾素華村的士兵。」

聽到這句話以後，國王覺得伯爾尼茲山人以下犯上，對他不敬。伯爾尼茲山人馬上向國王保證：我們這三個人比普通一支村民軍隊更強。請屈就一下，看看他們便知道了。」皇帝很快便知道他們沒有誇大，三位艾素華人真是強大的巨人。他們穿的衣服是野生動物的毛皮，熊的，狼的……，他們的武器是在山毛櫸小叢林裏砍下的。他們削去樹枝以後，把腿一般粗的樹幹像輕標槍似的扛著。國王的軍隊向敵營進發時，三位巨人便像行走的鐘樓似的，鶴立於士兵之中。

國王很快便覺察到，如果他要更多的山地人來，打仗的時候他們會互相阻礙，勝利就會推遲了。若要把敵人擊斃，或把生存者嚇跑，光是那三個艾素華人的木棒已經足夠了。

於是國王對那些巨人說：「你們隨便選擇報酬吧，我衷心感謝你們的幫忙。」

艾素華人謙虛而莊重地說：「我們只希望陛下允許一件事：若將來我們鄉有一百人入伍從軍，我們可以配戴光榮的皇鷹徽號。至於我們自己，則只有一個願望：夏天時，希望陛下允許我們在農村的湖邊走得口渴時，可以在布尼根的菜田，也就是這帝國的屬地，每人拔掉三個胡蘿蔔拿走，手裏一個，腰帶裏兩個。」

國王仁慈地允許他們的請求。從那天起，巨人便經常吃那多汁的胡蘿蔔。至於艾素華人配戴皇鷹徽號的事——艾素華鄉永遠人口太少，送到戰場去的士兵從來不夠一百人。

聽說，在因特拉肯附近麥頓村那兒，有觀察力的旅者會在一所房子的一隻窗的彩色玻璃上，找到一幅關於這古代故事的圖畫。畫中描繪的是一隻巨大的熊，牠腰帶裏帶著幾個胡蘿蔔。

with their giant cudgels were all that was needed to cut the enemy to pieces and put to desperate flight the few who had managed to survive the slaughter.

Thereafter the Emperor summoned the men from Iseltwald and said: "Choose what you will as your reward. Your service has earned our infinite gratitude."

The men from Iseltwald replied with dignified modesty: "We request only one thing of His Majesty: that he give our village licence to carry the proud imperial eagle in its coat-of-arms as soon as we have one hundred men we can send into battle. For ourselves, we have but one wish: that His Majesty give each of us licence to dig out three carrots from the vegetable patches in Bönigen (which are on territory of the realm) whenever we get there all thirsty from the long walk on a hot summer's day along the lakeshore from Iseltwald; that is, a carrot to hold in the hand, and two more to stick into our belts for later."

The Emperor graciously granted their demands, and from then on the giants frequently refreshed themselves with the juicy carrots. But as far as the privilege for Iseltwald to bear an eagle in its coat of arms is concerned, the village was ever to remain too small to send a hundred able-bodied mercenaries to battle.

By the way, observant travellers have reported seeing a stained-glass window in a house in the village of Matten near Interlaken which probably has some bearing on this old tale: the window shows a mighty bear wearing a couple of carrots in its belt.

失去的溫暖　Lost Warmth

In times long gone by, the slopes of Mount Langenegg in the canton of Bern used to be covered in vineyards that produced a most excellent wine. But then, as so often happens, the folk in the valley grew presumptuous and dissolute and less and less deserving of such easily earned bounty.

One day, a mountain gnome suddenly appeared in the neighbourhood and went around giving the following warning to anyone who was willing to listen: "At the moment, Mount Langenegg has a fine vineyard," he told the godless folk. "By the time I come again, it will be pastureland. And if I have to come a third time, all I'll see will be a glacier."

The people weren't given much time to mock at his wise words. An icy breath fell over the land, cooling the warm glow of the sun. Grapes and other fruit no longer ripened. Soon the whole area could only by used to graze cattle.

These days, people think with horror of the next change prophesied by the gnome.

很久以前，伯爾尼州的長峰山上有很多葡萄樹。用那裏的葡萄做酒，很是好喝。不過，住在那兒的人越來越自大放任，不太珍惜他們來得太易的一切。

一天，一位山精靈來到這個地區，他警告那裏的人說：「現在，長峰山有很好的葡萄園，不過我下次來這兒時，這塊土地只能用來放牧。我第三次來的時候，在這兒只能見到冰川。」

人們聽到山精靈這麼說，只放聲大笑。但是過了一段時間，寒冷的風來了，冷卻了太陽溫暖的光芒，葡萄和其他水果都不能成熟。沒過很久，這塊土地就只能用來放牧。

目前，住在那兒的人都很害怕——山精靈最後的預言會應驗嗎？

惡城　The Wicked City

伯爾尼州的西門谷現在是瓦森堡、澳泊威爾和別的小村子的所在地。

　　古時候，那裏有一個很漂亮和富有的城市。一天晚上，一個很窮、衣衫襤褸的小侏儒來到這個城市，他敲每個房子的門，求人家施捨。無論他到那裏，人們都表現得冷漠和輕蔑，只有城外一個很窮的人家，讓小侏儒進他們的茅舍來，與他一起吃了一頓便飯。善心的那家人，是一個老頭兒和他的女兒。

　　吃完飯以後，小侏儒拿一個鋤頭，在茅舍的周圍挖了一條溝。善良的老頭和女兒感到奇怪，但他們只是微笑，沒有阻止他。小侏儒把溝挖完以後，山裏突然傳來雷聲，整個城市戰慄起來。土地、岩石，都像大海一樣崩塌，把這自私的城市，及它所有的財富與冷酷無情的居民都埋葬了，只有善良好客的老人一家及他們的茅舍安然無恙，因為，侏儒挖的那道溝保護他們。

In the Simmen Valley in the canton of Bern, just where Weissenburg, Oberwil and other small villages are now situated, there is said to have once stood a big and wealthy city. One day, a ragged little man turned up there late in the evening, and went from house to house begging for alms. But wherever he went, he encountered nothing but indifference or cold scorn – except in one poor cottage just outside the great city. There a poor old man and his daughter, without much ado, invited the strange beggar to partake of their meagre meal. Whereupon the little man immediately seized a pick and with great zeal set to digging a ditch around his benefactors' cottage.

The old man and his daughter stood by, smiling indulgently as they watched the bedraggled little dwarf at his frantic work. But the manikin had hardly finished when they heard a thundering roar coming from the mountains, and a great black surge of earth and rocks came tumbling down onto the selfish city, burying it together with all its riches and its hard-hearted citizens.

Thus the wicked city was punished. But the little cottage and the hospitable old man and his kind daughter were spared, thanks to the ditch the manikin had dug.

牧輪曲的來源
The Origins
of the 'Kuhreigen'

In the evenings, when the sun starts going down behind the mountains, bathing their eternal snows in a red glow, the herdsman steps out in front of his chalet and, using a milk-funnel to amplify the sound, sings his evensong. The sound swoops down across the slopes and pastures. It is followed by the 'Kuhreigen', a tune the herdsman plays on his horn to call his cows home. With its long drawn-out melancholic succession of notes, the music has a magical effect on cows. But it also strangely affects human beings. It echoes back from the mountainside, filling the air with the sound of yearning.

Here now is the story of the origins of the 'Kuhreigen' and of why a herdsman started to play it.

Once upon a time, in the lofty mountains above the valleys of the Bernese Oberland, a herdsman named Res was tending his cows in their summer pastures. He had taken them up there in the spring. Every evening, after milking the cows, he made butter and cheese out of their snowy white milk. He lived all alone up there with his animals. So when he had done his day's work, he would go up to the fir tree near his chalet and sing an evening song for his sweetheart, who lived down in the valley near the lake.

One evening, Res was once again standing outside his chalet watching the full moon rise from behind the mountains, feeling the light breeze wafting across the pastures as night fell, when a strange feeling of

夜幕降臨，夕陽在山後落下，日落紅霞把全年積雪的地區染成了紅色，牧人拿著牛奶漏斗當作揚聲器，唱起一首黃昏之歌。歌聲飄揚，在山坡與草場上回響。之後，牧人用阿爾卑斯號角吹奏牧輪曲。他就是用這首曲調來引牧牛回家的。牧輪曲是一闋比較緩緩而憂鬱的曲調。音律有魔法一般的效果，不僅牧牛被它感動，人類也被它感動。山坡發出牧輪曲的回聲，整個地區充滿了思慕的聲音。

這裏講的是關於牧輪曲的來源，以及牧人開始吹奏這闋曲調的原因。

很久以前，伯爾尼谷上的高山，有一位叫德烈斯的牧人。每年夏天，他常常來這兒放牧，其實春天時，他已經把牛帶來。每個晚上，擠過牛奶之後，他便用白色的牛奶製造牛油與乳酪。就他一個人住在草場，伴著他的，只有牧牛。一天的工作完成以後，他就走到小屋附近的一棵松樹下唱起歌來，獻給住在湖邊山谷的愛人。

一個晚上，他又站在小屋前，看著月兒從山後升起來，他感到輕風隨著夜幕從牧場那邊飄過來，他心裏很抑鬱，也很想家。他返回屋子，在貯藏牛奶的房間裏喝了一碗牛奶，然後沿梯子爬上閣樓。他的床就在清香的乾草上。儘管他很憂鬱，可是一天的勞累還是讓他很快便睡著了。

半夜他醒過來，彷彿聽到有人打開了門，他感到房間裏吹起一陣涼風。然後，他清晰地聽到樓下有腳步聲，木板發出喀嚓喀嚓的響聲，好像有人在弄他的牛奶鍋。德烈斯悄悄的起床，從地板的縫隙往下面看。他吃驚極了，三個奇怪的男人把一個造乳酪的大銅鍋抬到爐灶上！灶已經點火了。他剛想開口問他們三更夜半在他屋子裏幹啥，就看到其中一個人把一百二十多斤的牛奶鍋舉起來，好像牛奶鍋輕如鴻毛似的。跟這樣的人打架有什麼好處呢？德烈斯想，只好一聲不響。

他還是很好奇，這三個奇怪的男人在幹什麼呢？三個男人中最健碩的一個有一張火紅的臉，血脈好粗，看起來像一根根的粗繩子。他長著蓬亂的鬍子，手腕上戴著一根皮帶，左手中指上戴了一枚很大的鐵指套。第二個男人是個臉色蒼白的少年，金黃色的頭髮披到他的肩膀。他從地下室拿來木碗子，把牛奶倒到鍋裏，牛奶一點也沒灑出來。

第三個男人交叉兩腿坐在爐灶旁。他穿緊身的草綠色獵人衣服，一聲不響地把

melancholy and homesickness overcame him. He returned to his hut, drank another bowl of milk in the small cool room where the milk was kept, and then climbed the ladder to the loft where he had his bed on a layer of sweet-smelling hay. Despite his melancholy, he fell asleep at once.

In the middle of the night he suddenly awoke. It seemed to him he had heard someone open the door of the hut, and he felt a cool draught of air come into the room. Then he distinctly heard the sound of footsteps on the floor below and the snapping and crackling of wood. It also seemed to him that someone was tampering with his milk pans. He got up silently and, looking down through the opening in the floor of the loft, saw to his dismay three strange men dragging the large copper cheese kettle to the hearth in which the fire was already burning. He was about to shout out in anger and ask the men what they thought they were doing in his chalet in the middle of the night, when he saw one of the men lift up the hundred-and-twenty-pound kettle as if it were a feather. There's no point getting involved with someone like that, he said to himself, and kept as quiet as a mouse.

Fascinated, he watched to see what the men were doing. The biggest of the three had a flaming red face with protruding veins as thick as ropes and a long shaggy beard. He was wearing leather wristbands and an enormous iron knuckleduster on the middle finger of his left hand. The second fellow was a pale lad with golden curls down to his shoulders. He fetched the shallow wooden bowls of milk from the cellar and emptied them into the cheese kettle without spilling so much as a drop. The third man sat cross-legged on the hearth-slab. He was wearing a tight-fitting, grass-green hunting jacket. Almost soundlessly he broke up branches and twigs and threw them into the fire, blowing into the embers to set them alight. After a while he took out a little bottle and poured a bright green liquid into the milk, which immediately curdled. Then he sat down on the hearth-slab again, crossing his legs and observing the movements of the others with his deep-set, gleaming eyes.

The giant walked heavily out of the hut, pulled up a young fir-tree by the roots, and after breaking off all the twigs, came back in and began slowly to stir the milk with the stripped trunk.

The pale youth took out a beautifully shaped alphorn and went to the door, which sprang open of its own accord. Mild night breezes and the pale bluish moonlight streamed into the room. And then Res heard a wondrous melody coming in from the warm May night outside, richer and sweeter than any music he had ever heard before. It was a passionate, mysteriously alluring strain. After listening for a while, Res realised that the horn blower was using the music to draw in his herds. The deep tones of heavy cowbells and the tinkling of silvery goat-bells started mingling with the tune played by the golden-haired boy. The music seemed to hover over the palely lit countryside, filling the air from earth to sky. The echoes thrown back by the craggy rocks wove themselves into the boy's melody. Lying on his bed, Res felt his heart burst with passionate longing.

When the pale, golden-haired youth returned to the hut, the others had already finished their work. The giant fetched three wooden bowls and poured the whey into them. How strange: the whey in the first bowl was blood red, that in the second bowl was grass-green, and the whey in the third bowl was as white as snow. All of a sudden the sound of cowbells could no longer be heard coming in from the meadows. The room was filled with an uncanny silence. Then the broad-chested giant with the red face shouted up to Res: "Come down here, little man! Choose a gift for yourself."

樹枝和嫩枝折斷，扔到火上，再向灰燼吹氣，點燃柴枝；過了一會兒，他拿一個小瓶子出來，把鮮綠色的汁灌注在牛奶裏，牛奶馬上凝結成塊。然後，他再交叉兩腿坐在爐灶旁，用深邃明亮的眼睛觀察別人幹活。

但見第一個男人腳步沉重地走到外面去。他連根拔起青嫩的雲杉，扯掉樹枝，用整個樹身慢慢地攪撥牛奶。

蒼白的少年拿出一支美麗的阿爾卑斯號角，靠在門上，門自動打開了。溫和的夜風與藍色的月光飄進房子。德烈斯聽到一闋美麗的曲調在暖和的五月夜中蕩漾。他從來沒聽過那麼甜美沉鬱的一首曲調，神祕、狂熱又不可抗拒。聽了一會，德烈斯忽然明白，吹號角的人原來是用這音樂來誘惑牧牛。牛鈴低沉的音調與銀色羊鈴清脆的鳴聲，與金髮小夥子吹奏的曲子混在一起，飄過暗色的田野，瀰漫於廣漠天地中。岩壁反射的回聲，再交織著小夥子的曲調。德烈斯躺在乾草上，狂熱的渴望讓他的心快跳出來了。

當那蒼白的金髮少年回到房子的時候，其他兩人已經完成了他們的工作。胸膛寬闊的紅臉巨人拿出三個木碗，把乳清倒進去。多麼奇怪，第一碗乳清是血紅色的，第二碗是草綠色的，第三碗是白色的。突然，草場上牧牛的聲音停了，不尋常的沉默充滿著房子。巨人向德烈斯叫道：「小夥子，你快下來選自己的禮物。」

德烈斯給嚇得不敢動彈，他感到四肢像鉛一樣的沉重。一會，他終於站起來，爬下梯子。那三個男子給他看那三個碗。

「你得吃一碗乳清。」巨人說，一面在火光中展示自己的肌肉。「紅色的液體是我給你的禮物。選這碗的話，你會長得強壯有力，成為巨人，可以戰勝所有敵人。還有呢，我會送你一百頭乳牛和一百頭黃牛，明天開始牠們會在這裏吃草。而且你參加摔跤比賽，會輕易把敵人摔倒。好好考慮吧，小夥子！」

然後穿綠色獵人衣服的男人溫和地說：「你還是喝我綠色的乳清吧，」他說，「它會令你靈敏和機智，賺很多亮閃閃的金幣。你聽聽這可愛的聲音。」獵人拿出一把金幣，扔在地板上，「你所有的朋友都會羨慕你這麼富有，村子裏最漂亮的姑娘都會喜歡你。」

然後那美少年說：「我的禮物是白色的液體。你喝了的話就會唱歌，會唱約德爾調和吹號角，像我剛才那樣子。我還會送我的阿爾卑斯號角給你。」

「噢，那我就不選強壯有力或財富

Res was so afraid he hardly dared move. His legs and arms felt as heavy as lead. But finally he pulled himself together and climbed down the ladder. The three men showed him the three bowls.

"Take a drink from one of these bowls," said the giant, flexing his muscles in the light of the fire. "The red one is a gift from me. If you choose it you will be as strong and powerful as a giant. You will defeat all your enemies. Besides that I'll give you a hundred cows and a hundred head of russet oxen. They'll be grazing on your pastures by tomorrow. And in the wrestling matches you'll throw all your rivals on their backs without the least effort. Think it over, young man!"

Then the green-clad huntsman spoke in his soft voice: "You'd do better to drink my green-coloured whey," he said. "It would make you cunning and smart. You'd earn lots of shining gold. Just listen to the pleasant sound!" At these words the huntsman dropped a shower of glittering golden coins onto the floor. "With such immeasurable wealth you'd be the envy of all your friends, and the prettiest girl in the valley would be yours."

Then the fair youth spoke. "My gift is the white liquid. If you drink it, you'll be able to sing, yodel, and play the horn just as you heard me do it now. Besides that, I'll give you my alphorn."

"I wish for neither strength nor riches. It's your gift I want," cried Res. And seizing the third bowl in both hands he emptied it at a gulp. It didn't seem to him to taste like whey, which is sour, but like pure, fresh, sweet mountain milk. As soon as he put down his bowl, the music of cow- and goat-bells rang out again through the night.

"You have chosen wisely," said the fair youth, giving him a friendly nod. "If you had chosen either of the other two bowls you would have put your life in danger. And I would have had to wait thrice three hundred years before I could have offered my gift to the alpine herdsmen again."

Res took the horn. No sooner had he laid his fingers on the smooth wood than the three figures dissolved into thin air, and he felt himself being lifted up and then laid down again on his bed of hay. He fell asleep at once, and slept soundly until the sun woke him. At first he imagined that the strange happenings during the night must have been a dream. But he was still holding the alphorn in his hands. He went out in front of his hut and began to play. Marvellous tunes poured forth from the horn, first softly, then louder and louder. Res cried out in joy and started singing and yodelling. And it all sounded as beautiful and enchanting as the music of the pale youth.

All the herdsmen were filled with astonishment at this beautiful morning canticle and wondered who could be singing. The music swelled until it filled all the valleys, sinking deep into the hearts of the mountain folk. And the 'Kuhreigen' exists to this day.

了，我選你的禮物吧。」德烈斯一面喊，一面雙手抓起第三個碗，一口氣把白色的液體喝光。它的味道不像酸乳清，反像更純，更甜，更新鮮的高山牛奶。喝完以後，牛鈴和羊鈴又在夜空中響起來。

「你選得很聰明，」那美少年點頭說，「若你選第一或第二碗，你的生命就會有危險了。我也要在三個三百年以後，才再可以向高山牧人送出我的禮物。」

德烈斯接過阿爾卑斯號角。當他的手指一碰到號角細滑的木時，那三個人就消失了。他感到自己被人抬起來，放到那乾草做的床上。他馬上睡著了，睡得很熟，太陽出來的時候才起床。起初，德烈斯以為昨夜發生的奇怪事情，只不過是他做夢而已，但是，他發現自己手裏確是握著號角，他明白那不是什麼夢境。他走出門外，開始吹奏。美妙的曲調從號角飄出來，先是輕柔，然後越來越高昂。德烈斯高興得大叫起來，開始高歌和唱約德爾調。歌聲跟那美少年的音樂一樣美，一樣醉人。

所有牧人聽到這麼美麗的早晨頌曲，都感到驚奇，很想知道是誰唱的。音樂越來越高昂，充滿整個山谷，深深打動了每一個牧人的心。

牧輪曲，便一直流傳到今天。

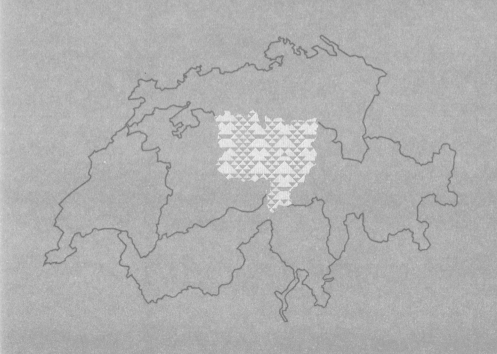

瑞士中部的傳說

Legends from Central Switzerland

賭照魂燈　The 'Lantern of the Dead' Gamble

首先要知道，過去有所謂「星期五發錢日」與「星期三發錢日」，這兩天，都是救濟基金給窮人發錢的日子。要得到這些錢，窮人必須為死去的人的靈魂祈禱。正因為這個理由，未得救贖的靈魂會在這樣的夜晚四處遊蕩，尋找人幫助他們脫離悲慘的命運。

接近一百年以前，曾有三個年輕紳士在施坦斯的「天使」客棧一起喝酒。一個是年輕醫生，另外兩個是大學生。他們邊喝啤酒邊打牌，聊得開心便開始吹牛。客棧的鐘敲響十一點，其中一個大學生瑟匹說：「咱們回家吧，今晚是『星期五發錢日』。」

「這和我們有什麼關係？」埃德華大夫插嘴道：「我們不是讀書人麼？民間種種迷信怎可以相信？我們又會遭遇什麼？今晚和每天晚上有什麼不同？我們都是學識豐富的人，明明知道死去的東西就是死了，回不來的啊。」

First of all you have to know that in former days 'Friday payday' and 'Wednesday payday' were the days the poor received their money from the paupers' fund. In exchange, they had to pray for the souls of the deceased. And that is why unredeemed souls chose those nights to roam about seeking someone to help rescue them from their sad fate.

About a hundred years ago, three young gentlemen were seated together in the Angel Inn in Stans. One of them was a young doctor, the other two were students. They drank their beer, they played cards, and then they started telling each other stories and showing off. It was eleven o'clock by the tavern clock when Sepp finally said: "Let's go home now. Tonight's Friday payday."

"What's that to us?" retorted Edward. "Aren't we educated people? How could you believe in such rubbish? What could ever happen to us? Tonight's a night like any other. After all, we're learned men: we know best of all that what's dead is dead and never returns."

So they spoke, rejecting traditional wisdom as pure superstition. They thought that people who had studied in Heidelberg and in Paris had no need to fear anything.

"Shall we try it out?" asked Stani. "Why don't we play another round? By the time we've finished, the witching hour will have come. Then, at the stroke of twelve by the tower, the loser will go alone into the charnel house and put out the light in the lantern of the dead."

"It's a deal," they all said, starting to play.

It was Edward, the doctor, who lost and had to prove his daring. At the stroke of twelve, the three men went out to the church together. Not a star in the sky. Total darkness. Except for a thin ray of light flickering through the crown glass panes of the charnel house. The men would fain have turned back, but their pride propelled them.

It must be explained that, in Stans, the lower charnel house is situated underground. To get there you have to go down a flight of steps. The people of the canton of Nidwalden are said to have had it built there so that they could use it as a place of worship if ever they were excommunicated.

Well, the three of them stopped at the top of the stairs. As usual, the charnel house door was open. Edward went down the steps. He could see the lantern of the dead in the rear of the room. Its light had been burning day and night for the past three or four hundred years at least, promising poor souls solace and relief. Skulls lay side by side along the walls. It was cold down there and Edward shivered as he crept towards the lantern. He opened its little door, took out the lamp, and blew out the flame.

A clap of thunder! Just one, and the charnel house door slammed shut. For a moment the two waiting men, paralysed by fear, could make no move. Then they tried to open the door, but it would not

他們這樣說著說著，把常理說成迷信。他們認為在海德堡和巴黎讀過書的人，什麼都不怕。

「要不咱們試一試，」斯塔尼建議，「再來打一場牌，打完了正好十二點。誰輸了，誰就在十二點整一個人去存屍所，把照魂燈吹滅。」

「說定了！」大家同意便開始打牌。

結果埃德華輸了，他得去証明自己的膽量。十二點整，他們一起到教堂去。天上沒有一顆星星。只有存屍所的砂玻璃窗透著燈光。三個人都想離開這個地方，只是這樣做，面子上太難看了。

這裏要解釋一下，施坦斯的存屍所建在地下，有一道臺階往下走。據說，下瓦爾登人特意把這座教堂建成這個樣子，以防被革出教門，他們也可以躲避在地下進行宗教儀式。

三個人於是站在臺階前。停屍所的門依舊開著。埃德華走下臺階，他看到照魂燈就擺在房間的末處。三四百年以來，這個燈白天黑夜一直亮著，照顧和安慰可憐的靈魂。裏面寒氣逼人，牆兩邊一個接一個的放著好多頭蓋骨。埃德華慢慢地向燈籠走過去，禁不住的發起抖來。他打開燈籠的小門，一口氣就把燈吹滅了。

突然響起一聲雷鳴。就只一聲，存屍所的門已經關上。兩個站在門外的朋友倉皇失措。他們想把門打開，卻不成功。他

們再使勁拉門閂，大力敲門，但門依然
打不開，可他們的朋友在深夜裏給關在裏
面。瑟匹趕去找司事，但是他也無法把門
打開。「這事有點古怪，」他說，「我們
需要找修士來。」

　　修士到來，開始祈禱。他不停地祈
禱。凌晨五時，當司事敲早禱鐘時，修士
趁第一下鐘聲再推門，門竟輕易地打開
了。埃德華走了出來，臉色蒼白，頭髮直
豎，臉孔帶著極度惶恐的神色。他一言不
發就回家了。

　　埃德華從沒向人提及當晚在存屍所
見到了什麼，但自那個晚上，他再沒有一
刻是健康快樂的。他逐漸消瘦，不到一年
就死了。他的兩個朋友也好不了多少。其
中一個在床上點蠟燭看書，起了火就燒死
了；另外一個遠離他鄉，死於一場決鬥
中。

open. They wriggled the latch, they knocked and they
banged on the door. All to no avail. Their friend was
trapped inside, and it was the middle of the night.
Sepp went and called the sexton. But he could not
open the door either. "There's something weird going on here," he said. "We'd better get one of the
friars to come."

The monk arrived and started praying. He prayed
on and on, tirelessly. Then, at five o'clock, the sexton
went to ring the bell for prayers. At the first stroke,
the friar went and tried the door again: it opened ef-
fortlessly, and Edward came out, deathly pale, his hair
standing on end, his face marked by fear and horror.
Without a word he went home.

Never did he tell anyone what he had met with in
that charnel house. But from that time on, he enjoyed
not a single hour of health or pleasure. Slowly he
wasted away. Within a year he was dead. The other
two young men fared no better: one of them was
burned to death after reading in bed by candlelight;
the other was killed in a duel in a foreign land.

The Bride
in the Treetrunk Coffin

樹幹棺材裏的新娘

In olden days, whenever someone had to be buried, people in Central Switzerland would hollow out a treetrunk and lay the dead person inside. These coffins are called 'treetrunk coffins'.

Once upon a time, at the beginning of winter – the wind had already brought the first flurries of snow – a young man from the upper village was on his way to visit his sweetheart. She lived in a fine farmhouse on the slopes of Buchs Hill. It was pitch dark as the young man walked up towards the house on the opposite side of the valley, and he was most astonished to see there was no light coming from the parlour. "What's going on?" he wondered. "Can it be that someone else is poaching on my territory? Well, if so, it's a good thing I've found him out."

Carefully he crept up the steps to the forecourt, from where he managed to get a view into the parlour. What he saw nearly took his breath away. On the floor in the middle of the room stood a treetrunk coffin. Four candles stood around it, their light shining out dimly to where he was standing.

The lad stared. Was he dreaming? In the coffin lay his sweetheart, stiff as a board and waxen-pale. He broke into a cold sweat. He couldn't believe it, yet there she lay before his very eyes. Not a sound

昔日，瑞士中部每有人死了需要埋葬的時候，人們就把一椿樹幹鑿空，然後把屍體放在裏邊。這些棺材叫做「樹幹棺材」。

很久以前，冬天剛開始，泡沫似的雪花剛從天上飄下來，上村的一個年輕人想見他的愛人。她就住在北茲山坡上一幢美麗的農舍裏。他從峽谷對面的山，沿著山路往山上走。他走近農舍的時候，已經黑得伸手不見五指了。教他奇怪的，是愛人的客廳沒有亮燈。「怎麼回事？」他心裏嘀咕，「不會有人在偷東西吧。幸好我發現了！」

他躡手躡腳，爬上了梯級，站在前院，往客廳一看，他給嚇得魂不附體。屋子正中的地板上擺著一副樹幹棺材。棺材周圍點著四根蠟燭，昏暗的燭光照到他站立的地方。

年輕人呆呆地瞪著那副棺材，他在做夢麼？棺材裏躺著的，是他蒼白僵直的姑娘。他額上冒著冷汗，不肯相信，只是她的確躺在眼前。四周一片死寂，唯有蠟燭的火焰輕微地躍動。

年輕人不忍再看下去，又不知道是否應該敲門喚醒裏邊的人，還是乾脆離開。終於，他像來的時候一樣，輕手輕腳地走下臺階，返回上村去。

年輕人的一個表哥是教堂的副牧師，名叫諾爾。年輕人決定向表哥求助，問點意見。不久，年輕人已經坐在表哥的書房裏，把經歷的一切告訴他。表哥靜靜地聽著，沉思片刻後說：「不，我沒聽說那家有人死了。若有，他們一定會通知我。不可能！而且也沒有人生病。但聽著，我現在跟你說的話，你要保密。你所見到的一切應該是一個預兆，這個姑娘與你不相配，她不適合你。相信我的話，回家去吧。」

年輕人聽從表哥的勸告。此後，他再沒有去那屋子找他的愛人。那個姑娘不久以後嫁給了另一個人；年輕人卻一輩子沒有結婚。

could be heard. Nothing stirred. The candles flickered faintly.

The lad couldn't bear to look any longer. He couldn't decide whether to wake someone or simply run away. Finally he crept down the steps as quietly as he had come and returned to Buchs.

He decided to seek help and advice from a cousin of his who was the parish curate and whose name was Rohrer. Soon he was sitting in his cousin's study telling him everything. His cousin listened in silence, bethought himself and then said: "No, there's been no news of a death in that house as far as I know. I'd certainly have been informed. No, and there's no one sick there either. But listen to me, and keep what I tell you to yourself. What you saw is a sign that that girl is not the one, not the right woman for you. Believe me. And now go home."

The lad took his cousin's advice to heart. He never went courting at that house again. Soon afterwards the girl married someone else. The lad remained a bachelor to the end of his days.

The Young Herdsman
from Oberrickenbach

鹿溪上村的牛郎

A long time ago, the upper farm in Oberrickenbach was owned by a wealthy farmer. It belonged to him alone. As for his herds – rather splendid herds they were too! – he sent them to pasture on Sinsgau Alp every summer.

It was a dairyman called Kaspar who, together with a young cowhand, took care of things on the alp. From time to time the farmer would also go up himself to make sure that everything was in order. The dairyman had been with the farmer for many years. But Veeri, a sixteen-year-old stripling, had been hired that spring. Red Veeri – as they called him because he had a shock of hair as red as beech leaves in autumn – was a strange boy. He had twisted opinions and strange desires. "You know," he would say to the dairyman, "you know what? I wish I had a pile of money, a whole basket of crown thalers and gold doubloons. That's what I'd like to have."

"And then?" asked the dairyman. "What would you do with it?"

"I'd buy two of the finest farms in Stans, and then I'd straightaway be elected president of the canton."

"Well, well, not bad," teased the dairyman. "Don't you think, Redhead, you'd be better as a handsome ensign with the hussars? Your ginger hair is redder by half than a cavalryman's jacket."

They spent many an evening together in this way, and the dairyman would chaff Veeri whenever he became too arrogant.

很久以前，鹿溪上村最上的農舍住過一個富有的農夫。農舍全屬於他，他的牛群——很棒的一群牛——每年夏天都在昕斯高牧場放牧。

一個名叫卡斯琶的奶農和一個牛郎一起監管牧場，有時農夫自己也上來檢查一下是否一切妥當。奶農已為農夫工作了一段很長的時間，可是威利，一個十六歲的小夥子，這年春天剛被雇用。人們叫他「紅色威利」，因為他的頭髮紅得像秋天山毛櫸的紅葉。他是個奇怪的男孩。他的思想有點歪，欲望也奇特。譬如他跟奶農這麼說：「你知道嗎？我真想有一大堆錢。整整一個籃子的塔勒和金幣。我就是想要錢！」

「然後呢？」奶農問，「你用這個錢想幹什麼？」

威利答道：「我會買施坦斯最漂亮的兩幢農舍，然後立刻當選縣長！」

「哈，不錯嘛！」奶農嘲笑他，「你這個紅髮小鬼，當一個英俊的輕騎兵小軍官不是更好嗎？你的紅頭髮比騎兵的馬甲更紅哩。」

像這樣他們一起度過了好幾個晚上，每當威利太狂妄，奶農就會嘲笑他。

到了秋天，他們倆搬到山坡下的小牧場。一天，他們的主人上牧場來看他的牲口，然後對奶農說：「明天施坦斯的豬官要來這裏，他想看看小豬。小豬看起來很不錯。你把牠們養得很好。卡斯琶，他會付出一個不錯的價錢，你要檢查一下是否一切妥當。」

這天晚上，奶農對威利說：「瞧，威利，明天會有人帶著一個厚錢包來，裏面裝著很多錢，你朝思暮想的都是這個吧。所以我們有這麼一句話：他像豬官一樣有錢！買豬的時候，他們整個錢包都裝滿了錢。」

威利這時一言不發，但假如奶農夜裏不像旱獺一樣睡得那麼香，他可能聽見威利在床上翻來覆去。

第二天，威利懶懶散散的發呆，直到奶農叱喝他，「你幹嗎像生了根似的開站，威利？去，趕快去看羊和山羊，牠們走向山澗去了，要是在這幾天有任何一隻跌死了，可真不合我的心意。快跑，去看看牠們。」

威利往山坡那裏跑，那是牲畜吃草的地方。他到了以後，就躺在草裏繼續做白日夢。他看不見眼前的美麗山巒在晨曦下閃閃發光。他想的除了錢還是錢。他身旁

One day in autumn, after they had moved to the lower part of the alp, the farmer came up to take a look at his livestock. He said to the dairyman: "Tomorrow, the pig-dealer from Stans will be coming by. He wants to see the young pigs. They're really not bad. Kaspar, you've fed them well. He'll pay a decent price for them. Make sure that everything is as it should be."

That evening, the dairyman said to Veeri: "Well Veeri, tomorrow someone with a great fat money pouch will be coming up here. With as much money as you've always wanted! It's not for nothing people say: He's got money like a pig-dealer. They carry bags of money on them when they go out to buy pigs."

Veeri didn't reply. But if the dairyman had not been sleeping as soundly as a marmot, he would have heard Veeri tossing and turning all that night.

The following day, the boy hung around until the dairyman shouted at him: "What do you think you're doing, standing around gawping? Go on, hurry up and go and tend to the sheep and goats. They've wandered off down to the gully. I wouldn't like it at all if one of them were to fall to its death, now in our last days up here. Go and run after them."

Veeri ran down the slope to where the animals were browsing. He lay down in the grass and went on dreaming. He didn't see the splendid mountains bathed in the morning light. All he saw was money, money, money. Beside him in the grass lay the catapult he used to shoot at goats if they ventured too close to the edge of the gully. He was an exceedingly good shot. Not long since, he had hit a billy-goat right in the eye from a distance of more than twenty metres. The sheep and goats were scared of him and his pebbles. But today there was no need for fear. Today

Veeri wasn't paying attention to the animals. He just sat there dreaming.

Listen, footsteps! Someone is climbing up. You can hear his stick striking the stones. Veeri crouches down and watches. Who's coming? Who is it? Veeri picks up his catapult and peeks through the grass. Now he sees the man climbing up through the forest. By my oath, it's the pig-dealer. Veeri ducks down into the grass. He hears the man panting with the effort of climbing the steep path. Now the man has stopped.

Whish! Something hits him on the forehead. "Holy Mother of God!" exclaims the man, throws up both hands and falls down, collapsing heavily to the ground. Spellbound, Veeri looks down, waits a moment. Then, seeing a trickle of blood running down the man's cheek, he hesitates another instant, before hastily snatching the dealer's pouch from his body. As expected, it's full to bursting with money. He runs into the forest to hide his booty. When he gets back, the man is dead. Veeri looks around to see if anyone is there. No. Far and wide not a soul. Summoning all his strength, the boy drags the dead man to the edge of the path and pushes him down the gully. He hears the corpse tumble from rock to rock. Then, suddenly, he's surrounded by nothing but eerie silence.

放著他的彈弓。山羊走得太近山澗邊緣的時候，他便用這個彈弓射牠們。他是個射擊好手。不久以前，他從二十多米的距離遠遠的射中了雄山羊的眼睛。羊和山羊怕他和他的石頭。不過，今天牠們沒有什麼要怕的，因為，今天他不理牲口，只呆呆地坐著，在做白日夢。

聽聽，腳步聲。有人從下邊爬上來。誰也能聽到有人的拐杖碰石頭的聲音。威利蹲下，埋伏起來。誰來？是誰？威利拿起彈弓，從草叢窺望著。他看見一個人穿過樹林走上來。天啊，是豬官。威利躲到草叢裏。他聽見人家氣吁吁，陡峭的山徑讓豬官喘不過氣來。現在豬官停住了。

吁！什麼東西打中豬官的額頭。「天主聖母瑪利亞！」豬官驚叫，高舉雙手，最後沉重地倒在地上。威利著了魔似的往下張望，等了片刻，當他看到豬官的太陽穴流出一行血時，他遲疑了一下，結果還是匆忙地把裝滿金錢的皮包從豬官的身上搶過來。他拿著贓物跑到森林裏，把皮夾藏起來。回來的時候，那個人已經死了。威利環顧四周，看看附近有沒有人。沒有。遠遠近近連人影也沒有。威利使勁地把屍體拉到山徑旁邊，將屍體推到山澗裏去，他聽到屍體下墜時碰到一塊又一塊岩石的聲音。然後，一片恐怖的死寂突然環繞著他。

送葬　The Funeral Procession

翁特瓦爾登州的男人都穿紅襪子，女人都穿白襪子的年代，鹿溪上村附近的田苔村曾經住過一個誠實可靠的人。一個冬天的晚上，他很晚才從狼席森走回家。月亮照著積滿白雪的峽谷。忽然，他發現一支送葬隊伍迎面走過來。走近時，他看到一匹馬拉著載著棺材的雪橇。棺材上坐著一個穿著一隻紅襪子和一隻白襪子的男人。在陪送的人群裏，他看到教堂的司事和神父，還有幾乎所有鹿溪上村的村民。送葬隊伍默默地走過，似乎沒有注意到路旁的他。

回到家，妻子發現他的臉色挺差的，便不斷問到底發生了什麼事，他只敷衍地答應明天解釋一切。正要躺下睡覺的時候，他發現自己穿了一隻紅襪子和一隻白襪子，原來，他早上太匆忙，無意中穿錯了妻子的一隻襪子。他嚇得大驚失色。現在他才明白那支幽靈般的送葬隊伍的真正意義：棺材上的人就是他自己。他把這個經歷告訴妻子，並派人請神父來他家，向神父懺悔自己的罪過。第二天早上，他便死了。

In the days when the men of Unterwalden all still wore red stockings and the women white ones, there was a good and honest man who lived in Feldmoos near Oberrickenbach. One late winter night, he was returning home from Wolfenschiessen through the moonlit snowy valley when, suddenly, he saw a funeral procession coming his way. As it approached, he could make out the horse-drawn sleigh with the coffin and, sitting on top of the coffin, a man who was wearing one red and one white stocking. In the crowd that followed he recognised the chaplain and the sexton, and almost the whole of the population of Oberrickenbach. The procession passed by, silent and unseeing.

When the man got home, his wife was struck by how haggard he looked. In vain did she plead with him to tell her what was the matter. He put her off till the morrow. However, as he was going to bed, he noticed to his horror that he himself was wearing one red and one white stocking: in his haste that morning he had mistakenly put on a stocking of his wife's. Now the meaning of that ghostly procession dawned on him: he himself was the man on the coffin. He told his wife what had happened, had the chaplain come, and contritely made his last confession. The next morning he was a corpse.

老雇傭兵講的故事 Tales Old Seldner Told

In his younger days, Richard Mathis Seldner had served as a mercenary in the Neapolitan army. Later, he lived as a poor devil, dependent on God's mercy and people's charity. In winter he'd tramp from one chalet to the other, and in the summer he'd help out on one or other of the alps. In the evening, after nightfall, he'd sit on the pile of logs by the fire, smoke his pipe and tell stories. "My grandfather," he once said, "was a Sunday's child. He saw more things than other people do. Once, in autumn, he had to go up to the Beckenried Alp. While walking up towards the chalet, he heard a furious rumbling sound. 'What's that?' he asked himself and looked into the house through a crack. And what did he see? There was a white foal standing there churning butter. Another time it was late at night and he had just come out from the forest of alder trees above Wolfenschiessen. There was a little cottage standing there that had been empty for as long as anyone could remember. From afar, he had heard jolly sounds of music. He was really curious to know who could be playing so prettily. He went up to the cottage and, looking in through the window, perceived five or six cats perched on the stove playing music.

It was the evening of payday, and as I said before: my grandfather used to see so many curious things."

裏察馬蒂斯賽拿年輕的時候，曾經在那不勒斯軍隊當過雇傭兵；後來卻變成一個可憐蟲，依靠上帝的憐憫和人們的善行過日子。冬天，他從一間牧場小屋走到另一間牧場小屋避雪；夏天，他偶爾在某一個牧場當傭工。當夜色降臨的時候，他一般會坐在火爐旁一堆柴枝上，點起他的煙斗，講他的故事。「我的爺爺，」他有一次這麼說，「他是個幸運兒，他比一般人多見過些東西。某年秋天，他去了貝肯列特牧場。他走近小屋的時候，聽到了隆隆的嘈雜聲。『怎麼回事，』他一面自言自語，一面從一條縫隙窺望屋裏的情況。他看到了什麼？一匹白駒站在屋裏，轉動攪乳器造牛油。還有一次，他深夜裏從狼席森後的櫸木林走出來。那兒有一幢小房子，很久沒人住過的了。離房子還有一段距離，他就聽到愉快的音樂聲。這倒讓他感到奇怪，誰在彈奏這麼好聽的樂曲？走近房子，他往窗裏張望，看到五、六隻貓坐在火爐上彈奏著樂曲。

發薪日的晚上嘛，我跟你們說過……我的爺爺見過不少怪事哩！」

卡斯特爾牧場的山精靈 — The Gnomes on Kastelen Alp

從皮拉圖斯山峰頂到赫期威爾村和艾根峽谷，都有住在那裏的山精靈的足跡，他們一會兒從地下隧道出現，一會兒又飛快地消失。他們身高不及兩呎，穿著綠色的外衣，戴著紅色的帽子。他們奇怪的腳像鵝爪，雪白的頭髮很長，銀色的鬍子長及地面。他們照顧小羚羊，養魚，也幫助牧民。不過誰一失言，他們就立刻報仇。

　　以前，皮拉圖斯山坡上的卡斯特爾牧場屬於一個富有的農夫，他叫克勞斯。有一天，瑪格達勒娜，克勞斯的一個窮表親的女兒，來找他幫忙，原來她母親患了病。克勞斯輕蔑地把她打發了，姑娘哭泣著下山。

　　途中，她遇見在附近的布潤棱牧場上工作的年輕小工，他可憐她不幸的遭遇，於是送給她屋中唯一剩下的小乳酪。姑娘本想繼續趕路，但是一場猛烈的暴雨把她留在小工的屋子裏好幾小時。終於，雷暴停了，姑娘走出小屋，卻在潮濕的草上滑倒了。她手中的小乳酪掉到地上，滾往深淵去，不見了。

　　她呆呆的站著，絕望地哭起來。這時候，有東西輕輕地拉著她的衣角。她驚訝地環顧四周，發現了一個小矮人，他戴著一頂紅色的帽子，穿著一件綠色的外衣，

The gnomes that used to live all over Mount Pilatus, from its crown right down to Hergiswil and the Eigen Valley, would sometimes suddenly emerge from their underground passages, only to disappear again as fast as they had come. They were barely two foot tall, wore green jerkins and red caps, had strange feet like those of a goose, and long snowy white hair with silvery beards flowing right down to the ground. They looked after the chamois and the fish and made themselves useful to the mountain dairymen. However, it took but an ill word for their vengeance to be provoked.

In those days, Kastelen Alp on the slopes of Mount Pilatus belonged to a rich farmer named Klaus. One day Magdalena, the daughter of a poor sick cousin of his, came to him to ask for help for her mother. Scornfully he refused and sent her back on her way. Weeping, the girl set off down to the valley.

On her way, she met the young farmhand from nearby Bründeln Alp. He took pity on her in her distress and gave her the only piece of cheese he had left in his chalet. But as the girl was about to set off again, a terrific thunderstorm broke out, so that she had to wait for several hours. Finally the storm abated, and the girl left the chalet. But she slipped on the wet grass, and the piece of cheese flew out of her hand down into the gully.

As the girl stood there, sobbing in despair, it seemed to her she felt someone pluck delicately at her skirt. Turning around in alarm, she espied a tiny manikin in a red cap and a green jerkin, and with a long flowing beard. He was carrying a piece of cheese on his frail shoulders and a bunch of fragrant alpine herbs in his hand. "I know how you've been treated," said the manikin in his little piping voice. "Now take these herbs and this cheese. You can cure your mother's sickness with the herbs, and the cheese will give you rich nourishment. As for your hard-hearted relative, he has already received his punishment."

The girl arrived home. She boiled the herbs and used the brew to cure her mother. Then she cut off a piece of the cheese, and it turned into glistening gold!

The same storm that had held Magdalena back in the chalet had also broken out over Kastelen Alp. It had struck the cliff above the alp, and rocks had come tumbling down over the splendid pastures, leaving in their wake nothing but a horrible wasteland. At the same time, one of the boulders had struck Klaus, smashing both his legs.

For a long time afterwards, the wretched man could be seen hobbling around the countryside, supporting himself on his crutches. But Magdalena married the kind farmhand, and together they bought Bründeln Alp.

有一束飄揚的長鬍子。他瘦弱的肩膀上托著一塊乳酪，手裏拿著一束芳香的阿爾卑斯野草。那小矮人是山精靈，他用微弱的聲音説道：「我知道你遭到了什麼。拿著這束野草和這塊乳酪吧。野草會治你母親的病，乳酪會給你良好的營養。你鐵石心腸的親戚已經受到了應得的懲罰。」

姑娘回到家中。她用野草煮了藥給母親喝，母親的病便治好了。當他們想把一點乳酪切下來的時候，乳酪竟變成了閃閃發光的黃金。

留住瑪格達勒娜在小屋中的那場大暴風，同時也刮到卡斯特爾牧場去。它搖動了牧場上的懸崖，岩石翻滾下來，掩蓋了美麗的牧場，把那裏變成一片可怕的廢墟。同時，一塊石頭擊中了克勞斯，把他的雙腿壓斷了。

從此以後，可憐的克勞斯拄著拐杖在野外四處亂走。瑪格達勒娜呢，她嫁給了樂於助人的小工，和他一起買了布潤棱牧場。

The Manikin
on the Anvil-Bench

砧石上的小矮人

接近一百年以前吧，來自下瓦爾登州施坦斯村的維塞爾布西格，要上皮拉圖斯山上的阿爾卑納赫牧場去，因為那裏的小屋有很多需要維修的地方。維塞爾帶著一名雇農到達牧場那天，牲口已經給趕到山谷去了。

他們把口糧放在一邊，然後準備工具。維塞爾是一個富有經驗的工匠，他檢查屋子一會，便對雇農説：「我看我們至少要在這裏幹活一個星期，大家馬上動手吧！」

他們修好一些東西之後，維塞爾便走出屋外休息一會，他環顧四周，突然發現屋子前磨鐮刀的砧石上坐著一個人——一個衰老、細小的矮人。他有一張土黃的臉，皮膚皺縮，頭髮雪白。他穿著有搭扣的鞋，白色的襪子，藍色的短褲和一件火紅的夾克。維塞爾呆呆地瞪著那個矮人，他不知道該説些什麼，只是覺得那矮人有點不對勁，心裏感到不安。他回到屋裏，問雇農外邊坐著的人是誰。雇農看了一眼，對維塞爾慢條斯理地説：「不認識。這個像伙真奇怪。來，咱們最好搬到下面的房子去。他可能會施魔法哩。」

後來，他們在春冒白牧場遇見了兩個來自敵對的上瓦爾登州的強壯漢子。上

One day – it must have been about a hundred years ago – Wysel Buäsiger from Stans in Nidwalden (Below-The-Forest) was told to go up to Alpnach Alp on Mount Pilatus to do some work on the chalet which was badly in need of repair. The day he arrived on the alp, together with the farmhand, the cattle had already been driven down to the valley.

They unpacked their provisions and set out their tools. Wysel, an experienced craftsman, looked over the house, then said to the farmhand: "I can see there's a whole week's work to be done here. Let's get started at once."

After they had done some of the repairs, Wysel went outside for a moment to have a look around. Suddenly he noticed there was a creature sitting on the stone bench of the anvil used for sharpening sickles and scythes. It was a tiny little old man with a yellowish brown face. His skin was wizened and his hair was snowy white. He wore buckled shoes and white stockings, short blue trousers and a bright red jerkin. Wysel stared at the manikin. He didn't know what to say, but there was something peculiar about the little man that made him feel uneasy. He went back inside and asked the farmhand if he knew the person sitting outside. The farmhand looked out and then said quite calmly: "No, I don't know him. He's a strange little fellow. Come on, let's move down to the lower chalet. He might be a sorcerer."

On Chrummelbach Alp they met two great strong men from the rival canton of Obwalden (Above-The-Forest). The men listened to their story and then said,

"Well for sure, we're not likely to be scared by a tiny manikin. Let's go and have a look. Perhaps we can do something to help."

When the four men arrived at the chalet, the little man was still sitting on the anvil bench. He eyed them all angrily, and the two men from Obwalden didn't even dare greet him, let alone talk to him.

Wysel went back to his work, but suddenly the manikin came in, sat himself down on a roof beam and started looking around. That was enough for Wysel: without waiting for evening to fall, he packed his bags, and set off again for the lower alp, together with the farmhand.

The manikin sat there sadly watching them go.

"You make sure you find another hut for when the animals and herdsman come back up to the alp," Wysel shouted back to him. "As for me, I'm going. To be sure, I'd earn a fine sum of money if I stayed here and finished my work. But I can't stand it – living in the same house as someone who hasn't got a shadow."

瓦爾登州人聽維塞爾講及那個小矮人，便說：「這麼一個小矮人，我們才不怕！咱們回去看看，我們或有辦法幫忙！」

他們一行四人走近小屋，發現那個小矮人依舊坐在砧石上，一動也不動，只憤怒地凝視著他們。兩個上瓦爾登州人早已喪失了勇氣，哪裏還敢跟小矮人說話。

維塞爾只好繼續在屋裏幹活。小矮人突然走進屋子來，爬上了屋樑，然後一直從上邊觀看維塞爾工作。維塞爾受不了，太陽未落山，他就把口糧收起來，帶著雇農往山下的牧場走。

小矮人依然坐在砧石上，看起來有點悲傷的樣子，目送著他們兩個。

維塞爾回頭向他喊叫：「你最好在人和牲口還沒有回牧場之前，去找別的屋子。我呢，我會儘快離開這裏。假如我留在這裏，把工作完成，我能夠賺一大筆錢，不過我實在受不了和一個沒有影子的怪物待在同一所屋子裏！」

妖怪伊貝斯　The Elbst Monster

住在瑞士最美麗的湖畔的居民，都知道好多神秘的傳説，譬如説湖的深處，有一尾奇怪的魚，牠頭上有閃亮的冠，像某些高山的蛇一樣。

也有一些奇怪的傳説是關於妖怪的。他常在烏裏州斯裏堡山的小湖活動，名叫「伊貝斯」。他從山上跳到水裏的時候，像燃燒的火球。有時他圍繞一個地方走動，就像一個熾熱的輪。他潛到水裏深處卻又像一條巨魚。他喜歡在晚上出沒——他出來之前總是陡然風浪大作。

他多在楚格湖附近出沒，他的出現是戰爭和瘟疫的預兆。人們説：「如果山居的人意外地殺掉魚形的伊貝斯，可怕的洪水便會襲擊周圍的地區，把不幸的居民淹死。」

The inhabitants of the shores of many of our most beautiful lakes used to recount many mysterious legends. They told of the strangest kinds of fish that lived in the watery depths, fish that wore glistening crowns on their heads, just like certain alpine snakes.

There are also strange stories about a monster that is said to lurk in or around the small lake on Mount Seelisberg in the canton of Uri. His name is Elbst. When he leaps from the mountain into the water he looks like a burning ball of fire. Sometimes, too, he circles the place in the shape of a fiery wheel. However, down in the depths of the lake, he usually looks like a monstrous fish. He particularly likes to come up in the evening – his emergence is usually announced by a strong wind whipping up the water.

This monster often used to roam around Lake Zug; his arrival there was considered to augur plague and war. It was said: "If a mountain farmer were inadvertently to kill the Elbst in his fish shape, a terrible flood would ensue that would devastate the surrounding areas and drown all the unfortunate inhabitants."

撒但之石 The Devil's Rock

The people in the Urseren Valley had tried several times to build a bridge across the Reuss River. Yet the terrain was so difficult that every attempt failed. A pact with the Devil seemed the only way out of their predicament. The deal was as follows: The Devil would build the bridge, and in payment he could claim the first creature to cross it.

In less than no time, the Devil had finished his work and now stood there awaiting his just due. But the Urseren folk are no fools. To get around their obligations they sent an old billy-goat across the bridge.

The Devil was furious. He dashed down to the valley and sought out the biggest rock he could find, intending to destroy the bridge with it. But the stone was so heavy that even he, the Devil, had to struggle with might and main to drag it up through the Schöllenen Gorge, and it was not long before he had to take a rest. As he sat there beside the path, totally exhausted, a frail old woman came up and started talking to him. She got him so entangled in the conversation that he failed to notice her make the sign of the cross on the rock. But then, when he wanted to continue on his way, he found he could not move the rock by a single inch. Perceiving that all his efforts were in vain, he flew into a rage and scurried off back down to Hell.

To this day the rock is still to be seen standing where the Devil left it. And as for the bridge, in the days of the horse-drawn mail-coach it was still used. But later, with the advent of the automobile, a new bridge was built beside the old one.

烏瑟棱谷的人民多次嘗試建造橫跨羅伊斯河的橋樑，但由於地勢太險峻了，無論用什麼辦法，他們都建造不成。跟撒但簽契約似乎是唯一的出路。契約是這樣的：撒但負責建造橋樑，可是第一個踏上橋的靈魂要給他。

一眨眼，撒但完成了他的任務，站在橋頭等待他應得的報酬。可是烏瑟棱的人也不笨，他們鑽空子把一頭老山羊趕過橋。

撒但十分憤怒，他衝下山，找全谷最大的石頭，想用它來把新建的橋砸壞。石頭那麼重，撒但用了很大的力氣，才把它推上舌樂能山峽去。他筋疲力盡，非休息不可。撒但坐在路旁的時候，一名瘦小的老婦人趁這機會跟他談起話來。老婦人引撒但談得起勁，趁他沒注意的時候，便用粉筆在石頭上畫了個十字形。撒但想繼續搬石頭的時候，卻發覺就算用盡氣力，石頭仍絲毫不動。最後，撒但只好憤怒地返回地獄去。

直到今天，那石頭仍蹲在撒但把它放下的地方。橋呢？汽車給發明後，人們在馬拉郵車那個時代用過的那座橋的旁邊，建造了一座新一點、大一點的橋。

The Spys Alp Ghost

斯
匹
司
的
鬼

In the middle of Beckenried village there's a house named 'Isrige'. Actually the name on its façade is 'Isenringen', but anyone who understands anything at all about old names will confirm that 'Isrige' is the correct term. For it means 'ours' or 'our own', and shows that the house used to belong to a freeman who paid neither rent nor taxes.

More than six hundred years ago, it was the house of the richest farmer in the region. They called him Härchi vo Isrige, Härchi being short for Henry. Härchi was so rich he didn't even know how much he owned. The finest farms between Boden and Niederdorf belonged to him, as did the whole of Mount Trischtälä and also Spys, one of the best alpine meadows in the country.

But it was exactly this alp that worried him. None of his dairymen had ever dared to stay up there for more than a few days. The few who did stay on, declaring they feared neither devil nor man, paid for their audacity with their lives: they were found dead in the mountain chalet. Someone had strangled them. They were blue in the face, their tongues hung out. It was altogether a ghastly sight. But who had done it? No one could say. The villagers searched the chalet and all the surrounding area but found no clues. The only thing they knew for sure was that it must have been someone extremely strong to have managed to overcome the fellows, who were far from being weaklings.

That is the reason why Härchi had not sent anyone up to Spys Alp for the past three years. It really was hard on him, and every time June came and he saw

貝肯裏德村子的中心有一座被稱為伊斯裏格的大房子；其實，房子的大門上名字是「伊申陵真」。對古名字有任何認識的人，都知道伊斯裏格才是正名，因為它是「我們」或「我們自己」的意思，表示屋主不需要付租金或稅款。

六百年前，有一家非常富有的農民住在那兒，人們稱當家的為伊斯裏格的哈爾希。哈爾希是亨利的別稱。哈爾希真的不知道自己富有到什麼程度，反正那個地帶最好的田地都屬於他，那一片山以及當地最美的高山牧場——整個斯匹司山都是屬於他的。

正是這個山上的牧場給哈爾希帶來了煩惱：沒一個牧民願意在上面多呆幾天。有一些自認不怕鬼的人，結果將自己的命丟在那裏，屍體是在山上的小屋裏被人發現的，臉色發紫，舌頭伸了出來，是被掐死的。這是誰幹的呢？人們將小屋翻了個底朝天，整個斯匹司搜個滴水不漏，還是沒人知道。大家唯一知道的，是這必然是個力大無比的傢伙幹的，不然哪能弄倒那些壯實的年輕牧農？

就是這個緣故，三年了，哈爾希再沒敢派人上斯匹司山。他心裏不大好受，每

the Beckenried folk drive their cattle up to Chlewen Alp, to Morschfeld and Bachscheite, when he heard the crack of the whips and the jingling of the bells, and saw the dairymen from Niederbau follow, then he thought he should be going up too with his cattle.

But it was impossible. Once a neighbour suggested that if he didn't want to go up to Spys Alp himself, he could send one of his farmhands. Härchi stared him in the face and remarked: "I wouldn't dream of it! The life and soul of a human being is worth more to me than a dozen alpine pastures."

After that, no one mentioned Spys Alp to Härchi any more – until the day Konrad Hummliger from Alsäle turned up. He was a young man, still almost a child really. But at sixteen he was big and strong for his age. His father had been a logger. He had been good at his work and had always found employment with good wages.

Konrad's father often worked in the forests belonging to Einsiedeln Abbey. Konrad used to go with him, and so it happened that he met the father cellarer. The priest noticed that Konrad was a bright young fellow and said to his father: "Hummliger, what would you say if we were to give your son an education?"

Old Hummliger scratched his head. "Well, that's a bit sudden," he said. He added that, what with seven children at home, he had no savings. He would have to think it over, and also he'd like to discuss the matter with the boy's mother. Meanwhile Konrad had been listening. What, he might become a pupil at the abbey school? He'd be an educated person! He could

年六月,當他看到北根列牧人把牛群趕上智利雲山,到莫斯非或巴詩艾,聽見揚鞭的聲音和牛鈴的鳴響,看到尼德堡的奶農徒步隨後,他便想,或許也應該把牛隻領到山上去。

但不成。有一次一個鄰居問哈爾希,要不要派他的一個雇農上山去?哈爾希看看這位鄰居説:「對我來説,一條人命要比十個牧場更值錢。」

很長一段時間裏,沒有人再提起斯匹司山,直到原居阿爾沙的康拉德出現。十六歲的康拉德看上去還是個孩子,但長得很高大健壯,他父親是個伐木工,有好手藝,所以有活兒,也能掙到些錢。

康拉德的父親常在修道院範圍的樹林工作,康拉德總是一起去。一天,他剛巧碰到管地窖的神父。神父覺得他是個聰慧的小夥子,便對他父親説,「漢姆力加,我們讓你的兒子受點教育,你怎麼看?」

漢姆力加搔搔頭,「唔,有點突然哩。」他還説,他家裏有七個小孩,所以一點積蓄也沒有;他要認真想想看,還得跟孩子的媽媽商量一下。康拉德在旁邊聽著。怎麼,他可以到修道院的學校念書?他將是個讀書人啊!他真是喜出望外。

那是聖誕節的時候。兩個月之後，康拉德的父親被一棵杉樹砸死了，從此家裏的日子沒法過下去。

一天晚上，母親對康拉德説：「孩子，家裏留不住你了，你得出去找工作，我會在家裏盡力照顧你的六個兄弟姐妹。」

康拉德耷拉著腦袋，他想起修道院學校，抬起頭對母親説：「媽，好吧，你覺得這樣最好便這樣吧。要是我能弄到些錢就送回家來。」

「唉，你是個好兒子。」他母親接著説：「你要能好好的，找到個藏身的地方我就心滿意足了。」

復活節那天，康拉德離開了家，下午到了貝肯賴德。康拉德直接上了哈爾希家，問他要不要雇農？

哈爾希上下打量了康拉德説：「我倒是喜歡你，可是我現在不需要雇農，我總是冬天的時候要人，你怎麼這個時候才來？」康拉德説起父親的去世和母親的愁苦。

「咳，是這樣啊！你看，就是我留你也沒有活兒呀。」哈爾希説。

「山上不需要人嗎？」康拉德問道。

「山上？那兒是需要人，你知道吧，我山上那兒鬧鬼，已經有三個雇農在那兒被掐死了，我還敢讓人上去嗎？」

「我沒什麼好怕的，」康拉德繼續説：「要是一個人老老實實做自己的事，相信上帝，不會出什麼事的。行行好，就讓我上山吧！」

think of nothing he'd have liked better.

That was round Christmas time. Two months later, old Hummliger was dead, struck down by a fir tree. Those were hard times for the family. In addition to their sorrow at the loss of their father, they suffered hunger and were worried about the future.

Finally, one evening, the mother said: "Konrad, you must go and seek your living elsewhere. I shall take care of your brothers and sisters as best I can."

Konrad let his head drop. The abbey school came to his mind. But then he raised his eyes and said, "Yes mother, if you think that's best. Perhaps I'll earn some money, then I can send it to you."

"You're a good lad," said his mother. "But I'll be quite satisfied if you find a suitable position and manage to look after yourself."

Konrad left home on Easter Monday morning and reached Beckenried by the afternoon. He went straight up to Härchi and asked him for employment as a farmhand.

Härchi looked him up and down. "I'd like to have you," he said. "But actually I don't need anyone. I hire all my people in the winter, not now. Why didn't you come earlier?" Konrad told him about his family, of his father's accident and his mother's distress.

"Oh dear, so that's why," said the farmer. "But you can see for yourself, even if I wanted to I couldn't find any work for you to do."

"Don't you need anyone up on the alp?" Konrad asked.

"On the alp? Spys Alp? Well yes, of course I could do with someone up there. But there's a problem: the place is haunted by an evil spirit. Three of my farmhands got strangled to death up there. That's why I don't want anyone to go. And that counts for you too."

"I'm not scared," answered Konrad. "It's my belief that if you do your duty and place your faith in God nothing can happen to you. Please let me go!"

The farmer hesitated. But finally he reasoned with himself: "Why not? Konrad's a good fellow. He'll manage all right."

So he agreed to hire Konrad from May Day to Martinmas (the 11ᵗʰ of November), the wages being a pair of rough drill breeches, a homespun shirt and a pair of wooden clogs.

Konrad would fain have gone at once. But the mountains still lay deep in snow. There was also a lot of work to be done in preparation for the move. A large cauldron was fetched from the cellar. It had not been used for the past three years. Konrad set to cleaning it. Härchi's daughter, Annie, brought him fine sand, and together they rubbed and scrubbed until it was shining bright as silver.

"Aren't you scared?" asked Annie.

"Scared? What's there to be scared of?"

"But Spys Alp is haunted! You must have heard. Three men have already been strangled. What if the ghost twists your neck! Oh my goodness, it's too terrible even to think of it!"

"Don't worry," said Konrad. "I'm not afraid. If I do everything in God's name, nothing can happen to me."

On hearing this, Annie was reassured.

"Look," said her mother to Konrad. "Here are the things you need for the cheese. You'd better check everything. See, some of the prongs in the cheese harp are loose."

Konrad mended everything and put his things in order.

"Are you sure you know how to make cheese?" asked Annie.

"Of course I do. My grandfather taught me. I helped him three summers long on Sinsgäu Alp. First you have to separate the curds from the whey, then you put the curds into the wooden mould. And then all you have to do is look after it, turn it regularly, rub salt into it, and the cheese will be fine. You'll see."

Little Annie felt rather proud of Konrad. She grew more and more fond of him. But she said nothing of this.

April went by and May came. The warm sun melted the mountain snow on the alpine pastures, and by June the migration could begin.

哈爾希想來想去，終於説服了自己：怎麼不？康拉德是個好夥子，他懂照顧自己的。

他於是同意雇用康拉德。這樣從五月頭到十一月聖馬丁節，康拉德給哈爾希幹活兒。哈爾希給他的報酬是一條褲子、幾件襯衫和幾雙鞋。

康拉德恨不能馬上就上山，可是山上的積雪還很厚，得等化了雪後才能上去，再説還得準備些帶上去的東西。哈爾希家的地窖裏有一口大鍋，三年沒使用了，康拉德高高興興的擦鍋子。哈爾希的女兒安妮給康拉德一些沙，他們一起將鍋擦得像鏡子一樣透亮。

「你不害怕麼？」安妮問他。

「害怕？有什麼好怕的？」

「斯匹司山鬧鬼呀！你一定聽過的。這個鬼整天在山上遊走，已經掐死了三個人。要是鬼哪天掐著你的脖子，天啊天！我想也不敢想啊！」

「你怕什麼，我幹的一切都是以上帝的名義，反正我是沒什麼好怕的。」

聽康拉德這麼一説，安妮心裏輕鬆了些。

「聽著，」安妮的母親對康拉德説，「你製造乳酪需要這些東西。你得檢查清楚啊。看，這乳酪叉有幾個尖子鬆了。」

康拉德把用具修理好，把一切收拾妥當。

「你真的曉得怎樣製造乳酪嗎？」安妮問。

「當然曉得，祖父教我的。我在星士高山幫了他三年。首先把凝乳和乳醬分開，然後把凝乳放進木模子裏，再小心看著便成，不時翻翻，灑點鹽，乳酪便會很好，瞧著吧。」

安妮越來越喜歡康拉德了，心裏很為他驕傲，可是她對誰都不說。

一轉眼已進入五月了，暖烘烘的太陽將山上和草原的積雪融化了，踏入六月，康拉德就要上山了。

哈爾希讓另一奶農幫康拉德扛著東西上山，安妮的母親給準備了一麻袋麵粉、熏豬肉、糖和鹽，外加一壺製膏藥用的燒酒。幹活兒的工具山上的小屋裏都有。在特烈殊谷放牛的老唯西給了他們五頭母牛和三頭公牛，還說有足夠的牛鈴和鞭子讓他們領隊上山。哈爾希伸出一隻手劃了個十字，但願上帝保護康拉德，安妮的母親囑咐康拉德萬事要小心，安妮把手伸給他，默默無語。

當天，那兩個夥子走到特烈殊谷；第二天一早，他們到了山上。康拉德走在最前面，身後跟著一頭帶著花環和鈴鐺的母牛，其他牛跟著走，走在最後的是隨行的奶農。蔚藍的天空，淺綠的森林，陽光將牛角染成了金黃色，將剛才還處在陰影下的斯匹司緩緩地普照在光輝和溫暖之中。

「那兒一定有很好的野乾草，」康拉德想著。牛群乖乖地向前走著，沒什麼蚊子，路上一切順利。

下午他們到達海支，老百陵格從農舍跑出來，看到他們，驚奇得一句話也說不出來。

Härchi appointed a young dairy hand to help Konrad carry everything up to the alp. Härchi's wife gave Konrad a bag of flour, a piece of smoked bacon, some sugar and salt, and a dram of liquor to use in poultices. All the tools and equipment he needed were already up in the chalet. Old Weysei, who herded cows in Trisch Valley, was giving them five cows and three heifers. He said he had enough bells and whips for the procession up to the alp. Härchi made the sign of the cross above Konrad's head and Härchi's wife said, "Take care of yourself, Konrad." And little Annie gave him her hand but was so moved that she couldn't utter a word.

That day, the two youths climbed up as far as Trisch Valley. On the following morning, they set off for the alp. Konrad led the way, followed by the leading cow with her crown of flowers and the big bell. Then came the other cows and the heifers, and finally the farmhand. The sky was blue, and the forest was clothed in the fresh green of spring. The sun bathed the tips of the Buochser Horn in gold, then glided slowly down the mountain slope, until her light and her warmth reached Spys Alp, that had been lying deep in shade.

"Plenty of wild hay there," mused Konrad. The cattle were walking well. There were no gadflies. The herdsmen made good progress.

When they reached Hegi, old Berlinger came out from the barn, speechless with amazement at seeing them.

"Well, well, well," he finally declared. "You are not thinking of going up to Spys, are you?"

"Yes, we are," answered Konrad. "It's high time the alp was used again. Such fine meadows!"

"Yea, and such a fine ghost haunting the place," shouted Berlinger, crossing himself and then running into the house, as though he had the devil at his heels.

Konrad laughed good-naturedly. They continued

on their way, and by midday they had reached the gate to the alpine pasture.

"Right," said the dairy hand. "As far as I'm concerned, you can go to the devil. I'm not going a step further. Farewell, Konrad." While saying this, he gazed at his companion as if it was for the last time. "Farewell. Here, take this bottle of holy water. It might come in useful."

Konrad thanked him, and the dairy hand disappeared even faster than old Berlinger before. Then Konrad opened the gate saying, "God bless us! … Come on cows, shoo, shoo!" And the cows slowly ambled into the meadow.

"Come on, start eating!" shouted Konrad. Strangely the animals didn't seem to want to start grazing, although it was a magnificent meadow, lush with thick green summer grass. But gradually they acquired the taste, and one after the other they started to feed.

Konrad carried his things up to the chalet. He soon found the key. It was hidden beneath the stone lintel of the doorway, just as his master had said. It was an enormous rusty key, which screeched as he turned it in the lock. Konrad pushed open the door, calling out: "May God bless this house!"

The door led straight into the only room, which was a kitchen, a parlour and a cheese dairy all in one. There were still cinders in the hearth. The spit was leaning against the wall. On the other side of the room Konrad saw a table and two benches. From the walls hung ladles of every size, a long-handled copper pan and a wooden rack to place the pan on, the so-called 'Pfannenknecht'. Konrad opened the shutters, swept away the cobwebs, and sunlight and fresh air came streaming in.

Behind the house, there was a hut that served as a milk pantry. It contained a wooden vat and a nice flat trough with a waste pipe. But it was dark and freezing cold inside, and Konrad was shivering as he

「怎麼啦，」他終於説道，「你們不是想到斯匹司山吧？」

「正是啊，」康拉德回答，「該是時候再好好利用斯匹司山了，草地那麼美。」

「對，鬼也很美哩。」百陵格喊道，一面劃十字架一面飛奔進屋子裏，好像魔鬼追在後面似的。

康拉德好脾氣的笑笑。他們繼續上路，中午時分便到達高山草原的柵門。

「好了，」奶農説：「現在我得回頭了，你自己多保重吧。」他一邊説一邊看著康拉德，好像是再也見不到他似的，隨手掏出一小瓶聖水，遞過去説：「這東西會保佑你的。」

康拉德接過瓶子道了謝，奶農轉身就消失了，比先前的百陵格跑得更快。康拉德打開柵門時，説了聲：「上帝保佑。牛，走吧，呼呼！」牛慢慢地湧了進去。

草長得非常茂密。「吃吧吃吧，」康拉德喊著，奇怪的是牛不吃。過了一會兒，牛聞到了草香，漸漸地開始吃草了。

康拉德扛著東西走向小屋，依主人的指示找到了放在石門楣上的鑰匙，鑰匙有棍子那麼大，生了鏽。康拉德打開門，朝屋裏望了一眼説道：「上帝保佑這屋子！」接著就踏進屋來。

小屋就這麼一間，既是廚房又是正房，得在那兒做乳酪。灶裏還有灰，烤肉的鉛絲一根根的靠著牆。屋子的另一端放著一張桌子和兩條板凳，牆上掛著大大小小的勺子、一個長柄銅鍋和鍋架。康拉德打開窗戶護欄，揮掉蜘蛛網讓屋子通通氣。

小屋後面另有一間存放牛奶的屋子，屋裏有一個大木桶，還有一個飼料槽。剛從陽光裏進來的康拉德覺得這屋子像冰窖一樣冷。

「得去看看牛棚。」康拉德對自己說。

牛棚緊挨著屋子。牛棚裏一塌糊塗，坑裏還有牛糞，拴牛的麻繩都腐爛了，飼料槽裏放著用來叉乾草的叉子也斷了。

康拉德回到小屋，爬上閣樓。他打開窗板，房間亮點，但一扇小窗子透進來那麼一小方塊的光，驅不去整個房間的黑暗。

「就在這裏掛十字架吧。」他這麼決定了，便回到柵門那兒拿鍋子，吊在火爐上，還捎來一點木頭。

太陽已照到牛角山的後面了，不一會兒天就要黑了。康拉德將牛趕回棚裏，牠們很溫順。他擠了奶，將奶倒進奶房的木桶裏，又將牛糞清掃一通，最後還給牛刷了個身，給棚裏鋪些新乾草。康拉德每幹一件事都要來一句：上帝保佑我的工作。

幹完活兒，康拉德閂上牛棚的門回小屋睡覺去。

這一覺睡得特別好，當康拉德醒來時，太陽已將山後面的天映紅了。

「嘿，我還活著。」說著，康拉德揉揉眼，在「上帝保佑」下起了床。不一會兒的工夫，他就擠好牛奶，將牛隻放出棚子，自己吃了早飯，還做好了第一塊小乳酪。康拉德將乳酪放進模子裏，上面蓋著木板，然後加上一塊石頭壓著木板，這樣做出來的乳酪樣子好看些。

一晃三天過去了，康拉德在第三天晚

came out into the sun.

"Now I'll have a look at the cowshed," he said to himself.

The cowshed was built up against the chalet. But things did not look as neat inside. The manure trough was still full of old dung; the ropes used for tying up the cattle lay rotting on the ground; and there was a broken pitchfork in the feeding trough.

Konrad went back inside the chalet and up the steps into the attic. There, he opened the shutters. The room brightened, but the little square of light from the one small window could not entirely dispel the darkness.

"I'll hang the crucifix up here," he decided. He went back to the gate, fetched the cauldron and hung it in the fireplace. Then he brought in some wood.

The sun had almost gone down behind Mount Horn. Evening came, and Konrad drove the cattle into the shed. They were docile. He milked the cows and poured the milk into the wooden vat in the pantry. Then he mucked out the shed, cleaned the animals and gave them fresh leaves. At each stage in his work he said, "God bless my work".

Finally he closed up the cowshed and went to bed.

He slept like a bear, and when he awoke the next morning the sun was already painting the sky behind the mountains red.

"Well, well, I'm still alive," said Konrad as he rubbed his eyes, invoking God's blessing as he got up. He milked the cows and let them out of the shed. After breakfast, he made his first batch of cheese and put it into the wooden mould, onto which he placed a heavy stone so that the cheese would keep its shape.

Three days had gone by in a flash, and as he climbed up to his attic on the third evening Konrad muttered to himself: "What's all this fuss about a ghost! I haven't seen the slightest sign of anything like that up here."

But there was a ghost. And Konrad was to encounter him the following day.

That morning, he was about to go down the steps from his attic when he heard a rustling sound coming from the milk pantry.

"Probably a mouse," thought Konrad. Then he saw the chalet door open and a grizzled old man come in. He had a long white beard and deep-set eyes that gazed out mournfully into the distance.

Konrad felt a cold shudder run down his spine. "He must be the one who strangled the three others. If he …!" His heart pounded as he thought of what might happen.

Meanwhile, the old man had come into the chalet. Only now did Konrad see that he was carrying a wooden pail. The man went to the cauldron, emptied the pail into it and then returned to the milk pantry.

"Anyone who works as hard as that can't be a murderer," mused Konrad, his fears instantly dissipated.

He went down into the room and lit the fire. The old man had emptied another pailful into the cauldron. They waited until the milk curdled, and then the old man stirred it with the cheese harp.

"He seems to know how to make cheese. Well, I'll let him get on with it," thought Konrad. But he didn't say a word.

He wondered who the man was, but he didn't ask. He went into the cowshed and found the animals were all still there, as calm and placid as ever.

"If that man really was a ghost, they'd have taken fright," he said to himself.

The old man was sitting by the cheese kettle, stirring energetically. After breakfast, he gestured to Konrad that the curd was ready and that he could start cheese-making. Then he went out, but by midday he was back again. Konrad said, "Let's eat together. God bless us!"

The old man ate no more than a few spoonfuls,

上去小屋的閣樓睡覺時心裏嘀咕著:「都讓這個斯匹司鬼給嚇的,我怎麼到現在還沒見到鬼呢!」

可是鬼還是來了,第四天,康拉德就遇到它了。

那天早上,當康拉德去奶房時,就聽見裏面簌簌地響。

「可能是老鼠吧。」康拉德心裏嘀咕。可是門大開著,只見裏面有一個白髮老人,他有一把長鬍子,一雙大眼睛深深地陷在眼窩裏,正用悲哀的目光看著遠方。

康拉德的脊樑骨一下子就涼了,「這肯定是那個掐死了三個人的鬼,要是他現在掐死我……」康拉德想著,心咚咚地快要跳出喉嚨來。

老人出了奶房走到小屋來,這時康拉德才看到他手裏拿著一隻木桶。那人將桶裏的奶倒進鍋裏,隨後拿著桶又回到奶房裏。

「像他這樣勤力幹活兒的人,哪裏會殺人呢?」想到這裏,康拉德心裏的恐懼已飛走了一半。

康拉德在灶裏點上火,老人提著桶進進出出,把奶倒在鍋裏,等到奶凝固,便用乳酪叉攪拌著。

「他還會做乳酪呢,就讓他做好了。」康拉德想,仍是一聲不發。

這老人到底是誰?康拉德心裏奇怪,但他沒有發問。他去牛棚看看,一切還是老樣子,牛也若無其事的。

「這老人要真是鬼,牛哪能這樣安靜?」他對自己說。

老人坐在乳酪鍋旁,用力攪拌。早餐

瑞士中部的傳說

後，他向康拉德示意牛乳凝固了，可以開始做乳酪了，然後便走出去。到了中午，老人走進屋來，康拉德對他說：「上帝保佑我們，吃飯吧。」

老人只吃了幾口，用悲哀的眼神看著康拉德，一句話也沒說。就這樣過了三天，康拉德有了勇氣終於敢開口了，他問老人到底是誰。老人望著康拉德，像是要把他看個透，接著說：「我是個老斯匹司人，七十年前死的，因為生前挪動了牧場的界石，被懲罰得做三百年的鬼，不得安息。每天夜裏我就變成了幽靈，還得扛著那些界石，只有在聖誕夜那天才能休息。現在你知道了吧。」

「你真是個可憐的人，我怎麼才能替你贖罪？」

「時間還沒到，我現在還不許對別人說。」

「那我就等著吧。你可不可以告訴我，那三個哈爾希的雇農到底是什麼一回事？」

斯匹司鬼忽然暴躁起來，他一跳老高，握著拳頭咆哮著：「那些人都是些無賴，對，他們都是無賴！」他大聲吼叫著，康拉德一下子又開始害怕起來。

斯匹司鬼的臉變得蠟一樣白，兩隻眼裏充滿了凶狠的神情。

「那些人一天到晚詛咒幹活兒，就想著怎麼偷懶，他們當然不能替我贖罪了，所以我把他們掐死了。」他的話像是用刀切著說的。他一邊說話，一邊還把細長的手指捏在一起，好像要把那三個可憐人再掐死一遍似的。康拉德不由兩手抱著自己

contemplated Konrad with mournful eyes and spoke not a word. It wasn't until three days later that Konrad summoned enough courage to ask him to tell him why, in God's name, he was so sad. The stranger looked at Konrad with piercing eyes that seemed to see right through him. Then he said:

"I'm old Spysler, the man from Spys. I died seventy years ago. But I'm doomed to wander around for three hundred years and can find no peace. I moved the boundary stones of the alp. Now I have to do bitter penance. Night after night, a burning spectre, I have to drag old boundary stones around. My only night of rest is Christmas Eve. There," he added heaving a sigh, "now you know."

"You are much to be pitied," said Konrad kindly. "I'd certainly like to redeem you. Tell me what I have to do."

"The time has not yet come for me to tell you."

"Well then, in God's name, I'll wait. But tell me one thing: What really happened to Härchi's three farmhands?"

At this the spectre fell into a rage. He leapt up, panting furiously and clasping his fists.

"They were scoundrels, vile scoundrels," he shrieked wildly, striking fear into Konrad's heart.

Then old Spysler grew deathly pale, and a sinister expression came into his eyes.

"They cursed their work, day and night. They lazed around, stealing God's time. Such brutes would never have been able to redeem me. So I strangled them." Thus he spoke, his words as sharp as knives. His lean fingers curled as though he was about to throw himself at the throats of the three miserable wretches. Instinctively, Konrad clutched at his own throat. What if the Spys ghost were to pounce on him?

"You don't have to worry, Konrad," said Spysler, as though he had guessed the young man's thoughts. "You're a good farmhand, and you do everything in God's name. If anyone can redeem me it's you."

At this Konrad immediately felt better. He quickly

said, "You only have to tell me …"

"Yes I know, but I can't talk yet."

The two of them lived together in peace and harmony for the whole of that summer. Konrad was glad Spysler was there. He found his work easy; the animals were happy and in the best of health, and the golden loaves of cheese in the attic gleamed appetisingly.

One day in August, they went up towards Mount Horn to make hay. From there you could see all the way down to Beckenried. There was the lake looking like a pool of lead, and on the meadow next to Isrige House laundry could be seen spread out for bleaching. Konrad thought he could make out a girl moving around among the sheets and towels. He felt a surge of warmth in his heart and gave a great whoop of joy. "Don't you sometimes feel like shouting and yelling?" he asked old Spysler. "Why don't you try?"

"I'm not in the mood, Konrad. In another fortnight you'll be going back down into the valley."

"Never mind. I'll be coming back again next year."

"But I do mind, Konrad. Please, don't leave me all alone up here. For the love of God, please take me with you!"

Konrad looked at him. Then he said, "As far as I'm concerned you can come. But what about the others, the dairy hand, the master and his wife, and little Annie? They'd all be scared out of their wits if they saw you. No, old dad, it's out of the question!"

"I'd keep absolutely quiet. No one would see me. Only you. I wouldn't harm anyone either. I promise." Spysler said no more. But his looks spoke words. "Have pity," they said.

Konrad nodded. "All right. I trust you. I'll take you down to Beckenried, and you can live with me in my room."

Spysler was as grateful as if he had just been rescued from a most terrible fate.

So it happened that when Konrad Hummliger came down from the alp, just before the annual fair

的脖子。如果斯匹司鬼突然襲擊他，那怎麼辦？

「康拉德，你不需要害怕。」斯匹司鬼說，彷彿猜到這年青人在想什麼。「你是個好雇農，做什麼都沒忘記上帝，要是有人能替我贖罪，那就是你了。」

聽到這裏康拉德心裏稍微鬆了口氣。他立刻說，「你告訴我便成……」

「我知道，但是我現在還不許說。」

整個夏季，一人一鬼平安無事地共處，康拉德很高興他不是一個人在山上。他覺得工作很容易。牛長得壯實，堆在閣樓上金黃色的乳酪發出誘人的香氣。

八月的一天，他們走上牛角山造禾草。從那裏可以一直望到貝肯裏德。那裏有一個像鉛造似的湖，在哈爾希家隔鄰的草原上，可以看見晾在外面漂白的衣服，康拉德覺得還看見一個姑娘在床單和毛巾間走動。他心中湧起一絲溫暖，不禁興奮地大聲歡呼起來。隨後他對斯匹司鬼說：「你試試也喊兩聲吧。」

「我可沒有興致喊什麼。康拉德呀，你還有兩個禮拜就要下山了呀。」

「哎，這沒什麼，反正明年我還要上來的。」

「沒什麼？康拉德，千萬不要丟我一人在這兒，你下山帶上我吧！」

康拉德看了看他說：「我倒是願意帶你下山，可是別人……擠奶的雇農、哈爾希、哈爾希的老婆和小安妮，他們看見你一定要嚇死了。不行不行，這肯定不行的。」

「我不開口，除了你之外沒有人能看

見我，我保證不碰任何一個人。」斯匹司鬼沒再說什麼，但他的眼光裏盡是哀求。

康拉德最終點了點頭，「好吧，我相信你。我帶你回貝肯裏德，你就和我一起住吧。

斯匹司鬼千謝萬謝，好像康拉德剛救了他一條命似的。

因此，當康拉德下山時，他身伴多了個隱形趕牛人。康拉德想趕在利列茲的周年市集舉辦前下山。那幾個在山上柵欄處等著接康拉德下山的雇農都沒察覺什麼，但他們都驚奇得幾乎不敢相信自己的眼睛。

「怎麼，你還活著？」

「不，我死了，我二十年前就死了，你真是個笨蛋。」康拉德笑道。由他這麼一說，他們反倒是安心了點。

貝肯裏德的人見到康拉德和那群牛時，沒有不驚訝的。哈爾希更是目瞪口呆，他老婆驚奇地舉起雙手，安妮則抓著圍裙的一角不停地拭眼淚。

「怎麼可能呢？看啦，康拉德……怎麼可能呢？牛長得結實呀，還有這麼多的乳酪！」

人們問這問那，康拉德不停地說山上的種種，唯獨斯匹司鬼的事他隻字不提，要是人家問起，他像個長者似的說：「現在不說這個，還不到時候。」

從此康拉德就和斯匹司鬼同住在哈爾希家的一間下房。斯匹司鬼多半蹲在一條板凳上，晚上康拉德回來後就向他說起那些牲口、他一天幹的活兒，還有哈爾希一家人待他怎麼好。康拉德可以一直在哈爾希家幹活兒，願幹到那天就那天，哈爾希說了。

in Reydlich, he had an invisible drover with him. Not even Härchi's two farmhands who were waiting for them at the gate noticed anything, although their eyes were popping out of their heads.

"What? You're not dead?" asked the dairy hand.

"You idiot, I've been dead for twenty years, dead as a doornail, can't you see?" laughed Konrad. At that the dairy hand felt better.

Everyone in Beckenried was not a little surprised to see Konrad arriving with the cattle. His master stood there open-mouthed, and his mistress threw up her hands in surprise. But little Annie had to wipe away a tear with the corner of her apron.

"My goodness, here's Konrad! What about that? The cows too, all healthy ... and look at all the fine cheeses!"

Everyone crowded round, and Konrad had to tell them about Spys Alp. He didn't even mention the Spys ghost, and when they asked him he simply replied like old Spysler: "The time is not yet come."

From then on the Spys ghost lived with Konrad in his little room. He'd sit on the bench all day, and in the evenings Konrad would tell him about the cattle, about his work and how well his master was treating him. He said that the farmer had told him he could stay at his farm as long as he wanted. So he did not have to leave at Martinmas as had been agreed. That was a good thing!

Then one fine day Konrad told Spysler that he had told Härchi all about him.

"You stupid fellow! You shouldn't have done that."

"I couldn't help it. Master heard sounds in my room. He asked me what was up. So I had to tell him. Or should I have lied to him?"

"On no, you mustn't do that," said Spysler. "But what did your master say?"

"He said he was satisfied I had done the right

thing. But he wanted to know how you can be redeemed. He wants to help you as far as he possibly can."

Now Spysler looked rather more cheerful.

"Tell Härchi I'll tell you all on Christmas Eve," he said.

Härchi was not quite satisfied with this news. He was the kind of person who likes to get matters settled at once. But now he had to wait, whether he liked it or not.

Christmas Eve came, and Spysler went with Konrad to the midnight mass in Buochs. On the way home along the lakeshore, they came to a wayside shrine. Here Spysler stopped, set down his candle and said, "Now I can talk."

It was pitch dark. A cold wind came whistling from across the lake, whirling up flurries of snow. But it did not blow out Spysler's candle. The flame continued to burn as if there were absolutely no wind.

"Listen, Konrad, I'll tell you now where the boundary stones stood before I moved them. The line goes straight up from the chalet to the fence; then, from the end of the fence for about six yards down as far as a blue stone with a cross carved into it. I'm afraid I covered the stone with moss. Seven yards further down, there used to be a fir tree with markings on it, but all that's left now is the stump. But next to that there's a juniper tree. From there the line continues for more than eight yards as far as a flat slab of rock. You can't see the cross on the rock any more, because I scraped off the top layer and threw it down the gully. From there you go as far as the old double-crowned ash. After that, the boundary's correctly marked. Now, I want you to tell Härchi to put back the boundary markings to where they were originally. And then he should also have communion hosts baked from his own corn. For each unbroken host he should have a holy mass read. If he does all that I'll be redeemed."

有一天，康拉德對斯匹司鬼説：「哈爾希知道你的事了，我原原本本都對他説了。」

「你不該説的，你真是個笨傢伙。」

「哎，不是我要説，哈爾希聽見屋裏有聲音，他問我來著，我只能告訴他，你認為我應該騙他嗎？」

「當然不要騙人了！哈爾希對你説什麼了？」

「哈爾希一點也沒有不高興，他對我很滿意，覺得我做得對。他還問能不能也幫你贖罪？只要他能幫上忙的，儘管説好了。」

斯匹司鬼現在看來開心了點。

「到聖誕前夕我才能説，你就這麼告訴哈爾希吧。」他説道。

哈爾希聽到康拉德轉告的話不大滿意，他歷來喜歡有什麼事就馬上解決，現在他必須等著，不管他樂意還是不樂意。

聖誕前夕到了。康拉德和斯匹司鬼去布茲城參加午夜彌撒。回家的路上，他們走到湖邊一個神龕。斯匹司鬼放下蠟燭，對康拉德開了口：「現在我可以説了。」

四周一片黑壓壓，陰冷的風從湖面嗖嗖迎面吹來，雪花在天空裏亂舞，可是蠟燭的火苗依然筆直地燃燒著，根本不理會風的存在。

「好吧，我現在就告訴你原先的邊界石在哪裏。邊界線從哈爾希家山上小屋一直伸到柵欄處，然後在柵欄盡頭直落六碼到一塊上面刻著十字的藍石頭，這塊石頭恐怕被我用青苔蓋住了；再往下走七碼原來是一棵杉樹，上面有標記的，但樹被我砍了，現在只能看見樹椿。它旁邊有一棵樅樹，往下走八碼多就能見到一塊扁平

的岩石，岩石上的十字被我磨掉了，石也
給我丟進溝裏去了。從這裏走到一棵老白
蠟樹那兒，邊界線就在那兒。你對哈爾希
説，讓他把地界標記放回原先的地方，他
也要用自己的玉米烘聖餐的聖餅，每個不
碎的聖餅他要做一堂彌撒。要是他這麼做
了，我的罪就贖完了。」

　　等到康拉德説過要做什麼來替斯匹司
鬼贖罪後，哈爾希一下子憤怒起來：「什
麼？什麼？新邊界！我買這塊地時就是現
在這個樣子，完全合法。我沒侵佔誰的
一分土地，我可不挪什麼地界標記！」

　　「這是為了給斯匹司鬼贖罪啊，他當
時挪了界石做錯了事，現在他自己不能贖
罪，這是有關他靈魂得不得到安寧啊。」

　　「他靈魂得到安寧？但是誰管我的名
譽了？難道我的名譽一文不值？」哈爾希
越説越激動。

　　「這和你的名譽沒關係。」康拉德
説。

　　「和我的名譽沒關係？你怎麼不明
白，沒有人會相信是斯匹司鬼挪動了地界
標記，所有的人都會説是我挪的，因為我
良心上有壓力，現在又挪回來了。」

　　哈爾希不停地搖頭，咕噥著好像説「不
不不」。康拉德還不死心：「但是……！」

　　「邊界的事別提了！我可以做彌撒，
你可以向斯匹司鬼説，但地界標記的事免
問！」

　　康拉德憂愁地離開了。斯匹司鬼聽罷
壞消息後搖搖頭。「光是彌撒不行的。邊
界一天不歸回原位，我的靈魂一天得不到
安息。」

　　又一個夏季到了，康拉德和斯匹司
鬼又上了山。這年的天氣非常糟糕，下了

Härchi was furious when he heard what he was
supposed to do to redeem the Spys ghost.

"New boundaries! I bought every bit of my
land perfectly legally. I bought the alp exactly as it is
marked now. I certainly shall not draw new boundary
lines."

"But if it means eternal peace for the Spys ghost?
He did wrong and cannot put it right himself. It's his
salvation that's at stake."

"His salvation, so what? What about my honour?
Does that count for nothing?" protested Härchi.

"It's got nothing to do with your honour," Konrad
answered.

"But don't you see? No one in the world will
believe the story of the Spys ghost. Everyone will say
it was I who moved the boundary markings in the first
place, and that I want to move them back because I'm
being plagued by my bad conscience."

Härchi kept shaking his head and mumbling
something that sounded like "no". But Konrad did
not give up.

"But ...!"

"Not another word about the boundary! I'll have
the masses read, you can tell Spysler that. But as for
the boundary markings, he can forget it!"

Konrad left him sadly. Spysler shook his head when
he heard the bad news. "The masses alone won't do.
My soul won't find rest unless the boundaries are put
back."

The next summer they went back up to the alp.
That year the weather was bad. A terrible hailstorm
broke out over Spys Alp and ruined all the grass. But
Spysler just laughed out loud, shouting at each clap
of thunder: "Ha ha, the boundary lords have come
at last!"

Konrad felt cold shivers down his spine.

The following week, Flower, their best cow, fell
to her death over the edge of the Fuilplatte. Konrad
went down into the valley to report the accident.

"Perhaps he'll notice now," he thought, as he went into Isrige House. But Härchi did not bat an eyelid. He received the news as if it were a normal accident, something you just have to accept.

Autumn came, and soon after the alpine fair it grew very cold. The feast of Saint Nicholas (on the 6th of December) was heralded by storms and snow.

Konrad had his lodger in his room again. Härchi was still very pleased with Konrad. Of course he was sad that Flower was no longer in the cowshed, and he could not quite forget the hailstorm. But after all, that was not Konrad's fault, he reflected.It never occurred to him that it might have been someone else's fault!

Konrad tried again to bring up the subject of old Spysler, but Härchi dismissed him saying, "You know my decision. It's still no. I'm not one to say yea today and nay tomorrow."

Konrad wondered what would have to happen for his master to swallow his pride. The answer was to come quite unexpectedly.

One night, someone knocked at Konrad's door. He jumped out of bed, lit a butter lamp and got dressed. His master was standing outside the door.

"Konrad," he said, "go down to Buochs and fetch the priest. Little Annie has a fever. Really bad. I'm at my wits' end."

Suddenly Konrad was wide awake. Annie sick? My little Annie, he said to himself, and then it suddenly occurred to him that he was very fond of her. My God, let her not die!

He lit a resin torch and went out into the dark night.

The priest in Buochs could doctor bodies and souls. At first he was rather annoyed to be woken up in the middle of the night. But then he agreed without further ado to go back with Konrad to Isrige House. He had taken along with him a little bag of herbs, and the brews and poultices they made out of them soon cured Annie's fever, and she fell asleep.

一場大冰雹，把所有斯匹司山的草都給毀了。但斯匹司鬼狂笑不停，對著外面的雷雨說：「地界大爺終於來了，哈哈哈⋯⋯」

康拉德覺得自己的脊樑骨一陣冰涼。

一個禮拜後，山上最壯實的牛「花兒」掉下富匹勒崖死了，康拉德急忙下山向哈爾希家報告，心想：哈爾希大概也意識到點什麼了吧。當他向哈爾希說了山上發生的事後，哈爾希眼皮子抬也沒抬一下，認為不過是一般的意外，沒啥特別，只有接受現實。

日子一天一天的過去，轉眼已是寒冷的深秋，聖尼古勞斯節（十二月六日）也在狂風暴雪中來臨了。

康拉德再跟他的房客一起在小屋裏生活。哈爾希對他沒有不滿意。當然「花兒」不在牛房他感到傷心。他也沒法忘記那場大冰暴，但想那畢竟不是康拉德的錯。他就是沒想到那可能是另外一個人的錯哩！

康拉德不時還是提起給斯匹司鬼贖罪的事，每次哈爾希都搖著頭，同一個神情：你是知道我的態度的，我不會今天說行，明天說不行，不行就是不行！

怎麼樣才能令哈爾希克服他過強的自尊呢？當康拉德左思右想不得法時，忽然發生了一件意外。

一天夜裏有人敲門，康拉德點上油燈，套上衣服開了門，一看是哈爾希站在門外。

「康拉德你快下山去布茲城叫神父來，小安妮發高燒，情況很糟，我不知道該怎麼辦了。」哈爾希急切地說。

聽到這裏，康拉德一下子完全醒了過來。安妮病了！我的小安妮！這時他才意識到自己是那麼的喜歡安妮。她可不能死啊！

康拉德點上一根松枝火把，出門走進黑夜中。

布茲城的神父懂得醫治肉身，也醫治靈魂。深更半夜被康拉德叫醒，他有點不悅，但知道有人病了，就帶上一小袋藥草隨著康拉德走了。安妮喝了神父調配的藥，敷了藥膏不久就退了燒。

但第二天夜裏，安妮的病情惡化了，康拉德又去請神父。路上，康拉德對神父說情況很糟糕，女主人擔心安妮恐怕不行了。安妮還是發高燒，迷迷糊糊的老是有幻覺，呢喃著斯匹司山什麼的。康拉德又對神父說起斯匹司鬼，當然還說到哈爾希不肯克服自尊的事。

他們半夜兩點到達哈爾希家。

「哈爾希在哪兒？」神父問女主人。「我得先替他治病。」

安妮的母親有點驚訝，但她不發一言推開起居室的門，這時哈爾希正跪在十字架前面對基督說：「我造了什麼孽，你要把我女兒帶走？我不是個好基督徒嗎？我救濟窮人，我每個禮拜天都到布茲城上教堂參加彌撒。你到底為什麼要帶走我的小安妮？讓她留在我身旁啊。只要安妮不死，你讓我做什麼都行。」

「我知道你該做什麼。」神父將雙手放在哈爾希肩上，哈爾希吃了一驚。「哈爾希，驕傲的人啊，將斯匹司山上的地界標記放回原處吧，一切便會回復舊時模樣了。」神父說。

「你別也來跟我說邊界邊界什麼的。誰管我的名譽、我的好名聲？」

「若你重視這些更甚於安妮的性命，那便無話可說了。你真的在乎人家說你什麼？上帝的意旨不是更重要嗎？」

But the following night her illness grew worse. Again Konrad had to call the priest. On their way to Isrige House, Konrad told him that things looked very serious and that his mistress thought Annie was dying. She was delirious with a fever and kept saying something about Spys Alp. Konrad also told the priest about the ghost and how Härchi could not overcome his pride.

They arrived at Isrige House around two in the morning.

"Where's the master?" the priest asked the mistress of the house. "He's the one I have to cure first."

The farmer's wife looked surprised. But she said nothing and pushed open the door to the parlour. There was Härchi, down on his knees in front of the crucifix, speaking to our Holy Saviour: "What have I done for you to take my little Annie from me? Am I not a good Christian? I give alms to the poor. I go to mass in Buochs every Sunday. And yet you want to take away little Annie, my only child! Please let me keep her. Tell me what I should do so that she doesn't die."

"I know what you need to do," said the priest. Härchi was startled. But the priest laid a hand on his shoulder and continued, "Härchi, you proud man, reset the boundaries on Spys Alp and everything will turn out well again."

"Don't you come talking to me about that cursed boundary too. I can't. My honour and my reputation won't let me."

"Well if your reputation is worth more to you than your daughter Annie, so be it. But isn't it all the same to you what people say? Isn't God's will more important?"

"Well, if you look at it like that I suppose you're right. Yes, let people say what they will. If only little Annie …!" And proud Härchi started to weep like a child.

But the priest hurried to Annie's bedside to give her Extreme Unction. He anointed her with the blessed oil, and then he and Annie's mother and Konrad remained for a long time beside the bed, praying. Then the priest said to the mother:

"Now only God can help. But Härchi's cured. And I think that your daughter will soon be better."

He was right. Annie fell into a deep sleep. She was no longer plagued by frightening, delirious dreams, and slept soundly. By midday her fever had almost gone and she looked much better. The priest came regularly, and his potions worked well. His patient grew stronger by the day.

Then Härchi said to Konrad, "Tomorrow you can take the flour to the monastery in Engelberg. And on the way, hand in this letter to the head alderman in Buochs. It's about the boundary markings. You can tell Spysler that everything is being done as he wished."

How happy Konrad was!

Everything went according to plan. The boundaries of Spys Alp were reset. The monks in Engelberg made hosts out of the flour, but only three of them came out unbroken, so Härchi had three masses celebrated, the last one on Whit Monday. That evening all of them – the master and his mistress, little Annie, the priest, Konrad and the dairyman – had their meal together in the best parlour. They recited the rosary for Spysler. As they were praying, he suddenly appeared before them, his eyes shining, his robe as white as the hair in his beard. Then, slowly, the apparition faded until it was gone.

A little later, a wedding was celebrated in Isrige House. No need to tell whose wedding it was! In any case, there was enough room in the house for Konrad's mother and brothers and sisters, who were all very proud of their clever big brother.

「好吧，這麼説來你或許是對的，管人家説什麼去吧，只要小安妮⋯⋯」驕傲的哈爾希像個孩子一樣號啕大哭起來。

神父趕到安妮的床前，為她行臨終聖禮，給她塗聖油。安妮的母親和康拉德留在床邊禱告。神父對安妮的母親説：「現在就讓上帝來幫我們吧！哈爾希給治好了，我想安妮會好起來的。」

就像神父説的那樣，安妮睡得很沉很好，噩夢和幻覺都消失了，到中午時燒也退了，精神好多了。神父按時來，他的藥很有效，安妮漸漸康復了。

哈爾希對康拉德説：「明天你去把麵粉拿到英格堡的修院，順將這封信交給布茲市議會的議員吧，是關於邊界標記的。你告訴斯匹司鬼，説一切都會照他的意思去做。」

康拉德聽後非常高興。

該做的事都一件件辦妥了，斯匹司山的邊界給從新劃定。英格堡的僧侶用麵粉做聖餅，但只有三個沒破，哈爾希便辦了三堂彌撒，最後一堂是在聖靈降臨節的禮拜一。那天晚上，大家——男女主人、小安妮、神父、康拉德和奶農——都聚集到哈爾希家最寬敞的一間屋子裏，為斯匹司鬼唸玫瑰經。忽然，斯匹司鬼出現了，眼裏含著淚水，他的長袍跟鬍子一樣的雪白；過了一會兒，他的身影越來越淡，最終完全消失了。

不久，哈爾希家裏舉辦了一場盛大的婚禮。誰的婚禮也不用説了。家裏有的是地方，康拉德的母親和六個兄弟姊妹都被接來一塊兒住，他們打心眼兒為康拉德的好心腸感到驕傲。

漢斯葛尼塞樂 Hans Gnyssäler

漢斯葛尼塞樂和兩個也從狼席森來的朋友到第萊博多去。第萊博多就是施坦斯山後面一個雅致的高山草原。他們想在那裏打狐狸。那時是冬天，雪很多。那個夜晚很明朗，月亮像黃白色的乳酪。三個獵人在高山一所茅屋裏過夜。那兩個朋友坐在壁爐前，木柴在爐中劈啪作響。葛尼塞樂站在窗口，上膛的獵槍在他的旁邊。他留心的注視著外面的一片漆黑，但直到半夜都沒見有狐狸來。

突然，他發現有人從山上的茅屋走下來。他腳步沉重地走在雪地上，背上架著很重的東西。

「你們快過來看，」葛尼塞樂說，「有人走下山來。」

另外兩個人來到窗前，以為只是隻狐狸。看清楚了，原來是個男人冒著雪走向山腳的茅屋。他們還看到那個男人把背著的東西放在地上，然後逐一的擺在牆前。這時，他們才發現那人背著的是木柴。

「這麼晚了，他想去哪兒？雪又那麼厚，」維斯說，「真奇怪。」他們看著看著，那個人突然消失了。

Gnyssäler and two other men from Wolfenschiessen were up on Diräbode Alp, a fine meadow just behind the Stanserhorn. They had come up to shoot foxes. It was winter. Everything was covered in a thick layer of snow, and the moon sat like a yellow-white cheese in the sparkling clear sky. The three huntsmen had taken shelter in one of the chalets on the alp. Two of them were sitting in front of the bright, crackling log fire. But Hans Gnyssäler was standing by the window. He had his loaded gun beside him and was peering out into the darkness. It was almost midnight, yet there was not a fox in sight.

Suddenly, he saw a man come out of the chalet higher up on the alp. With a seemingly heavy load in the carrying frame on his back, he started to trudge laboriously through the deep snow.

"Come and have a look," said Gnyssäler to the others. "Look! There's someone coming down the hill."

The two others came up to the window. First they thought it was a fox, but then, as he got closer, they saw it was a man coming through the snow on his way to the lower chalet. While they watched, he reached the building and, putting down his load, started to pile wooden logs neatly against the wall.

"What on earth can he be doing, in the middle of the night and in all this snow?" asked Wysel. "It's weird!" Then, as they watched, the man suddenly disappeared.

"We'd better look into this," suggested Gnyssäler. They went outside, intending to follow the man's tracks down to the other chalet. But, seek as they might, they could find no tracks. There was not a single footprint to be seen in the deep snow; and when they reached the lower chalet, there was also not a single log to be seen on the spot where the man had been piling up the wood.

They stared at each other in consternation. Shaking with fear, Wysel said, "Well, things like that do happen, you know. A soul can find no rest; he has to wander upon the earth because he moved boundary stones or a fence during his lifetime. May God help him if he is one of those poor souls!"

The three men went back home to Wolfenschiessen without having shot a single fox. And Hans Gnyssäler never went hunting foxes on Diräbode Alp again.

「我們去看看是怎麼一回事。」葛尼塞樂説。他們出去想順著那個人的腳印走到下面的茅屋，但是他們找來找去，找不到任何腳印。這麼厚的雪裏竟然一個腳印都沒有，而且到了下面的茅屋那人放柴枝的地方，也連一根木柴都看不到。

他們驚慌地注視著對方，其中一個朋友維斯目瞪口呆，戰抖地説：「這是可能發生的。一個人活著的時候把界石或柵欄移到別人的地裏，死了之後不得安息，就會在世上四處遊蕩。如果他是一個這樣可憐的靈魂，上帝該幫助他。」

他們三個人沒有打到狐狸就回家了，而且葛尼塞樂從此再也沒去過第萊博多打狐狸了。

艾嫩特布根的巫婆　The Ennetbürgen Witch

艾嫩特布根一個議員，不幸有一個寧願喜歡魔鬼也不喜歡自己老公的妻子。一天，久被折磨的丈夫忍不住把她告到政府去，說她是個狡猾的巫婆。

　　政府官員當然相信議員的話，便討論如何抓住他的妻子。他們以買木頭為藉口，讓一個人到議員那裏去，騙議員的妻子到城裏去。

　　約好的那一天，來了個人買六立方米木頭，他把木頭放到車上。議員對妻子說：「你不是還想買雙鞋嗎？為了一雙鞋不值得叫鞋匠來這裏，你乾脆親自去施坦斯挑一雙你喜歡的鞋子吧。」妻子同意了。議員又說天氣不好，太冷，叫她不要穿舊鞋，最好穿拖鞋，坐在車子的木頭上到城裏去。她又同意了。最後議員說，「還是用條繩子把你拴在車子上吧，因為拉車的牲口還小，跳蹦蹦的，路上坑坑窪窪的又不好走，我不想你掉下車呢！」她再一次同意丈夫的提議。

　　車子一到達施坦斯，人們便點燃車上的木柴，把車上的一切，包括巫婆，都一起燒掉了。

　　你看，這個女子救不了自己，因為她的魔法消失了：她沒穿鞋子，不能踩在地上，碰不到地面，所以施展不了法術。

One of the aldermen of Ennetbürgen was unfortunate enough to have a wife who preferred to consort with the devil rather than with her own lawful husband. This so vexed him that he could no longer put up with the situation, and so he reported his wife to the authorities, telling them she was a cunning fiend.

Of course they believed him, so they contrived a plan to catch her out: they would send a man to the house to buy wood, and he would trick the woman into going back to town with him.

On the appointed day the man arrived, bought two cords of firewood and loaded them onto his cart. Whereupon the alderman said to his wife: "Didn't you say you needed a new pair of shoes? There's no point having the cobbler come here for just one pair. Why don't you go to Stans yourself and buy a pair you really like?" His wife readily concurred. Then her husband suggested that, as the weather was so nasty and cold, she could put on slippers instead of her old shoes, and ride in the cart on top of the wood. Again she agreed. Finally the alderman said, "We'd better tie you to the cart with a rope. The horse is rather young and sprightly and the road's very steep and bumpy. We don't want you falling off!" Again the woman agreed to her husband's suggestion.

Once the cart had arrived in Stans the men set fire to the wood, and everything, including the witch, was burnt to a cinder.

You see, the woman could not save herself, for her magical powers had forsaken her: without shoes she could not put her feet to the ground, and without touching the earth a witch cannot perform her witchcraft.

田野的獵人　The Huntsman
in the Field

Jaggi, the clerk from Aennerberg, had always been regarded as a good huntsman. But in his later years his luck seemed to have forsaken him. Why was this? Let Christen the blacksmith, who was also a hunter, tell the story.

One December night, Jaggi went up to the little field on Birge Hill to go hunting. The ground was sparsely covered by a thin carpet of snow and the moon was shining so brightly that you could see each blade of grass and each little twig. He got to the refuge and settled down to await his prey. He had not been waiting long before he espied a fox coming up towards him from the marsh. He levelled his gun at it. But suddenly the fox rose up and ran on towards him on its hind legs. "Say your prayers, you idiot," Jaggi muttered to himself. "I'll get you."

He aimed. The shot rang out, and Jaggi distinctly saw the fox collapse and fall to the ground. But when he got to the spot – no fox. Jaggi walked in the direction the animal had come from – no tracks in the snow!

The incident unsettled him. Two days later, he went back to exactly the same place.

安納山的史裏伯亞高年青的時候被視為一個好獵人，但年紀大了，他的運氣就變了。為什麼呢？就讓史密德何裏施特告訴你吧，他也是個獵人哩。

有一年的十月，亞高到比爾格山的田地打獵，那時有很多雪，而且月光明亮得很，連一片草葉、一根樹枝都看得清清楚楚。亞高躲藏妥當等候獵物，待了不久便看見一隻狐狸從沼澤那邊走過來。握搶瞄準時，他發現狐狸突然用兩條後腿走路。他呢喃道：「怎麼祈禱都保護不了你。你逃不掉的！」

他瞄準狐狸，一聲槍響。他看見狐狸被子彈擊中倒下來。他忙跑過去，卻看不見什麼狐狸。他往狐狸來的方向跑，雪裏也沒發現狐狸的足跡。

他覺得很奇怪。兩天後，他又去那個地方打獵。

剛到那裏，他看見一個人走過來。月光很亮，眼睛不會騙他。真的是一個大男人走過來，但是他的領子上只有脖子，沒有頭。亞高被嚇得脊背上冷一陣熱一陣。他不敢再看那個人，但是他還是看見了那個人把頭夾在自己的胳膊下。亞高直站在那裏，嚇得全身癱瘓。最後他敢動了，就飛奔回家。

從此以後，亞高打獵的運氣就變得不好了。

He had not been waiting long before he suddenly saw coming towards him in the bright moonlight – it was so bright he couldn't have been mistaken – a tall man with only the stump of a neck emerging from his collar. There was no head! An icy shudder ran down Jaggi's back. Then he broke into a sweat. Not bearing to look, he yet perceived that the man was carrying his head under his arm. For a moment he stood there, paralysed with fear. Then he turned on his heels and ran off as fast as his legs could carry him.

Since then, Jaggi the clerk has never had any luck at hunting.

Cream Greta

Not far from the village of Andermatt in the district of Urseren at the foot of the Gotthard, you can see an enormous rock. It is of a milky colour and is shaped like a small house. And indeed, in ancient times, on the exact spot where the rock now stands, there used to be a little house that was inhabited by an old woman. The village people called her Cream Greta. For, although she had only one small cow, she somehow managed to sell as much cream as a farmer with a herd of fifty cows feeding on the lush grass of the rich mountain pastures. People wondered how she did it.

One day one of the neighbouring farmers could contain his curiosity no longer. He crept into Cream Greta's cowshed and hid in the grain bin. When the old woman came in to milk her cow, the man peeped out through a crack in the side of the bin to see what she would do.

She set a large empty milk pail on the floor in front of her. She poured a little cream from a small jug into the pail. Then she moved her hands in a sorceress' blessing and chanted the following rhyme:

Witches' craft and farmers' skill
With frothy cream this pail shall fill

Immediately the pail was filled to the rim with the finest white cream. The old woman hoisted the pail onto her shoulder with a laugh. She was in the best of spirits as she left the cowshed.

The man had seen enough. He remained in the

離烏瑟棱區安德馬特村不遠有一座山叫聖哥達，它下面的山谷裏有一塊岩石。岩石的顏色像牛奶，外形像一個小房子。以前在那個岩石的地方是一座房屋，住著個老太太，村子裏的人叫她「奶油格萊特」。雖然她只有一隻小牛，但是她能賣很多奶油，跟一個有五十頭牛的農夫一樣，牛還是在肥沃的草原放牧哩。人們都想知道是怎麼回事。

有一天，鄰居之中的一個農民禁不住好奇心，溜進了奶油格萊特的牛棚，躲在一個飼料槽裏。老太太來擠奶時，農民從木板的裂縫向外偷看，想知道她幹什麼。

他看見老太太把一個很大的空奶桶放在前面，然後從一個小罐子倒一點奶油，像巫婆一樣揮動著手唸唸有詞：

巫婆魔法農夫技
奶油填滿一桶子

擠奶桶馬上就滿滿的裝了最好的白色奶油。她笑著把桶放在肩膀上，高高興興地出門去了。

bin just long enough to memorise the spell and then climbed out, ran home to his own cowshed, locked the door, fetched an empty milk pail and placed it in front of him, just as he had seen Cream Greta do. But he decided one pailful of cream was not quite enough. So he changed the spell. Waving his arms he muttered:

Witches' craft and farmers' skill
With frothy cream ten vats shall fill

Cream came gushing in. In less than a second the pail was full. But the cream continued to bubble and flow.

"Enough," shouted the man, trying to drop his arms. But they kept making the magic gestures, as though a spell had been cast on them. In next to no time, the cream had come up over the rim of the food bin, then as high as the windowsills and over the top of the man's head, drowning him in its thick white flood. Still the river of cream continued to rise, bursting through the door into the hayloft, pouring out through the shingles in the roof. On and on it surged, running in rivulets down the walls of the house, growing thicker and thicker, deeper and deeper, until finally the whole building was ripped from its foundations and borne down into the valley on a milky white, shimmering stream. Cream Greta could be seen perched on the rooftop, shrieking with laughter.

老太太離開後，農民還呆在那兒，牢記著她的咒語，然後爬出來，跑回家進了自己的牛棚，鎖上門。他跟奶油格萊特一樣，也把一個空奶桶放在前面。但是他嫌一個桶子的奶油太少了，所以改了那個咒語，搖著雙臂呢喃道：

巫婆魔法農夫技
奶油填滿十桶子

馬上就滿滿的；但是，奶油還不停地流出來。

「夠了，」他喊道，想垂下兩臂停止，可是他那雙手臂彷彿受了魔咒般，又提起來施法。很快奶油浸到飼料槽、牛棚的視窗，然後淹過他的頭，最後濃稠的白色液體把他溺斃了。只是，奶油仍繼續流出來，湧向打穀場的門，從木板屋頂的隙縫中滲出來。它越來越濃，越來越深，小河一般從屋子的牆上流下來。整個房子給

"There's one who won't try to copy me again," she screeched in scorn. She did not notice the black clouds gathering in the sky. Complete darkness descended on the valley. Then, with a rumbling roar, the foehn storm rushed in, bending the trees and tossing the farmhouse up into the air like a rag ball. A gust of wind seized the witch, and she was hurled through the air, her skirts fluttering, her hair streaming out wildly behind her. As the terrified villagers watched, the house was whirled around a few more times before landing in a meadow with a thunderous crash and the rattling of a hundred milk pails. There it remained standing, a great milky white block.

It is said that Cream Greta still sits in the middle of the stone, keeping watch over the greedy farmer. She is to guard him until the day of the Last Judgement. Then, when the angels blow their trumpets, the white rock will burst asunder and the two bewitched creatures will be set free.

連根拔起,順著閃亮的白色奶油河漂流。奶油格萊特坐在她的屋頂上,開懷大笑。

「他再也不會摹仿我了。」她嘲弄地尖聲喊道。可是她沒發現山谷上烏雲密佈,天空突然變暗,一聲雷響之後刮起狂風。風把樹吹得東歪西倒,農舍也被刮到空中。巫婆被狂風吹到屋頂上,頭髮和裙子也在風中翻飛。給嚇壞了的村民看到那個房子上下飛旋,最後隨著一聲巨響,及一百個牛奶桶的碰撞聲,掉到一個草地上,最終變成了一塊奶白色的巨石。

據說,大石頭裏的奶油格萊特看守著貪婪的農民。直到最後審判日來臨,天使吹喇叭的時候,那個大岩石才會裂開,那兩個被施魔法的人才會被解咒,重獲自由。

The Gnome
on Mount Stanserhorn

施坦斯山的山精靈

施坦斯山的其中一個山坡叫做石山，這個地方住著山精靈。這些小人給山坡的奶農和地主的幫忙不少，所以很受歡迎。

離石山不遠有一個高山牧場，名叫「奧伯福」。奧伯福下面有另一個高山牧場，名叫「呂提馬特」。夏天的時候，石山的一個山精靈經常去奧伯福和呂提馬特的小屋休息，弄點吃的，也幫幫高山牧場的人各種各樣的忙。他餵牲口還幫忙割乾草。高山牧場的人很慷慨地招待他，他漸漸成為他們最好的朋友。

那山精靈有一個習慣，就是總愛坐在火爐旁一張石頭椅子上。一天，一些輕浮的人想捉弄他。他們看他從山上下來，就把他平時坐的石頭椅子燒得火熱。他來了，坐到石頭椅子上，給燙得直跳起來。從此，那山精靈再也沒回來了。

There is a slope on Mount Stanserhorn that is known as Steinberg, or Stone Mountain. This slope used to be inhabited by gnomes. The little fellows tended to be very helpful, so they were looked on as welcome visitors by the dairymen and landowners in the region.

Near Stone Mountain, there is an alp which is called Obfluh, and another, lower down, called Rüti Meadow. During the busy summer season, one of the gnomes of Stone Mountain often used to stop for a bite at the chalets in Obfluh or Rüti Meadow, and then he'd help the herdsmen at their varied tasks. For example, he'd tend the cattle and help make hay. In return, the herdsmen hosted him generously. In time, the gnome came to be one of their most trusted companions.

The gnome had his own particular seat next to the hearth in the chalet. One day, some thoughtless fellows played a trick on him. Seeing him approach down the steep mountain slope, they quickly heated up the stone slab he used as a seat, until it was blistering hot. The gnome came inside, sat down, jumped up, went away, and was never seen again.

達裏維橋的魔鬼　The Devil on Dallenwil Bridge

Once upon a time, a very long time ago, nearly every evening at dusk, a man could be seen standing at the head of the bridge across the Aa near Dallenwil. (There's a bridge there to this day.) No one knew who he was. There was something foreign and uncanny about him. So when he was there, no one dared to cross the bridge.

Then a couple of men from Dallenwil made up their minds to show the weird fellow what was what.

One evening, just as it was starting to grow dark, the lads went to the bridge and accosted the stranger: "What do you think you're doing here? Are you collecting bridge tolls? Since when does this bridge belong to you? You've got no business here. So clear off!" And they leaped at the unearthly creature, meaning to beat him up. But he made a lunge at them with arms like mighty claws, shouting: "I'll stay here as long as I like. If any of you thinks he can challenge me, he's welcome. Let him show his

很久很久以前，有一個人經常在太陽快下山的時候站在橫跨阿伊河的達裏維橋頭。誰都不知道他是誰。他看上去像外來的，樣子有點怪異，所以他在的時候沒人敢過橋。

幾個達裏維的人決定要讓那個奇怪的人知道這裏的規矩。

一個晚上，當天快黑的時候，他們去到橋上問那個陌生人：「你在這兒幹什麼？收過橋稅嗎？從什麼時候開始這條橋屬於你了？這兒不是你說了就算，快滾！」他們衝向那個幽靈似的傢伙，想痛打他一頓。但是他那好像巨爪似的手臂向他們撲過來喊道：「我想在這兒呆多久就呆多久。如果有人想跟我打架，那就試試，看他膽子有多大。如果他贏了，我馬上就走，如果我比他厲害，那麼他就屬於我了。現在誰敢過來？」

勞倫茲，小夥子中最高最壯的一個說：「我來對付你，你嚇唬不倒我的。」話剛說完，他像老虎似的撲向那個陌生人。

就這樣，兩個人打得不可開交，作生死之戰似的；兩個人都把對方摔倒在地上，骨頭摔得格格作響。時間越長，勞倫茲越感到吃力。當那個幽靈般的人把他拖過石路逼近河邊的時候，他鞋子上的釘子和地面磨擦出火花。

另外那些人看著這場毆鬥，越來越感到不安。眼前的這個場面並不讓他們樂觀，其中一個人喊道：「勞倫茲，你還撐得住嗎？」

「不行了，」他說，「上帝幫我啊，不然我就死定了。」

就在他說完「上帝幫我」這句話後，傳來一聲巨大的雷響，勞倫茲就翻滾到地上。這時，周圍的光變成綠黃色，大家看到一個像煤球一樣黑的魔鬼從橋上跳進阿伊河裏，那正是它剛剛想把勞倫茲扔進去的地方。

大家把失去知覺的勞倫茲帶到家裏。勞倫茲那雙爬山靴上的新鞋釘都斷了鈍了，鞋底也磨穿了。

mettle. If he defeats me, I'll go. But if I turn out to be stronger than him, well then he'll be mine. Come on then, who fancies a fight?"

Lorenz, the biggest and strongest of the lads, replied: "I'll take you up on that. You can't scare me!" And he threw himself at the fellow with all the fury of a wildcat.

It was a matter of life or death. They wrestled and they struggled. They threw each other to the ground, grappling with each other until you heard the cracking of bones. The longer it lasted, the more Lorenz lost ground. The nails in his shoes threw up sparks as the spook dragged him over the stones, closer and closer to the riverbank.

The others watched the fight with increasing unease. They did not at all like the way things were turning out. One of them shouted to his friend, "Lorenz, can you keep it up?"

"I can't," he answered. "Without God's help, I've had it."

But as soon as he uttered the words 'God's help' there was a loud clap as of thunder. Lorenz was sent whirling through the grass, the light all around turned yellowy green, and then they saw a coal-black devil leap from the bridge into the Aa, just where he had tried to throw Lorenz.

Lorenz was carried home, half unconscious. The new hobnails in his mountain boots were all broken and blunted, and the soles were quite burnt through.

艾梅頓的女巫石 — The Witches' Rock in Emmetten

If you take the road to Seelisberg and then, turning right after the school, take the rather steep little road that zigzags up towards the vast Emmetten alpine pastures, you will reach the narrow Kohl Valley. In the middle of this valley there's a flat meadow, and in the middle of this meadow there's an enormous rock.

Originally, this rock stood high up on Oberbauen Alp. Then, one day, the god-fearing Emmetten folk built a chapel, dedicated to the Holy Cross, down in the valley on the banks of the Tschäderibach (Babbling Brook). But the coming and going of pilgrims, the solemn sound of the Angelus bell ringing out through the calm of the valley and up the mountain roused and startled the witches who lived among the rocks and in the caves above the chapel. They were angry with the people for disturbing their peace, and all that devotion and the veneration for the Holy Cross infuriated them. They resolved to wipe the chapel from the face of the earth. The brook, which flowed through a deep gorge near the chapel, would come in very useful for their plan. The witches decided to dam it, so that the waters would attack the foundations of the building and make it collapse.

Immediately they got down to work. An enormous rock from Oberbauen Alp was loaded onto the shoulders of an old hag who, bent double beneath

從學校通往茲利斯堡的大街往右拐,再順著那條陡峭但寬闊的山路朝艾梅頓草原走,就到達狹窄的煤山谷。這個小山谷中央差不多平坦的草地上,有一塊石頭。

這塊石頭原本在很高的歐伯保恩的高山牧場上。艾梅頓的人篤信上帝,他們在山谷柴德里巴賀小溪旁建了一座朝拜神聖十字架的小教堂。這個小教堂蓋好了,虔誠的人經常去祈禱,萬福的鐘聲迴盪在山谷裏、山頂上,驚動了教堂上方住在石堆岩洞裏的女巫。那些人打擾了女巫寧靜的生活,她們很生氣。人們對神聖十字架的崇拜也惹惱她們,所以她們決定讓小教堂消失。不遠正好有一條從深溝流出來的小河,這正好派用場。女巫決定築壩攔住小河,讓河水沖毀教堂的基石,令它倒塌。

她們馬上著手做這個困難的工作。她們把一塊歐伯保恩高山的巨石放在一個老女巫的肩膀上，她扛著石頭蹣跚地走下山坡，背都給壓得彎下來了。到了局非圖裏的懸崖邊，她遲疑起來，不知道怎樣繼續。她大著膽子扛著大石猛跳下去，竟跳了二百米，安全地落在懸崖下一塊扁平的石頭上。她的腳陷進石頭裏好幾吋。從此來到這個地方的小孩子，沒有一個不崇拜她那勇敢的一跳，並且要和她比比腳的大小。

老女巫繼續把大石頭扛在肩頭上，接下來的路很順利。那時已經是夜晚，神聖十字架教堂的萬福鐘在山谷下發出寧靜而虔誠的聲音。老女巫一聽到鐘聲，就失去魔力，重重的石頭把她壓扁了。直到今天，她還被壓在那塊石頭下面。有的時候，行人還可以聽到她的歎氣和呻吟。只是，從那天起誰都不能移動這塊石頭，巫婆的計畫徹底失敗了。

her heavy burden, started staggering down the slope. When she reached the edge of the cliff at Küpfitürli she hesitated, not knowing how to continue. But then, holding onto her rock, she took a great flying leap and landed safely on her feet on a level slab of rock two hundred metres further down. On landing, her feet sank several inches into the stone, leaving such a clear imprint that, to this day, not a boy from Emmetten can pass the spot without marvelling at her bold leap and measuring and comparing the old hag's footprints with his own.

From there, she continued without obstacle, still bearing the mighty rock on her rugged shoulders. Evening descended, and the godly sound of the Angelus bell rang out serenely from the valley. But at the sound of the bell the witch lost all her magic powers. Collapsing under the massive weight of her burden, the poor old hag was crushed flat. Her body was pressed deep into the ground. And there she lies to this day, banished beneath the mighty rock. From time to time, a passerby might hear her groaning and moaning. But from that day on, no power could move the stone, and thus was the witches' plan confounded.

The Ancient Lords of the Mountains

Insofar as they have not been completely forgotten, the woodwoses are generally considered to have been the first inhabitants and therefore the rightful owners of our high Alpine pastures. They kept cows and engaged in dairy farming and cheese production long, long before the ancestors of today's mountain folk populated the region. And then people of our kind came and robbed them of their pastures and herds, forcing them to retreat into the inaccessible mountain clefts. Thereafter, in their unquenchable thirst for vengeance, the woodwoses would send down devastating tempests and thunderstorms from their mountain retreat. It was to protect themselves from these elemental forces that men later built holy chapels high up near the glaciers and the eternal snows.

According to legend, the place name 'Scheidegg' (on Mount Rigi above the Lake of Lucerne) dates back to those distant days when the mountain herdsmen were still threatened by the sorcery of their embittered forerunners. Those giant men – so tall their heads touched the clouds – with flaming eyes the size of hundred-pound cheese loaves, could still often be seen wandering around among the mountain chalets. They would leave behind them a terrible smell of sulphur. Once, a herdsman by the name of Klaus encountered some of them while he was tending his herds on the upper Geschwände Alp. The stench was so strong that it knocked him down, smiting him with paralysis in all four limbs.

Strangely enough, it was the mountain dairyman Florentin who found the cure for Klaus's paralysis. Florentin had been courting Klaus's daughter against the will of her stern father, and it was precisely on the

如果人們不善忘，當會記得山妖原來是阿爾卑斯山的原居民，也是這些高山牧場合法的主人。很久以前，遠在現代山民的祖先在這裏聚居以前，山妖已經善於做牛奶和乳酪。然後我們這些人來了，搶去他們的牧場和牛，山妖被迫離開，藏在山中的洞穴裏。自此，他們為了報仇雪恨，會從山洞那兒發動狂風暴雨。人們為了保護自己，於是在冰川及雪山旁建造神聖的教堂。

當時的牧人非常害怕山妖的巫術。傳說沙得格（位於琉森湖上的瑞吉山）這個地名是從那個時候來的。現在你仍不時可以看到重達一百磅的巨人在村子的周圍出沒，他們的眼睛火紅，頭差不多碰到雲端。他們走過時還會留下一種硫磺味兒。有一次，一個叫克勞斯的牧人在加司尉德山放牧時遇到他們，他們強烈的臭味立刻令他暈倒過來，四肢癱瘓。

很奇怪，竟然是一個叫夫洛倫汀的奶農找到治克勞斯癱瘓的解藥。夫洛倫汀早跟克勞斯的女兒相愛，不過克勞斯一直反對。就在夫洛倫汀和克勞斯女兒偷偷見面的地點，他發現了含有解藥的神奇水源，不久克勞斯便完全康復了。

終於，夫洛倫汀跟克勞斯的女兒結婚了。他們給新建造的房子起了一個名字，叫「沙得格」，就是「分離角」的意思，用以紀念他們原本沒有希望的愛情。

雖然山裏的巨人不再是威脅，人們還是決定做點預防措施：在加梳，高山平原的牧人建立了一個兄弟會，保護他們的是牧人的守護神溫得林、馬賽魯斯和安東尼斯。每年七月二十五日聖約伯節，會員會在卡泊裏山上慶祝，他們開心地跳舞、摔跤。他們興高采烈之際會插入一場表演，提醒大家和阿爾卑斯山山妖可怕的相遇和戰鬥。表演是這樣的：兩個牧人戴上面具，披著青苔和羊齒草，裝扮成一對兇悍的山妖夫婦，四處跳躍狂奔。

spot where the two lovers had their secret tryst that he discovered a miraculous spring of healing water that soon completely cured old Klaus.

Subsequently, Florentin and Klaus's daughter got married. They named their newly built house Scheidegg, which means "parting corner", in memory of the original hopelessness of their passionate love.

Although the terrible encounter with the mountain giants had come to a good end, they decided to insure themselves against future harm. Down in Gersau, together with the other users of the alpine commons, they founded a fraternity under the patronage of Wendelin, Marcellus and Antonius, the patron saints of herdsmen. Every year on St Jacob's Day, which is the 25th of July, the members of the fraternity celebrate their feastday with jolly dancing and wrestling. Suddenly, though, the festivities are rudely interrupted by a scene intended to remind everyone of the terrible encounters and conflicts with the old woodwoses: Two herdsmen wearing masks and clothed in moss and fir fronds appear and prance around, giving a realistic impression of a fierce woodwose and his wild woman.

無畏的牧人　The Intrepid Cowherd

Behind the village of Escholzmatt in Entlebuch Valley there is an alp which, in ancient days, used to be haunted. At the very mention of it, the herdsmen would tremble and glance anxiously behind their backs. Of those who had been up there with their cattle, there was not one who had not lost at least one of his best dairy cows in the course of a summer.

Anyone looking down onto the haunted alp from the slopes above could see signs that one or several ghostly herdsmen were at work there. In the morning the cattle were driven out to pasture, in the evening they were taken in again, and smoke could be seen rising from the chimney of the chalet. But no human being was to be seen, not a master, not a man, not a boy.

One day, an audacious young cowherd turned up in the district. He was quite fascinated by the haunted alp and wanted to go up and find out its secret. The other herdsmen sought in vain to hold him back. They particularly warned him against going into the chalet. No one who had gone in had ever come out alive! But nothing could stop the young lad.

"I want to see those ghostly churns with my own eyes," he said.

The next morning, to their dismay, his friends saw him confidently make his way up to the alp.

Sammy – for that was the bold cowherd's name – reached the chalet at about midday. Deathly silence reigned. Not a breath of wind. Not a bird in the sky. The branches of the big fir tree beside the hut were motionless. The blades of grass looked rigid. The spring water ran soundlessly into the cattle trough. As

據説，恩桃伯谷的伊曹茲密村附近一家高山牧場過去曾鬧鬼。住在附近的牧人只要提起這個牧場，總會不安地往身後看一眼，渾身發抖。在這個地方放牧的牧人，一個夏天下來沒有誰不曾丟失過一兩條最好的奶牛的。

從附近的山嶺往鬧鬼的牧場看，總能看到幾個幽靈似的牧人在牧場上工作，他們白天在草地上放牛，晚上把奶牛帶回牧場。小屋的煙囱裏可以看見冒出的煙，但從來沒見過一個人，沒有主人，沒有男人，也沒有男孩。

直到一天，一個很有膽量的牧人來到這個地方，他被這鬧鬼的高山牧場迷住了，想去找尋它的秘密。其他的牧人拼命勸告他，想讓他改變想法，但都是白費心思。他們特別告誡他千萬不要進那個小屋，因為沒有一個人進去後還能出來的。這個年輕小子還是決定冒險一試。

他説：「我只想親眼看看那些幽靈一般的牛奶桶。」

第二天清晨，我們這位勇敢的牧人滿懷信心地走向牧場，他的朋友只能無能為力地目送他漸漸走遠。

這位勇敢的牧人名叫薩穆爾。經過一

早上的跋涉，中午他終於到達這個鬧鬼的牧場。只見房屋四周死寂一片，沒有風，沒有鳥，屋旁那棵大紅杉樹的樹枝紋風不動，就連草也是僵直的。他走近小屋的時候，鞋釘踏在石上也沒發出聲音，只隱約聽到泉水輕聲地從岩石裏冒出來，湧進已經盈滿的水槽裏。薩穆爾忽然害怕起來。

他從矮窗往房子裏望，喊了幾聲可是沒有人回應，彷彿有魔咒把這幢房子周圍的一切變成靜止不動，甚至連牛棚上也沒有一個蒼蠅。

薩穆爾往門口走去。大門有魔法似的，靜靜地自動打開。他跨過門檻，走進屋子。壁爐裏的火是燃著的，火上還放了個乳酪鍋，似乎準備做乳酪，薩穆爾卻聽不見木柴在火中發出的劈啪聲。

「嗨，出來吧！我不怕你！」他大叫道，他想鬼牧人應該就藏在乳酪鍋後面。可是，依舊沒有回音。

薩穆爾繼續往裏走。他貼近牆邊走，看見屋子中間有一個桌子，桌子上擺好了盤子和勺子，而且有好幾種乳酪。薩穆爾再大叫，可還是沒人理他。

一個床鋪擺放在牆邊的一角，被子挺乾淨的，床前還拉著簾子。薩穆爾想，無論如何要查清楚到底是誰住在這裏，於是他躺到床上去，把簾子拉上。

果然，沒多久他就聽見腳步聲吧嗒吧嗒地走進了屋子。他好奇得很，從簾子的一個洞往外窺望：一個嚇人的妖怪進了屋子，它的腳和手像馬蹄，可是臉孔（如果可以把它叫作「臉孔」的話）像馬的頭蓋骨，鼻孔還噴著火，真是恐怖極了！怪獸

Sammy approached the chalet, he could not even hear the clatter of his hobnails on the stones. Suddenly he felt a hint of fear.

He peered into the chalet through the low window. He called out. No one answered. The building and its surroundings all seemed to be under the same spell. Trapped in the frozen silence, nothing moved – not even the fly on the door of the cowshed.

Sammy went up to the chalet door. It opened soundlessly, as if by magic. He crossed the threshold and stepped into the room. The fire in the hearth was lit, and the cheese kettle hung over it ready for cheese making. But Sammy could not hear the crackle of the burning logs.

"Hey, come out. I'm not scared of you," he shouted, imagining the dairyman to be hiding behind the kettle. But there was no answer.

Sammy went further into the room, keeping close to the wall. There was a table there, laid with plates and spoons and various sorts of cheese. Again Sammy called out, again there was no answer.

In a niche in one wall there was a clean-looking bed with a curtain.

"Somehow or other I'll find out who lives here," thought Sammy. He lay down on the bed and drew the curtain.

He did not have to wait long before he heard the sound of feet shuffling towards the chalet. He peeped inquisitively through a hole in the curtain. A gruesome monster was approaching. It had the legs and hooves of a horse and the most hideous face – if it could be named a face at all. In fact, it looked more like a horse's skull, with flames coming out of the nostrils. The monster trotted into the room, went up to the table and counted the plates.

Then with a fearsome roar he cried, "Everything is ready for the funeral feast. But where is the plate for the man in the bed?"

He dashed to the bed, tore open the curtain and grabbed Sammy by the arm.

"Get up and eat," he shouted, dragging the brave

cowherd to the table.

"Now I've had it," thought Sammy. But he kept his composure and said: "I haven't done anything to deserve this meal. So I shan't eat."

Thereupon, the monster sat down at the table and gobbled up all the food himself. Then he fetched a shovel, a pickaxe, a candle and a milk measure and threw them all down on the floor at Sammy's feet.

"Pick those things up and take them down to the cellar," he shrieked.

"I will do no such thing," answered the intrepid Sammy.

So the monster bent down and picked up the things himself.

"Now come down to the cellar with me," he thundered.

"All right," answered Sammy. "But you go ahead."

Down in the cellar the monster pointed to one of the four corners. "Start digging!" he bellowed.

"I haven't buried anything, so I shan't dig anything up," retorted Sammy.

The monster had no choice but to get down to work himself with shovel and pick. He laboured until he had dug out an enormous pot.

"Pick it up," he screamed, so loudly that the roof beams shuddered.

"I'm not picking anything up!" replied Sammy.

The monster picked the pot up from the ground. "Here," he shouted. "Carry it upstairs."

"I carried nothing down. I shan't carry anything up," answered the young man.

The monster hoisted the pot onto his shoulder and staggered heavily up the steps. When he had reached the room, he let the vessel drop with a crash onto the table, grunting, "And now remove the lid."

"I never put the lid on, I shan't take it off," said Sammy.

So the monster removed the lid himself. Sammy stepped back in amazement. The pot was filled to the rim with glistening pieces of gold. The monster

快步走進房間子，跑到桌前計算著桌子上的盤子。

然後他咆哮道：「喪宴準備好了，但躺在床上那人的盤子在哪兒？」妖怪衝到床前，扯開簾子，一把抓住薩穆爾的胳膊。

「站起來，吃東西！」他叫喊著，把薩穆爾硬拉到桌前。

薩穆爾心裏想這下完了，但嘴上卻鎮靜地説：「我沒做什麼值得吃這頓飯，所以我不吃。」

妖怪不理薩穆爾，自顧自的吃喝桌上的食物。吃完飯以後，妖怪拿來鐵鍬、鎬、一根蠟燭和一個量奶器，扔在薩穆爾的前面。

「拿起來放到地窖去！」他尖聲叫道。

「我一個東西也不拿。」薩穆爾無所畏懼地回答。

妖怪沒法，只好自己彎下身子去撿工具。

「那跟著我去地窖。」它大聲喝道。

「好吧，」牧人回答，「但你先走。」

在地窖裏，妖怪指著其中一個牆角吼叫道，「在那邊挖！」

「我又沒在那裏埋東西，我不挖。」薩穆爾反駁道。

妖怪只得自己用鐵鍬與鎬開始挖。挖著，挖著，他挖出一個大壺。

「撿起來！」妖怪一聲震天價響，連屋樑都抖動起來。

「我什麼都不撿。」薩穆爾回答。

妖怪從地上撿起大壺。

「把壺拿到樓上去！」妖怪高聲嚷道。

「我什麼都沒有拿下來，所以什麼都不會帶上去。」薩穆爾回答說。

妖怪只好自己把壺扛在肩膀上，搖搖晃晃地爬上樓梯。到達房間之後，他把壺「嘭」的一聲扔到桌子上，咕嚕直叫：「現在揭開蓋子！」

「我從沒蓋上蓋子，因此不會揭開蓋子。」薩穆爾說。妖怪自己取下蓋子。薩穆爾往後一退，大吃一驚：壺裏裝著滿滿的金幣！妖怪把所有的金幣倒在桌子上，並且分成大小相同的三堆。

「這三堆金幣中，其中一堆給你，第二堆給窮人和那些沒有食物的人，第三堆給那些被我所害的人的寡婦和孤兒。」他對薩穆爾說。「你現在選其中一堆。選對的話，你不僅能解救我，而且你將來的生活會很幸福；選錯的話，我就把你變成肉醬，而我得繼續當鬼，尋找我的救主。」

薩穆爾毫不遲疑，兩臂把三堆金幣湊成一個堆，說：「其中有一堆是對的。」只聽一聲巨響，房屋震動，妖怪突然消失了，變成一個金色頭髮的年青牧人，他的臉開心得發亮：「哎，我終於自由了！從今以後，牧場、牛群、工具和所有金幣都是你的了！」說完他轉身就走。

薩穆爾把所有金幣都裝進一個空的牛乳桶裏，高興地走回村子。其他的牧人看見薩穆爾安全地回來，震驚得連眼睛和嘴巴都合不起來。薩穆爾把帶回來的金幣按照妖怪的指示分發出去，從此過著幸福快樂的日子。

poured them out onto the table and then separated them into three equal piles.

"Of these three piles one belongs to you, one is for the starving poor, and the third is for the widows and orphans of my victims," he said to Sammy. "Now you choose one of them. If you make the right choice, you'll be happy for the rest of your life, and you'll also redeem me. But if you make the wrong choice, too bad for both of us. You'll be reduced to pulp, and I'll have to continue to haunt the place until I find my saviour. "

The cowherd did not hesitate. With a broad gesture he quickly swept all the gold into one heap, crying, "One of them must be the right one."

A clap of thunder shook the house. Suddenly the monster had disappeared. In his place there now stood a fair-haired herdsman who was beaming with happiness. "At last I'm free," he said. "And now all this is yours – the alp, the cattle, the dairy utensils, and all the gold." Then he turned on his heels and was gone.

Sammy put all the gold into an empty milk can and returned to the valley in good cheer.

The other dairymen were flabbergasted to see the young man return all in one piece and laden with riches. He divided up the money exactly as the monster had instructed and lived happily ever after.

女巫與雇農 The Witch and the Farmhand

There once was a young farmhand who never enjoyed a sound night's sleep. He did not have to work too hard and he was well fed, and yet he grew thinner and thinner.

For every night he was visited by a witch who came to his room. She would prise up a floorboard near his bed and change it into a halter, which she then threw around the young man's neck, thereby turning him into a horse. She mounted the horse, and off they galloped.

She always dismounted at the same place, tied the horse to a small tree and then went away. Before the bell for matins rang out, she would return and ride the horse back home.

One night, however, as he was standing under the tree, it occurred to the horse to take off his halter: apparently there was still a human brain within his head. Once the halter was removed, he instantly regained his human form. He waited under the tree. As soon as he saw the witch approach, he flung the halter at her. In a flash she was overpowered and he had slipped it over her head. Now it was she who was the horse.

The farmhand rode her home, put her in the stable, called his master and, showing him the strange beast, said, "Look what a splendid horse I've bought."

"Not bad," said his master.

At that, the farmhand took the halter from the horse's neck, and immediately the master's mistress appeared before their eyes, stark naked.

She was subsequently burned as a witch.

從前有一個年青的雇農，總是沒有機會好好的睡一覺，儘管他工作不怎樣辛苦，也吃著營養豐富的食物，但好像還是越來越消瘦。

原來，每天夜幕降臨的時候，都會有一個女巫來找他，把他床邊地下一個木板變成馬韁，套在他的頸上，於是他變成了馬，她就騎在「馬」上，疾馳而去。

她總是在同一個地方下馬，把馬拴在一棵灌木上然後離開。早晨的鐘聲響起之前，她會再回來把馬騎回家。

直到有一次，馬被拴在灌木上的時候，雇農忽然想到取下馬韁，顯然馬頭裏還有人的腦子。馬韁一取下，他立刻變回人形。他在樹下等著，當女巫回來的時候，他立刻把馬韁擲向她，她躲避不及倒下了，他便閃電一樣把馬韁套在她的頭上。現在她變成「馬」了。

雇農騎著馬回家，把她關在馬棚裏，然後叫主人過來看一看這頭奇怪的馬：「你看，我買的馬是不是很不錯啊？」

「是啊。」主人回答說。

雇農這時從馬頸上取下韁繩，主人的妻子便全身赤裸的在他們眼前出現。

主人的妻子終於受了火刑，這是對女巫的懲罰。

女巫與她的丈夫 — The Witch and her Husband

一名男子的妻子經常在夜裏出去跳舞，可是很長時間他都不察覺，因為妻子出去的時候總把一把掃帚擺在他身旁的床上。一個晚上，那男子終於察覺了，於是靜靜地監視著妻子，只見她進了廚房，之後便聽不見也看不到什麼。早上起床時，妻子已經躺在他的身邊。

第二晚，那男子偷偷地隨著妻子起床，並從鑰匙孔往廚房裏看。他看見妻子穿上漂亮的衣服，戴上珠寶，就像一個未婚的姑娘一樣。穿戴完畢，她便從一個小壺裏拿出軟膏抹在一條小棍子上，然後把棍子放在煙囪裏喃喃地唸咒：

> 往上飛
> 不碰壁
> 到阿薩
> 停下來

一眨眼她就飛上煙囪消失了。

「我也懂這個。」那男子想，於是

There once was a man whose wife often went out dancing at night. For a long time he was unaware of her escapades, since she always placed a broom beside him in the bed before she left. In the end, however, he noticed. So he kept watch, but he only saw her go into the kitchen, and then he heard and saw nothing more of her. In the morning, when he awoke, she was back in the bed beside him.

The next night he sneaked out after her and looked through the keyhole into the kitchen. He saw his wife put on all her finery and jewels, and make herself up just as though she were still an unmarried girl. When she had finished, she took out some ointment from a little pot and smeared it onto a stick, which she then placed inside the chimney, at the same time mumbling the charm:

> *Out the top*
> *Without a knock.*
> *Down in Alsace*
> *There you stop.*

And in the bat of an eyelid, she had disappeared up the chimney.

"Well, I could do that too," said the man to himself. He grabbed the pot and smeared some of the ointment onto a stick, all the while saying:

> Out the top
> Um umm, umm knock!

(He had not understood the rest of the spell.) Immediately, he shot like a rocket up through the flue, only to bump his head so violently against the rim of the chimney that he fell back down onto the kitchen floor more dead than alive.

The following morning, the woman noticed the bruise on her husband's head, but she said not a word. Her husband did not say anything either. But he did not give up, and the next night he watched closely to see exactly what his wife was doing. Again he imitated her, but this time he said:

> Out the top
> Without a knock!

It worked marvellously, and he shot out of the chimney. But once up in the air he did not know in which direction to fly. So it wasn't long before he fell down, right into the middle of thorny bushes, and was dragged around through the undergrowth until it finally occurred to him to let go of his stick.

It was dawn by the time he arrived home. His wife was already awake. Seeing her husband all covered in scratches, she remarked derisively, "Anyone who wants to do what I do needs to go about it a bit more intelligently than you!"

從小壺裏取些軟膏抹在棍子上，並且學著說：

> 往上飛
> 啊啊啊碰壁！

那男子沒全懂後面的咒語。他立刻往上飛，頭卻碰到煙囪的邊緣，掉了下來，躺在廚房的地板上，昏迷不醒。第二天早上，他的妻子發現他頭上有個巨大的腫塊，但是他們誰都沒有討論這件事。那男子不願意放棄，第二天晚上，他小心地看著妻子怎麼做，再次模仿她說：

> 往上飛
> 不碰壁

這次成功了，他從煙囪飛到外面，但到了半空卻不知道要到哪兒去，因此很快便墜下，落到荊棘叢中，還被棍子拖著，穿過矮林。最後，他才想到要鬆開棍子。

回到家已經是早晨了。他的妻子起了床，看見丈夫滿身傷痕便嘲笑地說：「如果你想模仿我，就應該學聰明一點。」

Smoothly Through the Chimney

Once upon a time, a very long time ago, there were two rather strange women who lived in Birchi, in the first or second of the houses on the old road leading from Seedorf or Isleten to the Isen Valley. They had a very fine cherry tree. In fact it was the only one in the whole valley. And so it was quite natural that occasionally people would wheedle a few cherries out of the two women. But they never ate them, for they did not dare to: no one quite trusted the two women or their munificence.

很久很久以前，在貝池的地方，從斯多夫或伊斯力頓往伊信谷的老路上，第一和第二幢小房子住著兩個很奇怪的女人。她們有一棵很美麗的櫻桃樹，也是全谷唯一的一棵櫻桃樹，因此不時有人來問這兩個女人要些櫻桃。取得櫻桃的人一般不敢吃，因為大家都覺得這兩個怪婦人不會那麼慷慨。

One day, however, a young lad was bold enough to help himself from the bowl of cherries the women had offered him. No sooner had he eaten a couple, than he felt a compulsion to leave the parlour and go into the kitchen. There he saw two tiny female creatures at the hearth. They were frenetically stirring something in a pot and muttering the while:

Smoothly through the chimney
Up and out the top!

有一次，女人請一個年輕小夥子吃一盤櫻桃。他壯著膽子吃了幾顆，結果，他身不由己似的離開客廳走進廚房。那裏有兩個矮小的婦人站在爐灶前，一面發狂地攪拌著鍋子裏的東西，一面喃喃自語：

順利穿過煙囪
向上飛升出去

All of a sudden, the lad felt himself being lifted up into the air. He was whisked up through the chimney, out over the roofs and into the sky, across the great mountain ranges, on and on for thousands of miles till he reached some distant continent, where he was finally dropped into a thick prickly bush. He had no idea where he was or what to do. So he started to pray to the Mother of God for help.

突然，小夥子被提到半空，穿過煙囪，越過屋頂，翻過高峻的山巒，飛越千里，最後到達一個遙遠的大洲，摔倒在茂密的荊棘叢中。小夥子站在這塊陌生的地方，不知如何是好，最後只好向聖母禱告求助。

Suddenly a beautiful woman, dressed all in white, stood before him. With a gesture of the hand she showed him which way he should go. Then she disappeared again.

The young man roamed for three days and three nights before he finally reached a monastery he had never seen before. He knocked at the gate. He was made welcome, but none of the monks knew him and none could understand his language. So they led him to the head of the monastery. The worthy man was sitting on a fine chair. A great big book lay open on his knees. It was the *Weltbuch*. The young man explained to him that he was trying to find his way home and told him about the beautiful woman in white who had directed him to the monastery.

"Even if you live to be a hundred and walk for ten hours every day, you will never reach your country unless I bless you," declared the worthy man. Thereupon he raised his right hand in blessing and laid a holy amulet around the boy's neck.

The lad walked and walked for a long long time over hill and dale before at last he saw again his beloved Isen Valley with its green meadows and dark forests of fir.

All that, just for the sake of a couple of cherries!

忽然，他面前出現了一個穿白衣的美麗女子，她用手勢指示他該走的路後就消失了。

小夥子走了三天三夜的路，終於到達一個他從沒見過的寺院。他敲了門，僧人接待他，但是沒有人認識他，也沒有人明白他說的語言。僧人引介他見修道院的院長。院長坐在漂亮的椅子上。他膝蓋上翻開了一本書——世界之書。小夥子向僧人解釋他只是想找路回家，是一個穿白衣的美麗女子指示他來這兒的。

院長回答說：「就算你活到一百歲，每天走十個小時，你還是回不到你的國家。可是，如果我們為你祝福，你就能回家了。」僧人於是舉起右手為他祝福，並給他在頸上掛一個護身符。

年輕人走了許久許久，越過高山峽谷及種種障礙，終於看見他深愛的伊信谷青綠的草原和蒼鬱的林木了。

這都是因為他吃了幾顆櫻桃！

很久以前，哥順是一家高山牧場。現在叫馬司格堡的山上有個房子，夏天那裏住著三兄弟，一個當奶農，一個當牧牛人，另一個是雇工。他們工作不多，因為在草原吃草的牛群不需要特別打理，也不用餵飼。

有一天，他們雖然感到心境愉快，但又覺得很無聊。無所事事，於是他們拿來一塊木頭，開始雕刻木頭人，還裝點布，給它穿上衣服，放在桌子前。

他們覺得這個小木偶挺好玩的，就叫它小漢斯。他們三人吃乳脂時間木偶：「小漢斯，你也想吃嗎？」還把乳脂扔向它。吃米布丁時又問木偶，「小漢斯，你也來一點兒吧。」然後把一點布丁塗在它的鼻子和嘴巴上。過了不久，他們還拿一把勺子塞在小漢斯手裏，教它自己吃。好奇怪，小木偶開始自己進食了。他們先是大吃一驚，不久就習慣了，後來還繼續開它的玩笑。

有一次，他們打雅斯牌。奶農問：「小漢斯，你也想打嗎？」之後便把牌放在小木偶的手裏。起初木偶只是拿著牌，

In olden days, Golzern was an alp. In what is now Metzgerberg there was a chalet which, in the summer, was inhabited by three brothers: a dairyman, a cowherd and a farmhand. They did not have much work, for the cattle in the pastures needed little attention and never had to be fed.

One day, when they felt so high-spirited and so very bored that they hardly knew what to do next, they took a piece of wood and carved a rough head out of it. Then they dressed the figure in rags and set it down at the table.

They had great fun with this wooden doll which they named Hänseli or little Hans. When eating cream, they would ask, "Hänseli, would you like some too?" and then they would throw a dollop at the doll. When eating their rice pudding, they would ask again, "Hänseli, shall we give you a little too?" and they would spread some around his nose and mouth. After a while, they clamped a spoon between Hänseli's claws and showed him how to eat. And, believe it or not, the doll began to eat. That really frightened them at first, but they soon got used to it and continued with their pranks.

Once when they were playing cards the dairyman asked, "Hänseli, do you want to play with us?" and he stuck some cards into the doll's paw. To start with, little Hans only had to hold the cards and his partner picked out the right one and threw it onto the table. But in time, the doll played by himself without help. What fun! From then on he always played with them, and whoever was his partner was bound to win.

The doll ate well and grew big and strong. Every Sunday they had to take him up to the nearby slopes of Crottabiel to sit in the sun. In time he had grown so fat that, even with united efforts, the three of them could hardly carry him. Yet when they moved up to the Oberstafel pasture, they took the doll with them. And when they returned to Golzern they also took him back with them.

All in all it was certainly the dairyman who had the most fun with the doll. Then the summer was over; the green of the alpine meadows had faded, and winter had already posted its sentinels on the mountain peaks. So it was time to move down from the alp. When the cows had been rounded up and everything was ready for the departure, Hänseli also put in an appearance. But not to make his fond goodbyes.

Sternly and firmly the doll ordered the dairyman, as the headman of the three, to stay behind. He allowed the others to leave, but forbade them to look back before they had reached the ridge.

So the dairyman remained while the others set off with the cattle. When they had reached the ridge, they looked back, and saw that the doll was hanging a piece of red cloth out over the chalet roof. The next moment they realised, to their horror, that it was the dairyman's blood-drenched skin.

但當它對面的夥伴把正確的牌選出來，放在桌子上，木偶就開始自己打牌。多好玩！從那次開始，它每一次都自己打牌，誰是它的夥伴，誰便一定贏。

木偶吃的越來越多，也越長越大。每個星期天，三兄弟都把木偶送到卡羅特比的山坡上曬太陽。不久，木偶胖得連三兄弟合力也差一點抬不動了，不過，他們去奧伯斯他福時還是帶著它，秋天回來哥順時又帶著它。

三兄弟中，最喜歡尋木偶開心的是奶農。夏天過去了，高山草原的草逐漸枯萎，冬天的氣息在山峰上隱現了，是下山的時候了。當牧牛聚集好，大家準備離開高山牧場時，小漢斯也露臉了，但可不是要送別三兄弟。

小漢斯表情嚴肅地命令奶農留下，因為三人中他是領袖。它讓其他兩個兄弟離開，但要他們到達山脊之後才可以回頭看。

奶農只好留在高山牧場，他的兩個兄弟帶著牧牛離開。他們到達山脊後朝後看，只見木偶把一塊紅布掛在屋頂上。他們再看一眼，卻嚇得魂飛魄散，那不是一塊紅布，是奶農染滿血的皮膚！

來自威尼斯的陌生人 — The Stranger from Venice

羅伊斯河谷的高山牧場上，夏天通常有一個奶農、一個牧人和一個雇農一起幹活兒。

一天晚上，一位陌生人來了。那男人走進他們的房子，問可否讓他在這兒借宿一兩個晚上。

「當然可以，」奶農説，「房間倒是有的，唯恐先生對簡便的飲食和樸陋的臥榻不滿意。」陌生人回答説：「沒問題，我滿意，豈敢麻煩三位。」

他就留下過夜了。當三個人問那陌生人從哪兒來，他回答説來自威尼斯。

第二天清晨，那陌生人很早便起來，帶了一個背包便出門去了。他整天留在外面，晚上回來時，背包裝滿了石頭。他把石頭拿給奶農等三人看，説他就要回威尼斯去，還解釋説這些石頭在威尼斯可以賣很多的錢。

那天夜晚，奶農思前想後，自言自語：「哈，若我拿走幾塊石頭，他也不會發現，之後我可以去威尼斯一趟，看看這些石頭到底能賣多少錢。」

A dairyman, a herdsman and a farmhand were spending the summer months with their cattle up on an alp above the Reuss Valley, as is the custom.

One evening a strange gentleman turned up and asked them if they could put him up for a day or two. "Of course," assented the dairyman. "We've got more than enough space. But can you make do with what food we have and with the simple bed?"

"I'll be satisfied with whatever you can offer," said the gentleman. "Please don't put yourselves out."

So he stayed there for the night. And when they asked him where he was from he replied, "From Venice."

The next morning he got up early, strapped a bag onto his back, and was away all day. He returned in the evening, with his bag full of stones. He showed the stones to the men and told them he now wanted to go back to Venice where he would be able to sell them for quite a fortune.

During the night the dairyman thought things over and then said to himself, "Why don't I just take a couple of the stones? He won't notice. Then, later, I can go to Venice and see what I can get for them."

The following morning the stranger examined his stones again, but he did not seem to notice that some were missing. Then he paid the peasants generously, thanked them, took his leave, and set off for Venice.

In the autumn, after they had come back down from the alp and the worst of the autumn work was done, the dairyman said to himself, "Now I can take the stones to Venice." And he started out on his long march.

He had just reached the town of Venice when he heard someone calling to him from a window high up in a fine house. The dairyman looked up and recognised the stranger who had been up on the alp with them the previous summer.

"Well, well," shouted the gentleman. "So you've come with your stolen stones, have you?"

As you can imagine, the dairyman was alarmed. However, the gentleman smiled pleasantly and invited him to come up, telling him he had nothing to fear, nothing would happen to him.

Full of apprehension the dairyman went inside and climbed the stairs to the gentleman's apartments. The gentleman was most cordial. He set food and drink before his guest and told him to help himself. The dairyman did not wait to be asked a second time, but ate and drank with ravenous appetite. When he had finished, the gentleman told him where to go to sell his stones. There they would give him whatever the stones were worth.

So the dairyman went off, found the place, and received a very nice sum of money for his stones. He then went back to see the gentleman. The latter asked him if he did not wish to be back home as soon as possible. "Of course," replied the dairyman. "The sooner the better."

Thereupon the gentleman took him up to the attic. He opened the door to a small room. It was completely dark inside. The gentleman told him to go into the room. He was to spend the whole night in there walking up and down. He must not stop for a moment. Only when he thought morning was breaking should he open the door to the balcony.

Well, the man went into the room and did as he had been told. In the morning, when he thought the time had come, he opened the balcony door – and found himself standing at the window of his own house! He could see down into the valley and could hear the bells ringing for matins. That really had been very quick!

第二天早晨，陌生人仔細端詳了石頭，好像沒發現缺了幾塊。他慷慨地給奶農等結了賬，道謝一番，起身告辭，返回威尼斯去。

秋天到，三人幹完了最辛苦的活兒，從高山牧場下來時，奶農自言自語說：「我現在可以拿石頭到威尼斯去了。」他便上路。

當他到達威尼斯時，有人從一所漂亮的房子一隻很高的窗子裏呼喊他。奶農一看便認出那是夏天在山上結識的陌生人。

「那麼，」那位先生叫說，「你帶了偷來的石頭到威尼斯，是吧？」

奶農當然嚇了一跳，那位先生卻善意地笑笑，邀請他到房子來，説明不必害怕，不會有什麼事情發生在他身上的。

奶農忐忑不安地爬上樓去。那位先生對他很熱情，準備了飲食，勸他多吃。奶農於是狼吞虎嚥，吃個痛快。之後，那位先生指示奶農到哪幢房子兌換石頭，説石子值多少，他們便會給多少。

奶農便到那幢房子去，把石子賣到一個不錯的價錢。他再回到那位先生的住處，先生問他是否想早一點回家。「當然，」奶農説，「越早越好。」

於是那位先生領他上閣樓，打開一個小斗室的門。裏面一片黑暗。先生叫他進去，並要他一整夜不住來回地走，直至覺得已到了第二天清晨，才打開向陽台的門。

奶農走進房間，按照先生的指示不住的踱步。當他覺得時間到了，便打開陽台的門——卻發現自己正正站在自己房子的窗前，遠眺是河谷，教堂剛響起早禱的鐘聲。那真的很快便回到家哩！

好了！奶農成為富翁了。可是俗話說得有道理：「來得快，丟的易。」奶農就有如此的下場。他不懂管錢，錢很快從他的指縫間溜走，過了幾年，一切便都花盡了。他自然很煩惱。

他想起：「我只要瞧瞧能不能自個兒找到那些石頭，找到了再去威尼斯便成。」

於是他上山去，來到一個鋪滿怪石的地方。那些石頭都很特別，閃閃發光，又非常沉重。「這些很像樣了，可以帶到威尼斯去。」他對自己說。

他把石頭塞滿背包出發了。石子的重量差一點將他拽倒，他只好拿出兩三塊。「不需全部都帶上吧。」他想。

來到威尼斯，他又到那位先生的住處投宿，把石子再次換成一大筆錢。情況沒有改變，奶農仍然不懂理財，過了幾年又把錢花光了。

「不要緊，」他想，「只要回到上次找到石頭的地方，塞滿一大個背包帶到威尼斯去便成了。」

地方他是找到了，可是，那兒連一塊石頭都沒有。

Fine, now he was a rich man. But the saying 'Easy come, easy go' is not without pertinence. For that is what happened to the dairyman. He could not manage the money. It just slipped through his fingers, and after a few years nothing was left. That really annoyed him.

But then he thought, "All I have to do is go and see if I can find some of those stones myself. If I do, I'll simply head for Venice again."

So he went up to the alp and soon reached a place where he saw a strange kind of stone, all glittering and incredibly heavy. "That could be the right thing to take to Venice," he said to himself.

He filled a bag with the stones and soon set out on his journey. But he nearly collapsed under the weight and had to take some out. "I really don't need to take all of them," he thought.

In Venice he stopped for a bite at the gentleman's and again he received a nice sum of money for his stones. But he just could not keep it together, and in a couple of years it had all been dissipated.

"Never mind," he thought. "All I need do is go back to where I found the stones, fill a bagful and take them to Venice."

He found the place all right, but there was not a single stone there any more.

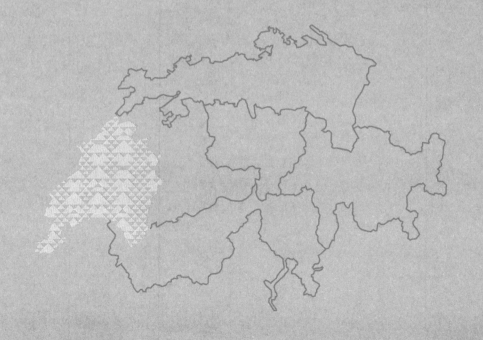

瑞士法語區的傳說

Legends from
French-speaking
Switzerland

人間天堂　Heaven on Earth

匈奴——或者是匈牙利吧，傳說經常把民族和他們遷移的路線都弄糊塗了——強攻了勃艮第的邊界後，也向日內瓦湖推進。夜空清澈澄明，燦爛的星辰倒映在平靜的湖中。來自東方大草原的野蠻騎兵，面對這樣的陌生景象都驚愕起來，他們看到天空就在腳下，以為無休止的侵略已經帶他們抵達世界的盡頭了。他們更以為自己已經越過世界的邊緣，來到天國，被閃亮的星星包圍著。

有的人說，這情景給匈奴人很大的衝擊，令他們拔腿便跑，直到安全抵達草原的家才休息。也有人猜想他們習慣了那神奇的景象，在這帶美麗的地方安家落戶。在這裏，可以同時看見頭上穹蒼和腳下湖水裏閃閃的星光。

After the Huns – or were they Hungarians? the old legends are most inaccurate about the different peoples and their migrations – had stormed the Burgundian frontier, some of them charged on as far as Lake Geneva. It was a clear night, and the black sky with its bright twinkling stars was perfectly reflected in the still waters of the vast expanse of water at their feet. The wild horsemen from the wide eastern plains halted, aghast at the unfamiliar sight. Seeing the sky at their feet, they thought their unbounded conquests had brought them to the end of the world. They even thought they had ridden over the edge of the earth and were now in God's heaven amidst the twinkling stars.

Some people say that this experience gave the Huns such a shock that they turned on their heels and did not rest until they were safely back in their homes in the grasslands. Others think that they became accustomed to the marvellous sight and settled as herdsmen in this blessed country where, in the quiet of clear nights, you can stand by a lake and see the stars shining simultaneously above your head and beneath your feet.

The Ship of Happiness
on Lake Geneva

In olden days, there could be seen on certain nights, near the shores of Lake Geneva, a bright ship that shone out like the sickle of the silvery moon. Drawn by eight snowy white swans, it would slide mellifluously through the waves.

The graceful woman standing on the deck was also clad in gleaming white. There were winged children frolicking gaily all around her – pious men thought they were little angels from heaven, people conversant with the writings of the learned poets said they were charming airy spirits or sylphs.

The enchanted ship never came to land. But it left its mark on all the shores from which it had been seen. The following summer, fields and meadows there were more fertile than anywhere else, and the trees blossomed in unusual splendour. As for the people who had actually caught sight of the shining ship with its woman in white, they soon had all their most secret wishes fulfilled.

從前某些夜裏，你可以看見日內瓦湖上一艘像銀色月光那麼亮的舟，八隻雪白的天鵝拉著它流暢地滑過波浪。

一名風姿超逸的女士站在舟上，她也穿著亮白的衣服；長著翅膀的孩子快樂地在她身旁嬉戲——虔誠的人把他們看作從天上下來的小天使，愛詩的人把他們看作可愛的空中精靈。

神奇的舟不會靠湖岸停泊，一次也不會，但它駛過的地方，那裏的農田和原野在接下來的夏天必比別的地方豐美肥沃，樹也長得特別茂盛。至於看過閃爍之舟和白衣女子的人，所有秘密的心願很快都會實現。

The Herdsman from Vaud and his Trip to Heaven

沃州牧人及其天堂之旅

遠古時代，我們的祖先還得和別的時代或別的世界的統治者分享土地的時候，一個叫奈麗娜的「黑仙女」熱戀著來自沃州的高山牧人米歇爾。奈麗娜熾烈的愛令米歇爾很不快樂，因為那青年已與鄰居的女兒薩羅美訂了婚，她金色的頭髮與紫水晶一樣的眼睛，比奈麗娜的黑魔法更有吸引力。

　　一天傍晚，黑仙女試圖奪取高山牧人的心。她對他說：「在地上，幸福很難找到，可是我可以幫你。」她向他保證，同時用魔杖碰一碰一朵高山玫瑰。玫瑰立刻變成舒適的小馬車，上百的燕子飛過來，黃金線把牠們繫在車前。高山牧人和黑仙女上了車，迅速地在空中飛越山脈。閃爍的山峰，黝暗的峽谷，蓋著銀色煙霧的山谷，在月光中光采熠熠的冰川，周圍的一切漸漸似乎都不存在了，只能看見星星在遙遠的夜空中。奈麗娜穿著雪白的裙子，站在她心愛的人旁邊，棕色頭髮裏的金星閃爍著。

　　可是，所有魔法都是徒然。儘管塵世的人會付出一切一睹這樣的景象，但米

In days of yore, when our ancestors still had to share the land with powerful creatures from other ages or from other worlds, there was dark fairy named Nerina, who fell passionately in love with an alpine herdsman from Vaud whose name was Michel. But her passion was to bring her unhappiness, for the young man was already engaged to his neighbour's daughter, whose fair hair and amethyst eyes appealed to him more than Nerina's dark charms.

One day the fairy was chatting with the herdsman and trying to win him over. "It's not easy to find happiness on earth. But I can help you find it," she assured Michel, at the same time touching an alpine rose with her wand. In a flash it was transformed into a comfortable little chariot. Hundreds of swallows flew up and were harnessed to it by golden threads. The youth and the fairy girl mounted, and in less than no time they were gliding swiftly through the air high above the mountains. Gleaming white peaks and dark ravines, valleys draped in silvery mists, and glaciers glistening in the moonlight – everything sank beneath them until only the stars were to be seen shining in heaven's vast dome. Nerina in her dress of white snow stood beside her beloved, and the golden stars in her brown hair sparkled.

But all the fairy's magic was to no avail. Although others might have given their soul to see such marvels, the herdsman remained indifferent. He did not feel the promised bliss. On the contrary, he could not stop thinking of his village, and there was no way the beautiful dark fairy could oust his fair-haired bride from his thoughts and from his heart. The magic trip soon seemed irksomely long, and he was filled with grief at being so far away from all the places and people he loved. He pleaded with Nerina to take him back to his chalet among the dark crags and told her there was nothing in the world he loved more than that tiny patch of earth that was his home.

His words filled the fairy's heart with pain. But she commanded the bearers of the airy chariot to take them back home immediately.

Later she managed a few more times to persuade the young man to engage with her on their marvellous night journeys, but she had lost the game. Michel resisted her allurements – unlike all the other mountain herdsmen in those bygone days, who would break faith with their peasant girlfriends as soon as they were assured of the love of one of the brown fairies.

Michel married his sweetheart Salome and lived with her humbly and happily in the same small house in which his ancestors had died. The legend does not tell if he ever missed his trips in the alpine rose chariot. But judging by everything that we have heard since, it is really quite unlikely.

歇爾仍然無動於衷。他沒有感到預期的快樂，相反，他禁不住想起家鄉；就是黑仙女多美麗，也不能驅去他心裏的金髮新娘。米歇爾覺得這次魔幻之旅實在太長了，他距離自己所愛的一切越來越遠，心裏怎會不憂傷？他懇切地請求奈麗娜帶他回到黑石叢中自己的房子。他說全世界沒有一個地方比那個小小的家更令他喜歡。

米歇爾的話令黑仙子很傷心，但她還是命令空中馬車的車夫馬上帶他們回家。

以後，奈麗娜曾幾次成功說服米歇爾與她重踏神奇的黑夜之旅——不過她心裏明白自己已經失敗了。米歇爾拒絕了黑仙女的引誘，他不像以往的高山牧者——他們一旦肯定了黑仙女的愛，就忘記了自己農村的愛人。

終於，米歇爾娶了他的愛人薩羅美，跟她樸素而快樂地在祖先住過的房舍裏過日子。他有沒有懷念高山玫瑰馬車的旅程呢？傳說可沒有告訴我們，但是從我們所知，這並不太可能。

汝拉森林的秘密 / Secrets of the Jura Forests

在汝拉山和阿爾卑斯山之間的林谷裏，有些寧靜的小屋子，屋裏保存了不少古老的傳說。在我們睿智的祖先遺下的大箱子中，則存放了好些古老的食譜，這是輕率魯莽的城市人所不知道的。

在納沙泰爾州偏遠的汝拉谷裏，人們很會做一種混濁的黃色飲料（黃色是因為其中的秘密成分），它的效果跟烈酒或濃葡萄酒不同。這種奇怪的飲料會帶出人體一種隱藏的力量，就連今天的專家亦不能解釋。這種危險的飲料源自某些久已消失的遊牧民族（他們的黑魔法很厲害），只要喝上一口就上癮，不能自拔。人沉湎於這種名譽甚差的飲料中，會不惜犧牲一切，只求快感，一杯一杯的，不停地把魔酒灌下肚子裏。明明知道會悲慘地死掉，也不肯放棄享受杯中魔液，每喝一次，酒癮就更深了。

一位來自納沙泰爾市的人聽到這神秘魔酒的傳聞，很是好奇；為了尋找這魔鬼配方，他走遍了汝拉的山林。最後，他走到偏遠山谷裏一座獵人的房舍，那兒一位神色陰沉的農民賣了一大瓶神秘魔酒給他。

The silent cottages in the wooded valleys between the Jura and the Alps still preserve many old traditions, and in big chests dating from the days of our wise ancestors there still lie many old recipes which it is just as well the careless and reckless city folk know nothing about.

In the canton of Neuchâtel, in the isolated valleys of the Jura, people know the recipe for a cloudy, yellow-coloured drink (the yellow colour comes from the secret ingredients) which has an effect quite unlike that of any schnaps or strong wine. The strange drink is said to release hidden powers within the drinker, something that even today's specialists cannot explain. Apparently just one taste of the dangerous potion, which originated in the dark arts of some now extinct nomadic race, can cause the most fearful addiction. Victims of the ill-famed brew will sacrifice everything just for the pleasure of pouring glass after glass of the charmed drink down their throats. Even the prospect of a dismal death does not seem too high a price to pay for the enjoyment of the magic potion. And each drinking bout increases their addiction.

Once there was a man from the city of Neuchâtel who, upon hearing the rumour of this mysterious herbal potion, became very curious. He roamed the Jura in quest of the devilish recipe. Finally he came upon a hunting lodge in an isolated valley where a grim peasant let him have a large bottle of the drink.

"The devil lives in the Jura. If he catches people like us, he wants more than just our souls – we also have to pay him a fee for transporting us to the fires of Hell." The man from Neuchâtel could not help remembering those words as he paid the grim fellow an exorbitant price for the bottle. However, he wanted to find out if the gruesome stories about the deadly mixture were true or if they were only old wives' tales to deter people from drinking it. So he paid up. And then he boldly started drinking one glass after the other.

Later, all he could remember was seeing the lodge and the forests disappear in a milky mist. In his drunken delirium he dreamed he had grown an animal hide, that he had shaggy paws with strong claws, and that he was tearing wildly through the thick undergrowth of the forest. Even at the time it seemed strange to him that his only sensation was one of intense pleasure. All his worries – about his business or his wife's fidelity, about impending war or the approach of old age with its attendant infirmities – all seemed to have evaporated. At a stroke he was no longer the pale stay-at-home of yesterday; he was strong and full of courage and enterprise. The forest with its thorny thickets suddenly seemed exceptionally beautiful, and the whole world was filled with a delicious perfume that he inhaled avidly.

After a night and a day, the man from Neuchâtel awoke out of a deep sleep. His head was heavy. Once again he felt weak and helpless.

"If I hadn't already polished off the whole bottle," he later said, "I wouldn't have hesitated to drink the

「魔鬼就住在汝拉山脈。他縱使抓住我們，得到我們的靈魂還不會滿足，他會把我們送往地獄，更要我們付運輸費哩。」納沙泰爾人付高價給那陰沉的人買魔酒時，心裏不禁想。只是，他太希望知道這種奪命酒的謠言是真的，或只是無稽之談，所以付過錢後，便毫不猶豫地一杯一杯地喝下去。

然後，他只記起房舍和汝拉森林沒入乳白色的煙霧中，精神恍惚地進入醉鄉，夢到自己身上長了獸皮毛，有毛茸茸的獸掌和尖銳的爪子，瘋狂地在森林茂密的灌木叢中跑來跑去。他覺得很奇怪：夢裏的他唯一的感覺，竟是強烈的快感；一切的憂慮——生意上的煩惱，老婆的不忠，對戰爭的害怕，對老及疾病之將至——都突然煙消雲散。一下子，他不再是個蒼白的人，不再老呆在家裏不愛出外，而是強壯、勇敢，又富有冒險精神的漢子。森林的荊棘灌木叢突然變得美不勝收。周圍瀰漫著一種迷人的香氣，他熱切地呼吸著。

這樣過了一夜和一天，這個來自納沙泰爾的人終於從沉睡中醒過來。他的頭很重，他再次感到軟弱無力。

「如果我沒有把整瓶魔酒喝光的話，」他後來說，「我會毫不猶豫地把剩餘的酒灌下肚子裏，只要能夠再做快樂的夢，便什麼都行，因為，夢裏我是多麼的強壯有力啊！」

他在汝拉狂飲做夢的時候似乎受了傷，雖然他沒發現自己身上有任何傷痕，可是他手上粘著結了痂的血。

當他看到報刊上報道那夜裏發生的事情，不禁大大吃了一驚。就在他受魔酒迷惑那夜，人們聽到了汝拉山邊區一頭巨狼可怕的嚎叫聲。狼在這個地帶並不常見。周圍村子的獵人拿了槍出去獵殺那頭狼，他們在森林灌木叢中找到了很多被野狼殺死的兔子屍體。儘管經驗豐富的獵人盡力四處追尋，可是仍沒法找到巨狼的蹤跡，只得空手而回。

至於那個從納沙泰爾來的人，雖然他仍然嚮往沉醉夢鄉的美妙感覺，但往後再沒受到引誘，沒再喝那種魔酒了。

rest of the devilish stuff – anything to get back to the realm of those blissful dreams in which I was strong and mighty."

Although he found no wounds on his body, it seemed as if he had injured himself during his drunken rampage up in the Jura, for there were crusts of dried blood on his hands.

Imagine his astonishment then, when he learned from the papers what had happened during his absence. The very night he had fallen under the spell of the magic potion, a mighty wolf had been heard howling on the borders of the Jura Mountains. Hunters from the surrounding villages had seized their rifles and started hunting for the predator, an animal seldom seen in the area. Deep in the forest among the thickets they found the remains of several rabbits the savage wolf had killed in its path. But, although they searched high and low, the experienced huntsmen finally had to return home empty-handed.

As to our man from Neuchâtel, although he continued to be haunted by the marvellous sensations and dreams of his drunken orgy, he managed to resist all temptation ever to drink of the magic potion again.

The Helpful Sprites in the Canton of Vaud

樂於助人的沃州精靈

The mountain folk of the canton of Vaud firmly believe in the existence of a kind of helpful sprite they there call 'servants'. (The word is the same in French as in English.) Rather like the helpful gnomes in the nearby German-speaking parts of Switzerland, these creatures are usually very friendly, are always ready for a bit of fun, and are well-disposed towards their human neighbours. They are particularly fond of fine cows and contribute a great deal to their general welfare. In the past they made themselves quite indispensable and knew a thousand ways of helping folk in their work on the alps or in the villages. Thanks to them, arduous tasks were made easy, and every day was like a jolly feast day – as long as one remained on good terms with them.

Out of gratitude for their reliable help in emergencies, people used to – and, it is said, still do in a very few places – place a bowl of good food on the roofs of their houses. You could then see little creatures come leaping through the thickly intertwined branches of the nearby trees. How charming it was to watch them – usually metamorphosed into kittens – eagerly gobble up the food!

However, towards the end of the era when such marvellous friendships were still common, people started losing their sense of gratitude. And thus it happened that, in a cottage where the little domestic sprite was in the habit of receiving a bowl of fresh

沃州的山中居民堅信，一種稱為「僕人」的精靈是存在的。他們樂於助人，有些像瑞士德語區之山精靈。他們通常友善開朗，愛嬉戲，對周圍的人類滿懷好意。他們最喜歡強壯的牛，對牠們的發育和成長作出了很大的貢獻。過去他們確實是不可缺少的，因為他們曉得各種方法幫助人類在山上或村裏工作；有了他們的幫助，各種艱鉅的工作都變得輕鬆容易，人類每天都像度過一個愉快的節日。

為了感謝「僕人」常常在人類危急時伸出援手，人們習慣每天把一碗好菜放在他們的屋頂上。聽說現在有一些地方仍有這個習慣。你可以看到小精靈飛快地穿過糾纏的樹枝，跳過來，小貓一般快樂地吃人類送給他們的食物。這個景象真好看啊！

以往，如此美妙的友誼是常見的；但人類開始失去感激之心，這樣的時代便慢慢地過去了。事情是這樣的：一座房舍裏的人習慣每天早上和晚上給家中的小精靈喝鮮奶，但某一天，他們決定中斷這古老的風俗。他們只想知道這玩笑會有什麼後果，卻萬萬想不到一個這麼可愛的小精靈，會對人類進行這麼殘酷的報復。

之後幾小時，什麼事情也沒有發生。然後，慢慢刮起一陣微風，使高山的花朵垂下頭來，使整個森林微微嘆息。

不多久，空氣狂暴起來。越來越厲害的狂風吹向狹窄的山谷，猛力擊打房舍，折斷了冷杉樹的枝椏。狂風暴烈的回聲響遍山川的每一個角落。軟弱的人類鑽進房舍裏逃避風雨的暴怒──沒有人猜到大自然肆虐，是因為小精靈要報復人類不再存感激之心。

第二天破曉時分，山居的人驚恐地發現牛棚空了，草地變了荒蕪一片。他們絕望地跟蹤牛群的足跡──牛是他們唯一的財產。他們穿過糾結的高山玫瑰叢，越過草原及永恆的積雪。

終於找到牛群了。牠們在狂風暴雨的恐懼中，盲目地跑越山野，互相踐踏。沒有了仙界守護者的保護，可憐的動物迷失了。在瘋狂的逃亡中，沒有一隻牛可以倖免於難。牠們不是在岩石上絆倒折斷了腿，便是掉到深淵下面去。牧人找到牛群的時候，牠們或已死了，或在垂死邊緣中掙扎。

milk every morning and evening, the occupants decided to give up the ancient custom. They were simply extremely curious to see what would happen. Never did they imagine that such a lovable little sprite could take cruel revenge on big human beings.

Indeed, nothing at all happened during the hours following their misdeed. Then a slight wind gradually rose, making the alpine flowers bow their heads and causing the forest trees to sigh.

Soon however the air grew more turbulent, the winds more powerful. Great blusters charged through the narrow valleys, beating at the houses with giant flails, snapping the branches of lone-standing fir trees. The howling winds could be heard resounding from every crook and cranny of the mountains. Weak humans crept into their cottages seeking shelter from the fury of the storm. Little did they realise that the raging of the elements was the sprite's revenge for man's ingratitude.

The following morning, the mountain folk were horrified to find their cowsheds empty, the nearby pastures desolate and deserted. In bitter despair they followed the tracks of their cattle – their sole earthly possessions – through tangles of alpine rose, across pastures, and over fields of eternal snow.

In the end they found their cows. Startled by the fierce storm, they had stampeded, rushing in blind panic through the mountain wilderness. Without a powerful guardian from the fairy world to protect them from the dangers all around, the poor animals were lost. Not a single one survived its frenzied flight without either breaking its legs on the rocks or falling down a chasm. By the time the herdsmen found their herd, the cows were all either already dead or gasping in the throes of death.

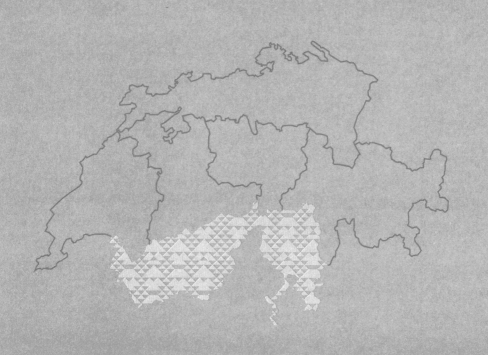

瓦萊斯州、提契諾州、保格爾谷的傳說

Legends from
the Valais, Ticino
and Bergell

我們發冷，老媽史密還在紡紗

We're Freezing, and Old Mother Schmid's Still Spinning

阿萊奇山谷距離冰川不遠的地方，很久以前曾有一所黑木小屋，裏面住了一個很虔誠的老寡婦。她常常為阿萊奇冰川裏可憐的靈魂祈禱。在冬天長夜昏暗的燈光下，她邊繁忙地紡紗，邊為了去世的人不停地祈禱。她通常不關上門，這樣，可憐的靈魂就可以進去她溫暖的房間暖暖身子。可是想進去，就必須得到老寡婦的許可。她睡覺前會打開窗戶，小聲喊道：「現在進來吧⋯⋯但別傷害我！」還會點起小蠟燭作夜明燈，然後才去睡覺。

不久，大門靜靜地開了，然後是房間的門，它們像被涼風吹開一樣。傳來很多輕輕走過地板的腳步聲，啪噠啪噠的，像很多人要走進房間擠在火爐旁邊。快到早禱鐘響的時候，寡婦又聽到同樣的腳步聲向大門那兒走去。

有一次，那個寡婦剛巧忙著紡紗，遲睡了一點，而外面已經很冷。突然，窗戶下有些什麼喊道：「我們發冷，老媽史密還在紡紗。」

In the Aletsch Valley, not far from the glacier, there once stood a small, black wooden hut which was inhabited by a pious old widow. She often used to pray for the poor souls in the Aletsch Glacier. And during the long winter evenings, while busily spinning in the dim lamplight, she would pray for them all the time. She also always left her front door unlocked so that the poor souls could come into her room and warm themselves at the stove. However, they had to wait for her permission before they could come in. Just before she went to bed, she would open a window and call softly, "You can come now … but do me no harm!" Then, leaving the stump of a candle to burn as a night-light, she would go up to her bedroom.

First the front door, then the room to the parlour, would open silently as though pushed by a cool draught. Countless footsteps would be heard pitter-pattering softly across the floor, like a mass of people crowding into the room to get near the stove. The following morning, just before the bells rang for morning prayers, the widow would hear the same steps scurrying back towards the door.

One day it so happened that the widow stayed up longer than usual at her spinning-wheel. It was extremely cold outside. Suddenly she heard someone shouting from below the window: "We're freezing, and old Mother Schmid's still spinning."

"I know," she answered, "but just let me finish spinning this skein of flax."

But before long the voice cried again, louder than before, "We're freezing, and old Mother Schmid's still spinning."

That made her cross. "All right. If you can't wait until I've finished, come in." But she forgot to add "do me no harm".

The front door and the parlour door burst open as if pushed by a strong gust of wind, and the footsteps of the invisible nocturnal visitors came pattering in, on and on, endlessly. The old widow was overcome with fear. She felt close to suffocation. But, because the room was so crowded with all the poor souls, she could not leave her spinning-wheel. It was the penalty she had to pay for having kept the dead waiting for so long out in the cold – at least, that is how she saw it.

The day came when old Mother Schmid lay dying. Her attendants asked each other: "What will the poor souls call out, now that their friend is dead?" At that moment they heard, coming out of the silence of the night: "We're freezing, and old Mother Schmid's still alive."

On hearing the voice, the dying woman gestured to show her contentment and then gave up the ghost. At the same time her attendants saw a brightness shining through the window. As they looked outside, they saw a procession of burning lights move away towards the glacier. On reaching the ice, the lights went out one after the other.

"Those," agreed the attendants, "are the poor souls with the night-lights which she used to leave burning for them. They're escorting their friend."

「我知道，」她回答，「但讓我先紡完這絞麻線吧。」

過了不久，聲音又響起，這次的聲量還大一點：「我們發冷，老媽史密還在紡紗！」

老寡婦不耐煩了，她說：「好吧，好吧，如果你們等不及我紡完線，現在就進來吧。」噢，她忘了說：「別傷害我！」

大門和房門「嘭」地打開了，像被大風吹開一樣，隱形的夜間訪客啪噠啪噠的湧進來，腳步聲越來越多，像沒休止似的。老寡婦真的很害怕，感到自己快窒息了。房間都被可憐的靈魂擠滿了，她沒有辦法離開紡輪。她想這該是懲罰吧，因為她讓死去的人等這麼久，要在屋外發冷。

老媽史密臨終時，照顧她的人互相問道：「可憐的靈魂的朋友要死了，它們現在會說什麼呢？」就在那一刻，他們聽到平靜的夜裏響起一把聲音：「我們發冷，老媽史密還活著。」

垂死的婦人聽到，作手勢表示感到很高興，然後就去世了。同一時間，照顧老寡婦的人看到一團強光從窗外射進來，他們望出窗外，看到一列燃燒的燈火往冰川移動，到達後又一個一個的熄滅了。

「這是可憐的靈魂拿著夜明燈護送他們的朋友，」照顧老寡婦的人說，「她習慣晚上給他們亮起夜明燈嘛。」

夜宴　Nocturnal Repast

當牛群從杜蘭冰川西邊的艾裏山下山時，一頭牛走失了。牧者回去找牛。找到了，便跟牛去高山的小屋過夜。

半夜他睡醒了，突然聽到一陣喧嘩聲，聲音越來越大，然後看到一群男男女女衝進小屋來，他們是鬼。

牧者害怕得幾乎不敢呼吸。

他們跳舞狂歡了兩三個小時，然後有人說：「餓了，我們可以吃什麼？」

「那邊有一頭牛，不錯哩。」第二個人喊道。

牧者蜷縮在床上，害怕得動也不敢動。

那群鬼把牛殺死，在火上烤了來吃。吃的時候，第三個人指著牧者說：「也給那個躺在床上的一口吧。」

接著把一片肉遞給發抖的牧者，不過他拒絕了。

「不吃便罰你。」他們說。他就聽話了。

然後他們把牛皮在地上張開。一個人把全部的骨頭放在一起，扔到牛皮裏面，把牛皮綑成一團，喊著：「露仙娜，站起來！」

牛站起來，那群鬼就消失了。

黎明時分，牧者把牛領到鄉村去。牛跛了，因為牠的後腿缺了一塊肉，那是給牧者吃了。牛的傷口很快便癒合了。

During the move down to the valley from the Alpe de l'Allée west of the Durand Glacier, a cow went missing. The herdsman went back to look for her. After he had found her, he took her with him to the alpine chalet to spend the night there.

Around midnight, he was suddenly woken by a rumbling din which gradually grew louder and louder until, finally, a throng of men and women burst into the hut.

The herdsman was so scared he hardly dared to breathe.

For two or three hours, the mob revelled and danced. Then one of them said, "I'm hungry. What have we got to eat?

"There's a cow over there which would do just fine," said another.

The herdsman cowered in his bed, petrified with fear.

They killed the cow, roasted it in the fire and started eating. During the meal, one of the creatures pointed to the herdsman saying, "Give the man in the bed a bite too."

A piece was offered to the trembling herdsman, but he refused.

"Woe to you if you don't eat it," they said. And he obeyed.

Then they spread out the cowhide on the floor. One of them gathered up all the bones and threw them into the skin, which he then folded up into a bundle. Then he cried, "Rosina, get up!"

The cow stood up, the spirits disappeared.

At the first light of day, the herdsman set off for the village with his cow. She had a limp, because the piece of flesh which he himself had eaten was missing from her hind leg. But the wound soon healed.

麵包乳酪吃不盡 | Enough Bread and Cheese

One day a farmer had to do down into the valley for several days. During his absence, a kind of dwarf known there as a 'Gogwärgji' looked after the cattle on the alp. The dwarf performed the job to the farmer's complete satisfaction, and he was very pleased with him and asked him what he would like as his wage.

The dwarf asked him to give him a loaf of bread and a cheese. "That will keep me in food for the rest of my life," he said.

That surprised the farmer. The creature might be tiny, but small people often have giant appetites. Even a dwarf would not go far on a single cheese and a single loaf of bread.

"How can you manage," asked the farmer, intrigued.

"Simple," answered the dwarf. "I cut a notch with my knife exactly in the middle of the loaf, and I do the same with the piece of cheese. Then I never eat more than half of either. In the night, they grow back into their original size again."

The farmer gave the 'Gogwärgji' another loaf of bread and another cheese and asked him to mark them as he had described. The dwarf willingly did this, then disappeared. But for the whole of that summer, the farmer ate from the same loaf of bread and from the same cheese. Every morning both were restored

一天，一位農民有事要到谷裏幾天。他不在的時候，一個葛維知族的小矮人來幫忙照顧高山牧地上的牲畜。小矮人做得非常好，農民對他很滿意，問他要什麼報酬。

小矮人要求一個圓麵包和一塊圓乳酪作為報酬，說：「這我就永遠有足夠吃的了。」

農民感到很驚異。雖然小矮人很小，但胃口通常很大，光是一塊乳酪和一個麵包，應該吃不了多久。

「你是怎麼辦到的？」農民好奇地問。

「非常容易！」小矮人解釋，「我用刀在麵包的正中央刻一道凹痕，乾酪也一樣，然後注意不要吃超過一半，夜裏它們便會長回原來的大小。」

農民給那葛維知族人另一塊麵包和乳酪，請他照樣子刻上凹痕。小矮人樂意地做了，然後就消失得無影無蹤。那個夏天，農民吃著同一塊麵包和同一塊乳酪，只要晚上不要吃超過一半，第二天早上它們就回復原來圓形的樣子，好像農民一點也沒吃過似的。

秋天到，農民請一些朋友來家裏吃晚飯。他拿乳酪、麵包和葡萄酒招待客人。他們通宵達旦，歡聚一整夜，早晨剩下的不過三兩個空瓶子、一些麵包屑和乳酪皮。

魔術破除了！再沒有什麼留下可以長回原狀了。農民這麼大意，他對自己很生氣。

to their round shape as though they had never been touched.

When autumn came, the farmer invited a couple of friends to a meal of bread and cheese and wine. They ate and drank until the early hours of the morning. In the end, all that was left were two or three empty wine bottles, a few crumbs and the cheese rind.

Now there was nothing left that could grow back again. No more magic!. How annoyed the farmer was at his own carelessness!

松樹林的神奇堡壘

The Magic Castle in the Pine Forest

In a secluded corner of the forest, there once lived a joiner called Jos together with his wife and his son. The latter had only just come of age, but he already had a sweetheart over on the other side of the Rhone. He visited her every Saturday evening, staying at her house – as was the custom in those parts – until every candle in the parlour had burned down.

His parents told him to put the girl out of his mind. But the boy would not give her up, whereupon his father threatened that the devil would take him if he ever again dared cross the bridge over the Rhone to go to his girlfriend's house. But his son answered that he feared neither death nor the devil and that he would never give up his girl.

Now the father was not the kind of man to give in to a son who as yet had hardly a hair on his chin. One Saturday, he fetched two goat-horns from the barn, dressed himself up as the devil and, at nightfall, went to the Rhone bridge where he lay in wait for his hardheaded son.

He had not been waiting long before he heard his son – who of course had no idea of his father's intent – approach with hurried steps. The man leapt into the middle of the path, his horned head lowered menacingly. His son stopped short. He called out three times but got no answer. So he took up a big jagged stone and knocked the devil down. He then continued on his way.

That evening he did not feel in the mood for merriment. So he soon bade his sweetheart farewell

從前有一個叫約斯的木雕工，他和妻子及兒子住在森林中一個偏僻的角落。他的兒子剛成年，有一個住在羅納河對岸的愛人。這小夥子每個禮拜六都去看他的愛人，留在她的家裏——這是當地的風俗——一直到客廳的蠟燭點完才離開。

木雕工夫婦要求兒子放棄那位姑娘，但小夥子不肯讓步。木雕工就威脅說，如果兒子再過羅納河橋去那姑娘的家，魔鬼就會把他捉去。兒子回答說他不怕死也不怕魔鬼，任何人都不可以阻止他去見那姑娘。

木雕工是不會向兒子讓步的，尤其兒子下巴連一根鬍子也未長出來。一個星期六，木雕工到草棚拿兩隻山羊角，把自己裝扮成魔鬼，夜幕降臨的時候，他在羅納河橋等待著他頑固的兒子。

不久，他的兒子匆促地走過來，毫不察覺父親的意圖。木雕工跳到馬路中央，把有角的頭往前凸出來，恫嚇兒子。他的兒子就站住了，呼喊了父親三次，沒有答應，便抓起一塊有棱角的大石頭，把「魔鬼」砸倒地上，繼續上路。

不過，今天晚上他在情人家裏也不是十分愉快，所以只呆了一會兒就走了。回家的路上，他在橋頭看到那倒楣的、魔鬼模樣的東西，仍然黑墨墨的躺在那裏一動也不動。他戰戰兢兢地看了它一眼，便一路上一聲不吭趕回家，回到家即馬上找父親。

他的母親吃了一驚，說：「怎麼，你沒看到他嗎？他裝扮成魔鬼模樣，去橋上嚇唬你啊！」

「那麼我把父親打死了！」兒子悲歎道，隨即放聲痛哭。

母子二人當晚把死者抬了回家，第二天，兒子便向法庭投案自首。

法官認為，如果他是一個這麼無畏的人，連魔鬼也不怕，那就要考驗他的膽量，以作懲罰。法官命令他天黑的時候走到叫阿賓活的松樹林裏去。原來，所有到那樹林的人都沒法回來。假若他運氣好，安然脫險，法官便會判他無罪釋放。

兒子說，如果有機會贖自己弒父的罪，任何處罰他都能接受。他同意進入松樹林，只希望森林的妖魔鬼怪會讓他痛苦一點。法官允許他披一條聖帶，袋子裏放一根聖燭和一本書。然後，那兒子就毫不畏懼地走進森林。

and set off back home. As he reached the end of the bridge he saw the misshapen, black, devilish creature still lying there motionless. Glancing at it fearfully he passed silently by, and as soon as he got back home he asked where his father was.

"You must have seen him," replied his mother, alarmed. "He dressed himself up as the devil and went to the bridge to give you a fright!"

"In that case I've murdered my own father," wailed the son, choking with grief.

They went to the bridge and fetched the dead man's corpse. And the following day the son gave himself up.

The judges decided that, since he was such a bold young man and feared nothing, not even the devil, he should receive a sentence that would put his courage to the supreme test. He was to walk through the pine forest known as Arbenwald in the dead of night. To that day, no one had ever come out of that forest alive. If he was lucky and managed to get through unharmed, he would be acquitted and that would be the end of that.

The son said he agreed to any punishment that might atone for his terrible deed. A walk through the pine forest was fine with him, he only hoped the forest demons would make him suffer. He was granted permission to wear a sacred stole, and to carry a holy candle and a book in his pocket. Then he marched off fearlessly into the woods.

Soon, blackest night was all around him. Not a single star shone in the skies. Rustlings and whisperings could be heard all around, as in any other forest. Moths fluttered past his eyes, brushing against his cheeks and his nose; glow-worms sent out their feeble lights; bats flitted past, swirling through the air; and an intoxicating flowery fragrance benumbed his senses. Soon the path disappeared, and he had to make his way through all kinds of rank growth, brushwood and brambles. Time and again he stumbled over the roots of trees.

About the time he felt midnight must be approaching, the thicket grew less dense, and he saw a shimmer of light in the near distance. He made for it, thinking he would soon be out of the forest and out of danger. Instead, he found himself standing in front of a vast, dimly lit palace which was built of the finest pinewood. The tall double doors were studded with silver. He wondered who could be living in this splendid forest mansion.

As the door was locked he knocked, not with his finger but with his whole fist. But no one came. He knocked a second and a third time, more loudly each time. Now the door swung open, and he stepped inside. But no one came to meet him. He found himself standing in front of another door. Again he had to knock three times before it opened. Then there was a third door, but this one opened silently at his first violent knock. Inside, he saw a dark, old-fashioned hall, dimly lit by a single small lamp.

The room was scantily furnished. A table with a chair stood in the middle. On the table there was a bottle of wine and a plate of bread and cheese. He sat down on the chair, lit his candle and, pushing the plate of food aside, opened his book and started to read. But he could not concentrate on the text. He kept reading the same page over and over again without understanding a word. His mind was on quite different things. He was anxious to know what would happen next. From time to time he looked round to see if anyone was standing behind him, but he only

不久，他就被漆黑的夜晚完全包圍了，天上連一顆星星也見不到。他周圍沙沙作響，像有人竊竊私語似的，跟其他樹林沒有分別。夜蛾在空中飛過，輕輕地掠過他的面孔和鼻子。螢火蟲發出微弱的亮光，偶爾一隻蝙蝠在空中迴旋，空中瀰漫濃郁醉人的花香。不久，他便看不見道路，只好用手撥開茂密的草叢、灌木叢和荊棘。走的時候，他被樹根絆倒了好幾次。

他感到已近半夜了。灌木叢越來越稀疏，他看到不遠處有閃光發出。他走過去，以為自己已經走出森林，度過了難關，卻突然見到一座極大，光線卻很黯淡的宮殿。它是由優質的松木築成的，高大的雙門全都釘有白銀裝飾。誰會住在這麼宏偉的一座森林大宅裏？他感到奇怪。

門是關著的，他就用拳頭——不用手指——敲門。沒有人來開門。他再敲門。他第三次敲門，這次敲得更厲害。門突然打開了，讓他進去。沒有人來迎接他。他又站在另一扇門的前面。他又敲了三次門，門才打開。再有第三扇門，這次他只用力敲了一下，門就輕輕地打開了。他看到門內是一個又陰沉又古老的大廳，廳裏只有一盞黯淡的燈。

大廳佈置得很簡單，中央是一張桌子和一把椅子。桌子上有一瓶酒、一盤乳酪和麵包。他在椅子上坐下來,點著了自己的蠟燭,推開那盤子食物,打開他的書讀起來。但是他心不在焉,看了一頁,又看了同一頁,還是一個字都看不懂。他急於知道將會發生什麼事,於是不時回頭看看有沒有人站在他的背後,但是他只看到大廳那四面陰暗的牆壁。周圍寂靜無聲。

突然傳來敲門的聲音。小夥子吃了一驚,一動也不敢動,亦不敢出聲。他心裏想:我敲門的時候沒有人回應,只得盯著門。門給敲了三次,發出一聲刺耳的「嘎」就打開了。宮殿震動了一下,燭光飄忽不定,三個炭黑色的巨人出現了,他們停住腳步,站在他的面前。他們一言不發,只示意他隨他們前行。巨人身旁是一隻很醜的黑狗,牠的眼睛裏好像燃燒著炭一樣,顏色不斷變化,一時發出紅光,一時閃出綠光。小夥子想他不應該留在那裏,就站起來。他不喜歡那隻狗,於是把他的聖帶脫下來,把狗拴在桌腿上。然後,他就把自己交托給守護神,跟著巨人沿一道很長的樓梯,走到地下一個墓穴去。到了之後,巨人抓起已經準備好的尖鋤和鐵鍬,示意他開始工作。

但是小夥子拒絕了,說:「我在這兒沒有埋藏什麼東西,也不會挖掘什麼東西。」

saw the four dark walls of the hall. Not a sound broke through the stillness.

Suddenly, there was a knock at the door. He was startled but made no move and held his peace. After all, no one answered when I knocked, he thought, staring at the door. At the third knock, the door flew open with a terrible screech. A shudder went through the palace, the candle flickered, and three coal-black giants appeared. They planted themselves in front of the young lad and, without a word, bade him follow them. With them there was an ugly black dog. It had eyes like fiery coals that glowed in changing colours, now bright red, now greenish grey. The lad decided he could not very well stay where he was, so he got up. But he did not like the look of the dog. He quickly took off his stole and used it to tie the beast to the leg of the table. Then, committing himself to the protection of his guardian angel, he followed the giants down the long staircase to an underground vault.

There they picked up a shovel and a pick and made signs he was to use them.

But he refused, saying: "I haven't buried anything here, and I shan't do any digging."

Thereupon the first of the giants grabbed the pick himself and broke up the earth with powerful blows.

The second giant picked up the shovel and signalled to the lad to remove the broken-up earth.

But he retorted, "I haven't hidden anything here, and I shan't dig anything out."

The second giant got down to work himself, and big, heavy stone slabs came into view. Now the third giant bade the lad raise the slabs. But he folded his arms saying, "I haven't covered anything up, so I shan't remove any covers."

At that, the three giants, with concerted strength,

managed to pull up the stone slabs, revealing three great metal pots full of gold and silver coins that gleamed as though they had only just been minted. The giants signalled to the lad to lift up the first of the money-pots. But he said, "I never placed anything here and I won't take anything out."

So they took out the pot themselves. And when he gave them the same answer for the second pot they took that one out too. The third pot was so heavy that they could not get it out in spite of all their efforts. At their pleading gestures, the lad gave them a hand, and with a great tug they managed to haul the pot out.

As soon as he had straightened up, the lad saw before him three white-clad, normal-sized men who had recovered the use of their tongues.

"Many thanks," they said. "Now we're redeemed. If you'd obeyed us just once, we'd have had to kill you; and a few years later we'd have been doomed to eternal perdition. For we've been waiting for several centuries for our redemption, in vain until you came. This money is yours. Give the first pot to the poor. Build a forest chapel with the second. And keep the third, the biggest, for yourself. Now go upstairs and release the dog, for he's the devil incarnate. If you had let him go with us, all our efforts would have been in vain and we would never have been able to dig up the pots. But before you untie the beast, don't forget to open the windows and the door. For he'll make such a ghastly stench that you might almost suffocate."

The three ghosts escorted the lad up the stairs, opened the door to the hall and then vanished. Our bold hero did as he had been told. After untying the dog, he struck it three times with his stole, so that it ran away howling, leaving behind such a stench that the young man felt as though someone were holding a lump of burning sulphur under his nose.

那麼第一個巨人就自己抓起尖鋤，用力地鋤鬆土壤。

第二個巨人拿起鐵鍬，示意小夥子把鋤鬆的土壤鏟掉。

他就說：「我在這兒沒有埋藏什麼東西，也不會鏟掉什麼東西！」

第二個巨人就自己動手挖出幾塊很大的石板。第三個巨人示意小夥子揭開石板。小夥子把兩臂交叉在胸前，說：「我在這兒沒有蓋上什麼東西，也不會揭開什麼東西！」

於是三個巨人合力把石板抬起來，地上露出三個巨大的鐵壺，裏面裝滿金幣和銀幣，閃閃生光，像剛鑄造出來的樣子。巨人又示意小夥子把第一個錢壺拿出來，但是他說：「我在這兒沒有放進什麼東西，也不會拿出什麼東西！」

他們就自己把錢壺拿出來。小夥子照樣拒絕拿出第二個錢壺，三個巨人又自己把壺拿出來。到了第三個壺，那個壺沉得三個巨人合力也拿不出來，於是他們請求小夥子幫忙。他就動手，猛一用勁把錢壺拿了出來。

小夥子一站直身子，便看到三個穿白衣服，有著正常人個子的男人站在他的面前。那三個男子開口說話。

「我們非常感謝你，」他們說，「我們得到解脫了。假若剛才你服從我們，就算只是一次，我們也要殺死你，過了幾年以後，我們就會陷於永恆的苦難中，萬劫不復。我們等待解脫，已經有幾百年了，直至你來我們才得救。錢歸你了，請把第一壺送給窮人，第二壺用來起教堂，第三壺是最大的，你自己要吧。現在請你上樓，把狗解開，牠是真正的魔鬼。假若你讓牠跟著我們，便一切都徒然，我們不會掘出錢壺的。別忘記，解開狗之前，你得把窗戶和門打開，因牠要發出使你呼吸不了的臭味！」

三個男子陪小夥子到樓上，打開大廳的門後，就消失了。我們勇敢的英雄按照指示行動。解開狗的時候，他用聖帶給牠三擊，牠便吼叫著離開了，只留下一股很強的臭味，讓他覺得有人在他的鼻子下拿著一桶硫磺。他感到暈眩，要抓著桌子定定神。幸好窗戶和門都開著，所以他只失去知覺一剎那而已。

他蘇醒過來，擦擦眼睛，發覺堡壘不見了。他站在松樹林的出口，身旁放著三個壺。經受得住這一次考驗，他自由了！

不過，他的腦子和四肢都很沉重，累得只想躺在草地睡上一會兒。他要有足夠的體力，才可以帶走那些財寶。他用左手摟著一個錢壺，右手摟著第二個錢壺，然後把第三個錢壺夾在兩腿之間。打了幾個哈欠，他就開始打著呼嚕，酣然入睡。

He felt faint and had to hold on to the table. But the door and the windows were open, so that he only lost consciousness for a brief moment.

On recovering his senses, he rubbed his eyes and saw that the castle had disappeared. He was standing on the edge of the pine forest. Beside him stood the three pots. He had survived the ordeal! Now he was free!

But his head and his limbs felt heavy with fatigue. He lay down in the grass, thinking to take a nap; for he would need all his strength if he wanted to carry away his treasure. He put his left arm around one pot and his right arm around the other, he clamped the third pot between his legs. And then he yawned a couple of times, before snoring his way blissfully into the land of slumber.

The Dance of Death

An hour's walk above the pretty parish of Unterbäch there lies a hamlet called Im Holz, which means 'In the woods'. It is made up of a few dark huts that are only inhabited for a few months in the summer. Nearby, in the snow-covered woods, a young lad from the parish was busy chopping wood. His mind was filled with sad thoughts, for it was only a month since his sweetheart, with whom he had danced through many a joyful evening, had died of a malignant disease.

Just before nightfall he piled up the logs, stuck his axe into a tree-trunk and slowly set off on his way home.

To save himself from the long climb down to the village, he had already spent every night of the week in his hut up there, and every evening he had cooked himself a bowl of hot soup. As always he lit the tallow lamp and stirred his soup over the fire. Then he went out and down to the cellar to fetch cheese and bread. As he came up, he noticed that the house opposite was brightly lit. He saw dark figures flying past the windows, and he heard strange music.

"What on earth's that?" he muttered to himself. "There's no one living there. Probably it's people from Unterbäch and Eischol who've got together secretly for a dance. I suppose they didn't tell me about it because I'm in mourning for Magdalena. And then also I haven't been down to the village all week."

He was starting to feel cold, so he went back into the house. He had his supper, put away his pewter plate and his wooden spoon, buttoned up his jacket and sneaked across to the neighbouring house to look through the window.

距離美麗的烏特拜赫村莊一個小時的路程，有一個由幾間黑色茅舍構成的小村落，叫作恩賀茲，即「樹中」的意思。那邊只在夏天的幾個月有人居住。附近大雪覆蓋的森林裏，有一個在教堂工作的小夥子正在砍木。他沉浸在悲痛的回憶中。一個月前，他的情人瑪格達勒娜因嚴重的疾病逝世了。從前他們常常一起跳舞，愉快地度過很多個夜晚。

夜幕降臨之際，他堆好砍下來的木頭，把斧子砍進一棵杉木幹裏，慢慢地走回家。

為了避免走漫長的路下山回村莊，他整個星期都在自己山上的茅舍過夜，而每天晚上他都給自己煮一碗熱湯。他如常點上蠟燭，在火上攪拌他的湯，然後他到地下室去拿乳酪和麵包。他再上來的時候看到對面的房子燈火通明。他看到黑暗的人影飛過窗戶，還聽到奇怪的音樂聲。

「這是什麼？」他喃喃自語。「這山上沒有人住，肯定是烏特拜赫人和伊斯初人在這裏暗中聚會跳舞。他們沒有通知我，是因為我還在哀悼我的瑪格達勒娜，而且我一個星期也沒有下山回村莊了。」

他開始感到寒冷，就又走進房子。喝完了湯，他把錫盤子和木勺子放到一邊，把外衣的扣子扣好，偷偷地走到隔壁房子，從窗戶窺探一下。

夜晚的天氣非常冷，一層灰色的冰遮住了窗戶，使他看不清楚。前門開著，於是他靜靜地進去，不要讓人家知道他來了。他走到裏面的門口，門也是開著的。

從門的窄縫，他看見桌子上的燈，一個在角落的小提琴手正彈奏舞曲，舞伴們親密地擁在一起，隨著音樂瘋狂地旋轉著跳舞。奇怪的是，不管小提琴手或跳舞者他都不認識。他們不是烏特拜赫的人，也不是伊斯初的人，他們全是他從前沒有見過的陌生面孔。他還發現那班人大都是古裝打扮的，穿著有扣環的鞋子、及膝褲和在腰間擺動的燕尾服。他沒有聽到他們在地板上跺腳的聲音。男人和女人的衣服上佈滿了白霜，褲子、裙子、領子和髮梢上則掛著細小的冰珠子。他們的手也像冰柱一樣。

突然他看到一張熟悉的臉。他幾乎發出一聲呼喊。

「這是什麼奇怪的聚會！那個有紅色長髮的姑娘，不就是我的愛人瑪格達勒娜嗎？我剛把她埋在墳墓下面啊！」

一股寒氣直透他的背脊，好像他站在冰河下，冰水淌了過來一樣。他轉過身來，趕快跑回自己的茅舍。他把大門和房門都關好後，馬上躺在床上，用被蒙住頭，但過了很久，他仍不感到暖和。他時冷時熱，不斷戰抖，總是回想起死亡舞會中他的情人。

突然門閂嘎吱嘎吱作響，有人輕輕敲門。他屏著氣傾聽。敲門的聲音大起來了，但是他沒有勇氣說「請進」。他在被子裏蜷得更緊。過了一會兒，他把頭伸出

But the night was bitterly cold and the windows were covered with a film of grey ice so that he could not make out anything clearly. Then he saw that the front door was open, so he crept inside very quietly, so as not to be heard, and went up to the inside door which was also ajar.

Peeping through the narrow opening, he saw lamps on the table and, in the corner, the fiddler to whose tune couples, locked in close embrace, whirled and twirled in a wild dance around the room. To his surprise, the lad did not know the fiddler or any of the dancers. They were not from Unterbäch and they were not from Eischol, they were all strangers he had never seen before. Now he noticed that most of them were dressed in old-fashioned clothes, that they were wearing buckled shoes and knee-breeches with tailcoats that flapped around their waists. Their stamping feet made no sound on the floorboards. The men's and the women's clothes were covered in frost; pearls of ice hung from their trousers and from their skirts, from their collars and from the tips of their hair. The fingers on their hands seemed to be pure icicles.

Suddenly his gaze fell upon a woman who looked familiar. He nearly cried out aloud.

"What strange company! And the one with the long reddish hair, isn't that Magdalena, my sweetheart, whom I recently buried down in the churchyard?"

A cold shudder ran down his back, as though he were standing below the glacier with the icy water gushing over him. He turned away and hurried back to his hut as fast as his legs could carry him. He bolted the front door and then the parlour door and jumped into bed, pulling the covers over his head. Yet he could not get warm. He was shaken by a fit of hot and cold shivers. All the time he could not stop thinking of his beloved in the dance of the dead.

Suddenly he heard the creaking of the latch. Then someone knocked gently at his door. Holding his breath he listened. The knocking grew louder. He did not have the courage to say "Come in". Instead, he just buried himself deeper under his covers. After a while he stretched out his head to get his breath and to check the door was still firmly bolted. Alas, at that moment it opened and Magdalena, his dead and departed truelove, stepped inside, the icy pearls on her dress jingling softly like little bells. The lad felt quite wretched and in his despair called out: "Jesus, Holy Mother of God! Who are you?"

An icy cold shadow bent over him and touched his lips. The ghost had been addressed. Now it could draw on the boy's breath and speak to him. Suddenly the lad's fear disappeared, and he engaged on a long conversation with his sweetheart.

First she asked him, "Do you recognise me?"

"Yes, you're my beloved, my own dear Magdalena," he answered.

"I am your beloved," she said. "I've come from the Aletsch Glacier and am doomed to dance here with the others to atone for all the forbidden dances I danced with you. But now you've talked to me, so I hope I'll soon be redeemed. Go down to the village tomorrow and do a good deed for my soul. That way you can speed up my salvation."

She talked about many more things, clasping him to her bosom and kissing him. For she stayed in his room until the bells for matins rang out from the village below.

Afterwards, the lad never said a word of what he had seen and heard to any living soul. He performed the good deeds Magdalena had asked him for and remained a bachelor all his life. Never again did he jest with a girl nor ever again fall in love.

來,呼了一口氣,看門是否還是鎖好。就在這時,門打開了,他死去的情人瑪格達勒娜進來了。她衣服上的冰珠子像細小的鈴鐺一樣噹啷作響。小夥子感到很沮喪,絕望地喊出來:「耶穌和瑪麗亞,你是誰?」

一個冰冷的陰影向他靠過來,觸摸他的嘴唇。鬼被招呼過,所以現在可以吸呼他的氣,並和他說話。小夥子的恐懼突然消失了,他和情人就進行了一次很長時間的談話。

首先她問,「你認得我嗎?」

「認得,你是我的情人瑪格達勒娜。」他回答。

「我是你的情人,」她說,「我是從阿萊奇冰河裏來的,我被判到那裏和別人跳舞,去贖從前和你跳禁舞之罪。但是你現在和我說了話,我希望很快就能得到解脫。請你明天下山去村莊為我的靈魂做一件好事,這樣就可以加快我的救贖了。」

她跟小夥子還說了很多話,二人並擁抱和親吻。她留在他的房間直到早禱的鐘聲從村莊響起。

小夥子沒有把他聽到和看到的事情告訴任何人。他依瑪格達勒娜所托,做了一件好事。他一輩子保持獨身,再沒有和別的姑娘玩兒,也沒有再戀愛。

火騎士 The Fiery Horsemen

遠古的從前，在冰河還沒有崩塌下來的地方，曾經有廣闊的綠色草原，高山山谷，還有幾座村莊和部落。在那些逝去的日子，甜美的果樹仍然茂盛，葡萄園亦隨處可見，可以釀造美味的酒。

傳說在土特曼谷的後谷底，有三個村莊：格魯本、邁登和布盧馬特。現在，夏天最好的幾個月也只有幾頭牛在吃草。

這三座村莊的村長都是騙子，喜歡偷用村民的錢，把錢暗藏在圓桶，埋在一個叫法芬，亦即「牧師」的小樹林裏。村民沒有發現他們交給鄉鎮的錢都流進了騙子村長的腰包。如有人敢提醒村長，説該是時候向村民交代一切開支了，就會有人打斷他的話，説他厚顏無恥，最好住口。所以一切照舊，一直到三個騙子死後下了葬許久，騙局才被揭破。

以後，人説在牧師樹林有一些古怪的事。有人在那邊見過那三個村長。他們因為無恥詐騙，被判永遠在樹林作鬼，以作懲罰，每一百年才可以露臉一次。

幾百年已經過去了。氣候變得陰冷。巨大的冰河逐漸形成，往前移動，流過了光禿禿的陡峭山崖，填滿了最後的小山谷。那三個村莊消失了，只留下遼闊的高山草原。有時候牧民會找到鋪馬路用的石塊，在有一些地方還能找到馬蹄鐵、窗框和石牆的遺跡。

有一個夜晚，一個來自邁登牧地的牧民走到山谷來。他在羅納谷給一隻病牛買

It was in the dim and distant past, long before the roaring avalanches came tumbling down from the glaciers and devastated the area with its green meadows and its high alpine valleys dotted with villages and hamlets. In those bygone days, rich fruit trees still flourished there, and even the grapevine thrived, producing an exquisite wine.

In the hindmost valley there used to be three villages: Gruben, Meiden and Blumatt. Nowadays, all that is to be seen are the cows grazing in the alpine pastures – and that only during the best months of the summer.

The mayors of the three villages were rascals who robbed the people, storing the money secretly in barrels which they kept buried in a small wood known as Pfaffenholz or Parson's Wood. The villagers did not notice that all the money they paid the corporation actually went straight into the pockets of the deceitful mayors. And if someone or other dared to remark that it was about time the mayor rendered account of his expenditures, the others shouted him down, saying he was a cheeky devil and would do better to hold his tongue. So nothing ever changed, and it was not until the fraudsters had all three long been dead and buried that the swindle finally came to light.

After that there were rumours of weird goings-on in Parson's Wood. Apparently the three mayors had been seen there. They had been doomed to haunt the place as a punishment for their outrageous fraud. And they were only allowed to show themselves once every hundred years.

Since then, many centuries had passed. The climate had grown harsher. Great glaciers had formed, advancing along the bare rugged cliff walls right into the hindmost valleys. The three villages had disappeared, leaving behind only vast alpine pastures. Occasionally herdsmen grazing their cattle there would come across bits of paving from the village roads. Now and then they would find a horseshoe, a piece of a window-frame or remnants of stone walls.

One day a herdsman from Meiden Alp was walking back up the valley. He had been down to the Rhone Valley to collect some medicine for a sick cow. Taking great strides he hurried along beside the roaring mountain stream. By the time he had reached Parson's Wood it must have been around midnight.

The long tramp had made him thirsty, so he crouched down to take a drink from a nearby brooklet. On straightening up again he saw, standing right in front of him, a man in old-fashioned clothing, wearing knee-breeches and a cocked hat. The man addressed him thus:

"Tomorrow, at midnight, you must come back here and wait for us. We'll appear before you then and on the following two nights at exactly the same time. If you manage to stand firm and not retreat by a single step we'll be redeemed. And then we'll show you the treasure we stole. For there are three barrels of gold hidden in Parson's Wood. The first and largest barrel will be for you. But you'll have to give the second to the church, and share out the contents of the third among the poor and needy."

Having spoken thus the spirit disappeared, and the herdsman continued on his way home. Now he rather regretted having given his word to return. However, when he woke the next morning, and while he was getting dressed, he kept thinking of the golden treasure the spirit had promised him. Then two men came and told him that both his sheep had been killed in a rock slide. Now the money would

了藥。他快步沿著湍急的溪流走著。他走到了牧師樹林的時候，大約已到了半夜。

因為這次旅程很長，他感到口渴，所以他在附近一條小溪邊蹲下來。牧民再站起來的時候，看到面前有一個衣飾古老的人，穿著及膝的褲子，戴著三角形的帽子。他和牧民打招呼說：「我是幾百年前騙山谷村莊的三個村長之一。我們因此受到了懲罰，得到解脫前要在這裏出沒。今天又流逝了一百年，獲允許說話。請你讓我們解脫吧！」

牧民上氣不接下氣地聽著。他性格善良，就答應給他們解脫，問該怎麼辦。

「請你明天半夜的時候來這裏等待我們。我們會向你顯現。往後兩晚也是一樣。如果你能經受住我們，一步也不讓，你就能夠給我們解脫了，然後我們會讓你看到我們從前偷走的財寶。我們在牧師樹林裏埋藏著三桶黃金。第一個最大的圓桶歸你，第二個圓桶你要交給教堂，第三個圓桶你要分發給窮人及有需要的人。」

說了這幾句話之後，鬼就消失了。牧民繼續走回家的路。他幾乎後悔答允回去牧師樹林，但是早上起床穿衣服的時候，他回想到鬼答應給他財寶。然後有兩個人前來，告訴牧民他的兩隻羊因山崩死了。現在他更加需要錢，所以他打算在約好的時間來到約好的地方掙那筆獎金。有了這麼多的錢，他就可以把整個高山牧地和牛群買下來，村民也會選他為村長。

快到半夜的時候，他上路了，比預定的時間早了一點到達沃淪橋。流水潺潺，石塊在河床翻滾的聲音，好像從沒有那麼的清晰。天空雲層很厚。

他等了不久，樹林裏突然湧出一叢火焰。在恐怖的隆隆聲下，出現了三匹烏黑黑的巨馬，牠們被口吐硫黃、身像胳膊一樣粗的蛇纏繞著。巨馬用後腿直立著，張開的鼻孔噴出長長的火舌。

牧民抓著橋的欄杆站住，怕得心裏怦怦直跳。他害怕馬會踩死他，或者蛇會殺死他。巨馬來到距離他三步的地方，直立起來，拐著彎消失了。

牧民嚇得好久才恢復過來。驚魂甫定後，他手插在褲袋裏走回家去。

第二夜，他又站在橋上。這一次他的恐懼少了一點，因為他知道只要站得牢，便不會受到傷害。突然地上一震，黑馬再次飛奔向他衝過來。這次騎在馬身上的不是蛇，是三隻熊，牠們齜牙咧嘴，揮舞利爪威脅著牧民。

他嚇得毛髮直豎，四肢發抖，但是他還是寸步不退，然後鬼和昨天一樣拐彎消失了。他鬆了口氣走上回家的路。

come in really useful! So he decided to return to the designated place at the designated hour and gain the prize. With all that money he would be able to buy not only the alp but also all the cattle on it, and then they would even have to elect him mayor.

Towards midnight he set off and reached the Vollen Bridge just before the appointed time. Below him the rushing waters roared and bubbled, and it seemed to him he had never before so distinctly heard the pebbles rolling around in the riverbed. The sky was overcast with a thick layer of cloud.

The man did not have to wait long. Suddenly a sheet of flame burst out from the wood, there was a fearsome thundering crash, and three coal-black horses appeared. They had snakes spitting fire and brimstone and thick as a man's arm writhing around their bodies. The giant animals reared, their dilated nostrils breathing out long tongues of flame.

The herdsman grabbed the railing of the bridge and held fast, although his heart was beating with terror. He feared he might be stamped on by the horses and killed by the snakes. But three steps in front of him the horses reared again, swerved off and disappeared.

It took quite a time for the herdsman to recover from his horrible experience. But then he put his hands into his pockets and set off back home.

The second night found him standing on the bridge again. This time he was a little less frightened, for he knew that if he stood fast he would not be harmed. Suddenly the earth shuddered, and the black horses came charging towards him. In place of the snakes there were three bears astride them, great creatures with wide-open snarling mouths and massive threatening paws.

The herdsman trembled all over, and his hair stood on end. But he moved not an inch. And when the ghosts veered at the last moment, as they had the night before, he gave a sigh of relief and made his way home.

One more night to get through and he would be the richest man in the whole valley and probably be elected mayor to boot! To be sure of not arriving too late he left early for the bridge. Black clouds loomed in the sky, lightning flashed, heralding the approach of a thunderstorm. A cold wind rose up, making him shiver. As he was just beginning to think the ghosts were not coming after all, a bolt of lightning shot out, striking the ground at his feet. This was followed by a deafening clap of thunder that nearly stunned him. At the same time, the earth quaked as though pounded by the hooves of a whole cavalry squadron. Here they came! In full gallop, fiery swords at the ready, three pitch-black horsemen rushed towards him. Wielding their swords, they plunged at him. Panicked, he let go of the railing and scarpered back up the valley as fast as his feet could carry him. He sensed, close at his heels the fiery horsemen. Panting with fear he raced on, but at the next bend in the path he stumbled and fell to the ground in a faint. He did not hear the horsemen's curse.

On awaking the following morning, he found himself lying on the dung heap next to his hut … next to what had been his hut. The building was gone. All that was left was a smouldering ruin. Lightning had struck the house during the night, setting it ablaze and killing his two cows. Now he had nothing left at all, and there was no future for him in the valley. How ashamed he felt, and how full of regret at having run away in such a cowardly manner when, with more staying powers, he could have become a man of immense wealth!

He left the region and nothing was ever heard of him again.

還有一個晚上，他就會成為山谷裏最有錢的人，並很快成為村長哩。為免遲到，他早一點來到橋上。天上黑雲密佈，還閃著電，好像雷雨即將來臨。冷風吹起來，使他發抖。他以為鬼不來了，突然雷電擊在他旁邊，響起震耳欲聾的雷聲，差不多使他昏倒過去。這時地面顫動起來，好像有騎兵隊要向他衝過來似的。對，三個穿烏黑衣服的人撥出火劍，全速向他跑過來。他們揮動著劍刺向他。牧民極度驚惶，不自覺放開了握著欄杆的手，向山谷逃去，能跑多快就跑多快。他身後緊跟著發火的騎士。他恐懼地喘著氣繼續跑，終於精疲力竭，在一個拐彎的地方暈倒在地上，聽不到騎士發出的詛咒。

早上醒過來的時候，他在自己茅舍旁邊的糞堆上躺著——應該說是以前茅舍的旁邊！茅舍沒有了，他只能看到一堆冒煙的瓦礫。雷電在夜裏把茅舍燒掉了，並且劈死了他兩隻牛。他現在一無所有，不能再留在山谷裏了。他有機會變成一個很有錢的人，卻沒有力量堅持下去，膽小地逃走了。他感到多麼的後悔和慚愧！

牧民最後離開了這個地方，消失得無影無蹤。

魯斯根的伯爵夫人 The Countess on Lusgen Alp

阿萊奇谷的冰河邊有一塊叫魯斯根的高山牧地。那裏有一些高山茅舍，八月份才有牛群在附近放牧。從那裏走過去，經過閃出青藍光的那段冰河，就到了一座給風雨剝蝕的山崖，山崖分成了成百上千的石板和岩石塊。這個地方，人們叫它「岩石海」。石塊散滿四周，有些是碩大的立方體，有些是角錐形，或者平板形的；有的直豎著，有的橫躺著，像巨大的石製桌子。老牧民傳說，自古在此地便藏有一批財寶。有人說曾在日落的時候看見過這些財寶，閃光的銀子雖然使他們眼饞，但是有一個惡魔，和一位穿雪白衣服的貴夫人在那邊看守著，他們就被嚇倒了。

有一次，一個星期日出生的窮牧民走到岩石海這邊找一隻迷路的羊，他不知道財寶和白衣女子的事情。突然，一隻有金翅膀的蝴蝶在他面前飛過，他一手抓過去想捉住牠，蝴蝶卻飛走了。牧民追著，蝴蝶就在石板的裂縫中消失了。牧民迅即忘記了蝴蝶，因為他眼前的石板上有一塊漂亮的棉布，布上放著不可多得的珍寶。

這些寶物的光澤使他眼花繚亂，他要用雙手遮住眼睛。突然他給嚇了一跳，離

Lusgen Alp is situated in the upper Aletsch Valley, near the rim of the glacier. If you go up as far as the highest alpine huts to which cattle are not taken before the beginning of August, and then climb down to the blue and green shimmering stretch of glacier, you will reach a spot where the changing seasons have broken up the rock into hundreds of thousands of individual slabs and cubes. Such spots are known as felsenmeers, which is German for sea of rocks. The stones are strewn all over the terrain; some are formed into massive cubes, some are shaped like pyramids, others like flat plates, some are upright, others lie flat like great stone tables. There are old herdsmen who maintain that the place conceals a treasure, hidden there since time immemorial. Some even claim to have seen it with their own eyes, at sunset; they had been drawn towards the sparkling, shining hoard of silver, they say, but then they had always been held off by an evil spirit: a fine lady in a snowy white dress sitting beside the treasure.

One day a poor herdsman, a child of fortune who knew nothing about the treasure or the woman in white, was just passing the felsenmeer in search of a lost sheep, when a golden-winged butterfly flew up in front of him. He made a grab for it, but it escaped his clutch and fluttered away. He chased after it, but it disappeared into a crack between the stone plates. Suddenly the herdsman forgot all about the butterfly, for he noticed that the stone slabs had been covered with a beautiful linen cloth on which lay masses of silver treasure, enough to satisfy one's heart's desire.

He was so dazzled by the treasure that he had to shield his eyes. But then he started in fear! Seated on the table, quite near him, there was a beautiful woman. On her left side lay a heap of gold, on her right a pile of silver coins. She kept putting more and more gold and silver onto the two piles, and was so preoccupied that she took no notice of the young man. Her heavy dark hair was bound into a large knot, and her apparel, spun of the finest silk, shone like the moon. Around her neck she wore a golden necklace that glittered like dewdrops in the rays of the morning sun. Now she raised her black eyes towards the man and beckoned to him to approach; but he shrank in fear from the blinding white marble figure.

He beat his forehead. Was he awake or just dreaming? "I can't run away from a woman," he said to himself. "That would be too shaming!"

So he approached, greeting her politely. Only now did he see that her dress was spangled with diamonds that glistened like ice crystals, scintillating in all the colours of the glacier and the rainbow.

The cold expression on the woman's face disappeared, giving way to a friendly smile. Her eyes shone like stars in the night sky.

He was about to ask her, "Your Highness, what do you want of me? I'm nothing but a poor herdsman." But then she stood up. His heart started thumping, and his whole body trembled like a blade of smooth-stalked meadow grass in a breath of wind. The words he wanted to say stuck in his throat. Overcome by

他不遠有一位漂亮的伯爵夫人坐在石板桌上。她左邊放著一堆黃金，右邊放著一堆銀子。她忙著把越來越多的黃金與銀子堆上去，甚至連那小夥子她也沒注意到。她黑色而濃密的頭髮結成了髻。她的衣服是用最精細的絲綢紡織成的，像月光一樣發亮。她頸上戴著一條黃金項鏈，像露珠在早上的太陽下閃閃發光。現在她抬起一雙黑色的眼睛，向牧民看過來了，也招手示意他走過去。他看著這白得耀眼，像大理石一樣的一個人，卻不禁毛骨悚然。

他拍拍自己的額頭。做夢嗎？「我不應該因一個女人而逃走的，這樣太丟人了。」他自言自語。

他於是過去向夫人客氣地致意，這才看到她衣服上佈滿了冰水晶一樣爍爍發亮的鑽石，閃耀著冰河和彩虹的各種顏色。

夫人冷淡的臉上掠過一絲客氣的微笑，眼睛像黑暗裏的星星般閃閃發光。

他正想問：「伯爵夫人，您想要什麼？我只不過是一個窮牧民。」她卻站了起來。牧民心裏怦怦直跳，抖得像微風中的嫩草，說不出話來。他感到極大的驚恐，轉身便跑，飛快跳過石板朝牧地跑去。

他一面跑，一面聽到身後響起雷聲和爆裂的聲響，好像整個山崖快要崩下來。

terror he fled, dashing and leaping across the flat rocks and boulders towards the alp.

Behind him he heard a thundering and a crashing as though the whole mountain were collapsing. After the terrible din had died down, he heard a sighing sound just behind him. But he did not dare turn his head before reaching his hut.

He lay awake all night. Again and again the figure of the countess appeared before his eyes, together with her immense treasure of silver and gold. He could not stop reproaching himself. "Look what you've lost, thanks to your childish timidity!" he repeated to himself again and again.

For sure, the countess would not have done him any harm. He was furious with himself, calling himself a coward and an idiot. He decided to set off at the first light of day, climb back up to the felsenmeer and prostrate himself humbly and contritely at the woman's feet.

Dawn had hardly broken when he started on his way uphill, all the while turning over and over in his mind what he would say to the woman with the treasure of silver and gold. In his mind's eye he already saw himself as a wealthy man. He would acquire the beautiful alp, then he would travel down to the Val d'Hérens where he would buy a fine herd of cows. Then he would be able to go to the big spring and autumn fairs in Brig with bags of money to spend.

He reached the felsenmeer well before midday. He would have to wait a long time until the setting

恐怖的隆隆聲消失了之後，他聽到沉重的歎氣聲，但是他不敢回頭看，只一直跑回茅舍去。

整夜他也睡不著覺，總是想到夫人的樣子和無窮的金銀財寶。他禁不住自責起來。「看你失去了什麼？這都是因為你幼稚又膽小！」他不斷喃喃自語。

夫人肯定不會傷害他。他生自己的氣，叫自己做膽小鬼、蠢材。他決定大清早出發，回到岩石海，謙卑地匍匐在夫人腳下，以表示自己多後悔。

天剛破曉，他爬上山，腦中練習著要對夫人說的話。她擁有那麼多的金銀財寶。在牧民心中，他覺得自己已經是一個有錢的人了。他要把美麗的高山牧地買下來，然後去埃陵爾谷買一批好的牲畜。春天和秋天的時候，他想帶一袋袋錢到布裏格的市場去花費。

到達岩石海時還未到中午，他還要等到夕陽染紅了西方。他於是離開那奇怪的地方到高山草地散步，打算黃昏才回來；到那時，伯爵夫人肯定已經坐在石板桌子上，或者正等待他哩。

sun coloured the western sky. So he left the bizarre place and went for a stroll across the mountain pastures, having decided not to return before the evening, when the countess would be sitting on the table, perhaps even waiting for him.

At sunset he turned back, leaping across the rocks and boulders to the place where he had seen the fine lady the day before. This time he would stand firm. But the stone slabs were bare. All he saw were the many grey, moss-covered blocks of stone which had probably been lying there for aeons. He heard the bells of the cattle grazing down in the valley, but up here nothing stirred. The sun sank behind the mountains, and night rose up from the Rhone Valley. Shadows like black drapes slid upwards along the cliff walls and the slopes, covering the chalets down below and coming closer and closer until he could no longer make out the individual blocks of stone. There was no point in waiting up here any longer. Sadly he wended his way down towards the valley, swearing never ever to tell anyone about what he had seen.

Every week he returned to the rock tables, until the autumn wind came sweeping across the pastures and the cows were led down from the alp. Never again did he see the countess, and yet he could not forget her. He became quite strange and was to remain a queer fellow for the rest of his life. He avoided his friends and was always wandering around on the alp as though looking for something, no one knew for what. And then he met an early death.

太陽落山的時候，他回到岩石海，跳過岩塊和大石，到他昨天遇到夫人的地方。這一次他不會逃跑。但是石板上什麼都沒有，只有長著灰色苔蘇的小岩石塊，好像自古已躺在那裏似的。他聽到山下吃草的牧群脖子上發出的鈴聲，但是山上什麼聲音也沒有。太陽在山嶺後落下去，黑夜從羅納谷升上來。影子像黑布一樣向上滑過崖壁和山坡，把遠處山下的高山茅舍都蓋上了，越來越近，他幾乎看不清個別的岩石塊了。在這裏繼續等待已沒有用了，他傷心地向谷底走去，發誓不再提及這件事。

往後每星期，他都會來到石桌旁，等待等待，一直到秋風拂過草地，牲口從高山牧地趕回來的時候才離開。他再也沒有見到伯爵夫人，卻忘不了她。他成為一個古怪的人，以後半生都如是。他避免和朋友來往，總是獨個兒在高山牧地上漫遊，彷彿在尋找什麼。沒有人知道他要尋找什麼。終於，他死去了，死的時候還很年輕。

勇敢的冷克婦女 The Brave Women of Lenk

山谷裏已經建立了很宏大的城市和教堂，不過山裏強悍的牧人還是相信他們自己的秩序和法則。他們經常搶掠山谷的鄰居。他們這樣做主要不是因為貧困，而是要表示他們多麼的勇敢。誰的力量大和詭計多，誰就能增加自己的財產。漂亮的女孩子都會被他吸引，無論敵人或朋友都會尊敬他。

有一天，瓦利斯人突然衝進冷克人西門谷上肥沃的高山牧場，迅速地把牛群搶走然後離去。那時只有女人和老人在茅舍裏，因為善於作戰的年輕人都往其他地方去了，他們正進行種種危險的活動。不管怎樣，牧場裏能走動的人都立刻衝出來，追趕無恥的敵人。

冷克人追趕了一段時間之後，就見到他們被盜的牛群平靜地在草地上吃草。瓦利斯人悠閒極了，他們快樂地喝酒、唱歌、開玩笑，慶祝他們的勝利。他們大概

Long after the establishment of powerful cities and churches in the valleys, the strong mountain folk still held on to their own laws and customs. They used often to raid their neighbours – more out of wanton pleasure than dire need. And whoever managed to increase his chattel the most – be it thanks to physical strength, skill at arms or guile – was sure to be the favourite of all the pretty girls in the region and to be held in high esteem by friend and foe alike.

One day, like a bolt from the blue, a gang of men from the Valais descended on the fertile alps belonging to the families of Lenk (at the top end of the Simmen Valley), and quickly went away again, joyfully driving before them whole herds of stolen cattle. Only women and old men had been at home at the time of the raid, because all the fighting-fit young men were away somewhere or other on their own dangerous adventures. Nevertheless, every single person who still had the use of their limbs rushed off in pursuit of their brazen foe.

Soon the people of Lenk caught sight of their stolen cattle grazing peacefully in a meadow: apparently the victorious Valais lads were in no hurry, and were celebrating their easy victory with wine and song and jokes. Perhaps they were so sure of their superiority that they even wanted to let their pursuers approach – so that they could make fun of the weakly women and decrepit old men.

But the crafty old men of Lenk sneaked up to their cows, surreptitiously took the bells from their necks and started to shake them gently, so that their jolly ringing continued to be heard in the pastures. In the meantime the women quietly drove the stolen herds back home.

Once the women and the cattle had got so far that even the most stupid of the Valais men had to admit that pursuit was in vain, the wise old men stopped ringing the bells, and burst into peals of laughter that re-echoed from the mountains all around.

From that day on, as a reward for their courage, the women of Lenk have been honoured with the privilege of being allowed to precede their husbands when leaving the church after mass.

自覺優勝,所以故意讓追趕他們的冷克人靠近,意圖嘲笑孱弱的女人和老頭兒。

不過,聰明的冷克老頭兒偷偷地把牛的響鈴解開,放在自己的身上輕輕地搖,那麼快樂的鈴聲便繼續在草原上響下去。同一時候,冷克的女人靜靜地把被偷的牛群領回家去。

冷克的女人和牛已經跑得很遠很遠了,瓦利斯人這才發現他們受騙。就是瓦利斯人中最笨的牧人,也得承認現在追趕冷克的女人是沒用的了。這時候,聰明的老頭兒停止搖鈴,笑得山谷裏哪兒都可以聽到回音。

從那天起,為了讚許勇敢的冷克婦女,她們得到了比男人早點離開教堂的權利。

夫爾卡山道的酒祭 Libations on the Furka Pass

有時候在夫爾卡的山裏，烏森和郭姆斯那兒，偶然可以在雪上看到一些奇怪的紅色斑點，像有人灑了血或者葡萄酒似的。

山裏的人總愛這樣解釋這個神秘的現象：從前的人習慣用馬走山道運貨，而他們都犯了嚴重的罪，就是沒把美味的義大利紅酒全數交給付了錢的瑞士商人，反而為了減輕負擔，把珍貴的紅酒一滴一滴的往自己乾渴的口裏灌。再加上他們無禮、傲慢又大意，關酒桶的時候常常不小心，關得不牢固，於是走到那兒，酒便滴到那兒。

上天是公正嚴明的，顯然無法容忍這樣不誠實的勾當——如此對待天賜的禮物實在太浪費了。所以，雪上那些斑點是馬夫的靈魂，他們註定永遠在寒冷中孤零零地贖罪。這樣對他們是很大的折磨啊，因為遑論多口渴，他們都永不能消解口中炙熱的痛楚。

人們路經這裏的時候，若袋子裏或背包裏有一瓶葡萄酒，一般會把幾滴倒在斑點上。那麼，可憐的鬼魂為報答這些人，會給他們指示方向，或當他們在危險的山路發生意外時會解救他們。

On the Furka Pass between Ursern and Goms, but also in other mountainous regions, you may occasionally come across strange red stains in the snow that look like red wine – or even human blood.

To explain this mysterious phenomenon, mountain folk will talk about the men who, in the olden days, used to drive their packhorses across the pass. Apparently they were guilty of a serious crime. For, instead of dutifully delivering all of the delectable Italian wine in their charge to the Swiss merchants who, after all, had paid for it, they would relieve their mules of quite a significant part of their load – by consigning the refreshing beverage drop by drop to their own thirsty gullets. On top of this, insolent and arrogant as they were, they tended to be very negligent. Thus, very often, they failed to bung the casks firmly, so that the wine dripped onto the mountain path wherever they passed.

Obviously, heaven in its justice could not permit such dishonesty nor such squandering of one of God's finest gifts to man. So, you see, the red stains in the snow are quite simply the souls of those dissolute mule-drivers, doomed to atone for their sins in eternal cold and isolation, suffering the torments of hell since, in their present form, they can never quench their aching, parching thirst.

And so it happens that, whenever they are on their way through the region and happen to have a bottle of wine in their pockets or in their rucksacks, the mountain folk always pour a couple of drops of the cordial onto the haunted spots. In return, the poor spirits render them useful services like helping them find their way or rescuing them after accidents on the dangerous mountain trails.

空中生活 | Life in the Air

Once, in the Onsernone Valley in sunny Ticino, there arose such a furious mountain storm that people feared it would tear the roofs from their mountain huts.

However, a cowherd who had served as a mercenary in the famous city of Venice, where he had learned a great deal about Venetian art, went out courageously to face the raging storm. He took out his long-bladed knife and, after mumbling some incomprehensible words into his black beard, suddenly flung the knife into the air right into the path of the howling storm.

After a few seconds the swirling winds had calmed down, as if by miracle. The people searched all around for the knife, but in vain. It was never found. But on the ground, not far from the spot from which the herdsman had hurled his knife, three drops of blood could be seen shining like red pearls.

After that the Onsernone Valley remained untroubled by storms for a very long time.

位於提契諾州的歐瑟諾谷向來陽光充足，但有一次卻刮起狂風，山中的人都害怕房子的屋頂會被山風掀掉。

那兒有一個牧牛人，他年青時在有名之威尼斯市當過雇傭兵，學過不少那裏的魔法。他跑出去勇敢地面對怒吼的風暴。他抽出長刀，對自己的黑鬍子嘰裏咕嚕地說了一堆不知什麼的話後，便把長刀用力地擲向空中風暴的來處。

不一會兒，空中的狂風像中了魔法一般停了下來。人們四處找那把長刀，但都白費力氣。地上呢，離牧牛人投刀不遠處，有三滴血像紅珍珠那樣閃亮著。

那次以後，歐瑟諾谷很長時間沒再遭受狂風吹襲了。

普魯爾斯位於查溫納上邊的麥拉河畔，那
兒位置好，礦產豐富，所以城裏的人都很
富有。人們在庫爾森林上邊的紅角山峰發
現了一個很大的銀礦，從此驢騾日日夜夜
不停地背著從山裏挖出來的銀塊，運到
冶煉廠去。人們還說那兒有些河裏滿是黃
金，每天早晚兩次，都可以從河裏淘出一
桶黃金來。普魯爾斯的居民甚至控制了南
方的絲綢貿易，所以這個城市又名「寶以
福」，就是「可愛的市集」的意思。

　　不久，普魯爾斯的居民開始忘記高山
生活的傳統美德了，他們的心越來越硬，
眼中只有金錢。他們開始看不起沒有錢的
人，不賺錢的事便不幹。想起他們的父兄
以前也是牧人，也像附近的牧人一樣穿著
粗糙的毛絨衣裳，他們竟然感到很羞恥。
結果，他們把最後一絲良心也壓下去了，
對這些以前的兄弟越發瞧不起，對他們的
態度比最卑鄙的暴君還要差。

　　1618年的情況就是這樣。普魯爾斯
的居民舉行了一個婚禮，趁機炫耀自己的
財富和地位。新娘、新郎和所有的客人在
黃金繡的帳篷下慢慢地走到教堂，然後用

The burghers of Plurs, a small town which used to stand on the banks of the Mera River above Chiavenna, had become very rich and powerful due to the excellent location of their town and also to its mineral resources. A vast seam of silver had been discovered near the top of Mount Rothorn above Churwalden; day and night endless files of mules could be seen transporting the ore to the smeltery. There were also said to be small streams so full of gold that twice a day, morning and evening, each yielded a full measure of the precious metal. The burghers of Plurs also controlled all the silk trade going south. Finally the town and its region became known among the people as Belfort, meaning 'Lovely Market Town'.

Soon the people of Plurs started to neglect the traditional virtues of alpine life and became hard-hearted and rapacious. People who had no money were mocked, and whatever did not bring in money was spurned. People even started to feel ashamed at being the descendants of simple farmers who, within living memory, had still worn coarse woollen smocks just like the herdsmen in the neighbouring alps. Concerning the latter, their former brothers, they looked down on them in scorn, and – perhaps to suppress any twinges of conscience – treated them worse than the vilest of tyrants.

Such was the situation in 1618 when a wedding in Plurs once again provided the occasion for the small town to make a show of its great power and wealth. Shaded by gold-embroidered canopies, the wedding procession wended its way through the town to the church. Afterwards the guests dined lavishly from silver plates and then, after the feast, strolled gaily along the banks of the Mera.

All of a sudden, from the nearby meadows, they heard a lamb bleating piteously for its mother. The wails of the poor little creature displeased the wealthy bride.

"Straying animals can be captured and slain," she cried, citing a law the people of Plurs were only too glad to observe. Considering it could only add to the general merriment of the nuptial party, they tied the lamb to four posts, skinned it alive, and then, tauntingly, returned the pathetic, blood-drenched, flayed creature to its owner.

But now the cruel, avaricious burghers had definitely gone too far. Suddenly fearsome cracks could be seen in the sides of the neighbouring mountains, deep fissures appeared in the ground, all around there was a rumbling and a quaking – enormous rocks in the cliff side shuddered into motion and, with a thundering crash, rolled down over the ungodly town.

Plurs, with all its palaces and noble mansions and its chests full of gold and silk, still lies buried beneath the debris. To this day the story of its fall is told as a warning to later generations. And greedy, grasping people dreaming of unfound treasure still dig in the deep rubble in quest of the fairytale riches.

純銀的盤子吃豐盛的晚宴，再愉快地在麥拉河邊散步。

突然，附近的牧場傳來小羊可憐的叫聲。牠迷路了，牠要找媽媽。富有的新娘覺得小羊的叫聲很討厭，打擾了她。

「按照普魯爾斯的法律，迷路的動物誰都可以拿回家宰殺。」她喊道。普魯爾斯居民覺得這樣做可以令婚宴更熱鬧，便樂於照辦。他們把羔羊牢牢的綑在四根柱子上，然後活生生地剝牠的皮，最後更訕笑著把沾滿血、剝了皮的小羊還給牠的主人。

這麼可怖的罪行是不可原諒的。突然，附近的山出現恐怖的裂痕，地面亦出現很深的縫隙，四周隆隆的震動起來。崖邊巨大的岩石搖搖欲墜，然後「嘭」的一聲滾下來，掩埋了整個罪惡之城。

普魯爾斯的豪華宮殿、官邸巨宅及一箱箱的金銀絲綢，都埋在瓦礫下面。直到現在，它墜落的故事仍然廣泛流傳，以警後世。貪婪的人則努力地挖掘，希望找到傳聞中的普魯爾斯財寶。

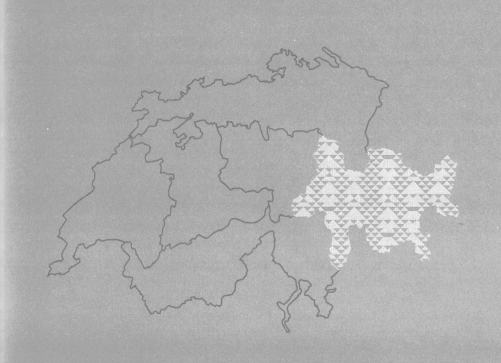

Legends from Graubünden and Glarus

格勞賓登州與格拉魯斯州的傳說

卡殊裏牧場的巫術　Witchcraft on Caschlee Alp

This is a story my father told me. It happened when he and his brother Vigilius were working as cowherds in Milar. That same year, two of their friends, the brothers Jakob Anton and Christian Deragisch, were herdsmen up in Strim. When summer came, they all drove their cattle up to Caschlee Alp. That was great fun, four herdsmen up on the Hexenplatte – or 'Witches' Paving Stone' – which is still there to this day.

"We had a great time, up there all day on the Hexenplatte, making fun of witches and their witchcraft," my father said. "Then, in the evening, we drove our cattle into the barn above our chalet, said our prayers and went to bed. We slept like kings. But in the middle of the night we were awoken by a fearful storm: great gusts of wind, crashes of thunder, jagged forks of lightning, hailstones hammering on the rooftop … We could hear the heifers running around like wild, mooing loudly and shaking their bells. Thoroughly alarmed, we rushed out of the chalet to herd our cattle. They kept running down towards the crags and Ondalusa, or down the steep sides of the ravine. Several of the cows were as red as fire, and they kept racing around, up and down the dangerous slopes – but they never fell over.

Then Jakob Anton Deragisch said, 'There's something funny about this. We haven't got any red cows with fiery horns and tails. Let's go back to our chalet and leave the witches to their tricks. They just want to get their own back on us because we

這個故事是我父親告訴我的。他跟他的弟弟維哲裏斯在妙勒牧牛。同一年，在史特林放牧的，是他的朋友雅各安東和奇斯頓杜拉吉斯兩兄弟。每年夏天，他們都領著牲畜到卡殊裏去。很有意思哩，四個牧者在一個叫「女巫石」的地方一起玩。這地方現在還在那裏。

「我們玩得很開心，整天在女巫石上開玩笑，嘲笑女巫跟巫術，」父親說，「晚上，我們把牛趕到小屋後的牛房去，然後一起祈禱。祈禱後便睡覺，睡得挺香甜。誰料午夜時天氣驟變：風開始吹，接著是響雷、閃電、下冰雹，直敲在屋頂上。小母牛開始亂跳，大聲叫喊，猛搖著鈴子。我們嚇得跑出小屋，想把牲畜放牧在一起，但牠們一直朝安大杜沙懸崖那裏走，直到陡斜的峽谷那邊。幾頭牛紅得像火一樣，在危險的山坡彈跳，卻沒有掉下去。

infuriated them by making fun of them and their witchery.'

We followed his advice and returned to our chalet. To be on the safe side, we sprinkled some holy water around, made the sign of the cross, lit a lantern and hung it in front of the house. It was midnight. We two older herdsmen were tired out from running around, and the young boys were exhausted with fear and crying, so we soon fell asleep.

Early next morning, as soon as we'd got up, we went to check up on our animals. They were all exactly where we'd left them the evening before! They hadn't been disturbed by lightning and hail. And down in the villages they told us it had been a lovely quiet night with a moon and stars.

Now we knew for certain who had plagued us that night: it was the gang of witches we'd teased and angered all that day. There and then we decided never again to make fun of witchery."

那時雅各安東跟我們説：『這可真奇怪！我們的牛不是紅色的，牛角和尾巴亦不是火燒的樣子。我們進小屋去，就讓女巫自己作法吧。我們剛才嘲笑她們和她們的魔法，她們生我們的氣，要報復啊。』

我們就返回小屋去。為了安全，我們還在周圍灑聖水，身上打個十字，也點起燈籠，掛在小屋前。我們兩個大的跑來跑去，快要累死了，兩個小的感到害怕，哭得厲害，也累了，所以我們很快便都睡著了。

第二天早上，我們起來立刻去看看牲畜。很奇怪，牠們就關在原來的地方，沒受到冰雹和閃電的騷擾。山谷下的村民説他們過了一個美麗安靜的夜晚，還有星星月亮。

現在我們知道誰整夜害我們了：就是女巫！只因前一天我們害她們生氣。自此，我們不敢再嘲笑所有跟女巫有關的事情了。』

野少女　The Wild Maiden

從前有一個人，每年春天總要早晚到山下的牛棚餵飼牛隻，但每當他來到牛棚，牛總是餵過了，牛棚也給整理得漂漂亮亮。有一個晚上，他想：「我真想知道誰給我餵了牛。」於是他躲藏在空的槽裏面。

　　早上門開了，一個漂亮的少女走進來。他發覺她是個野少女，那時代這樣的女孩為數不少。她給牲畜吃的、喝的，最後給牠們一束乾草，這樣就可以把鏈條放回牲畜的脖子上了。她去拿乾草的時候，他從槽裏爬出來，走到牛棚門口跟她攀談。他問她要不要喝牛奶，說她餵的牲畜怎樣也比他餵的好。她搖搖頭。

　　那個晚上，她還是回來了。翌日他對她說，她應該到他的家，因那兒有很多工作。她跟著他走，他給她看什麼要做的，怎麼做飯，及其他別的事情。她第一次做飯沒有加鹽，他便把鹽桶給她看。每一件事她都做得很好。不過她不跟鄰人說話，只跟他說話，而且只是必要的時候才說話。最後他娶了她，並生了兩個可愛的孩子。

There once was a man who, during the spring months, had to go up morning and evening to his cowshed in the lower pastures to feed his cattle. Every time he arrived, the animals had already been fed and the cowshed beautifully cleaned up. So one evening he said to himself, "I really would like to find out who's feeding my cattle," and he hid himself in the empty manger.

Towards morning the door opened, and a lovely young girl came into the shed. He saw that she was one of those wild maidens there were quite a lot of in those days. She fed and then watered the cows. Finally she started giving each cow a handful of hay, as you do before you place the chain around its neck. When she went out to fetch some more hay, the man climbed out of the manger and accosted her at the shed door. He asked her if she would like to drink some milk, after all, she had fed the animals better than he ever did. She shook her head.

But in the evening she was there again. Then, the following morning, he asked her to come down to his house as he had a lot of work for her. She went with him, and he showed her what to do, how to cook and all that sort of thing. The first time she cooked she forgot the salt, so he showed her the salt cellar. She did all her work very well, but she never talked to the neighbours, only to him, and to him only when it was really necessary. Finally they married and had two splendid sons.

One day he had to take some cattle to the market in Chiavenna. Before leaving, he gave his wife exact instructions how everything was to be done. However, while he was away, she finished all the work in the fields and got the harvest in before the fixed time, before all the other farmers. For she had noticed that there was going to be an early winter.

This annoyed the neighbours. So when her husband returned home, they complained: All his wheat and hay was already in the barn. Thinking his wife had done something wrong, he strode into the house in a fury and hit her in the face with the back of his hand. At that she said, "I'm not staying here any more." For before the wedding she had said he must never box her ears, especially not with the back of his hand.

She continued to look after the children. But her husband never saw her again. He never noticed when she attended to the children.

A few days later, winter came and covered everything with snow. And the man went insane with grief and mortification.

有一次，他要帶著牲畜到赤惠拿的市場去，所以先指示她事情要怎麼做。他不在的時候，她很快已經把田裏的工作做好，還提早把麥稻收割妥當——比預定的時間早，也比其他鄰居的早——因為她感覺到今年的冬天會早一點兒來。

鄰人都很生氣。他回來的時候，鄰人紛紛向他投訴。他看到穀物和乾草都被妻子安放在屋頂下。他以為她做錯了事，於是生氣地走進屋去，用手背打她的臉。她說：「我再不能留下來了。」因為婚禮之前她跟他說過，他永遠不可以打她耳光，尤其不能用手背打她。

她繼續照顧孩子，只是再不跟他見面。他也不知道她什麼時候來看孩子。

幾天之後，冬天就來了，雪把全部蓋住了。他傷心慚愧得發瘋了。

高山牧場的古怪事 Strange Goings-on on the Alp

泰拉密斯的農民加殿得到消息,說他的一頭牛生病了,他便趕回高山牧場去。可能他那天為了一些工作沒辦法早一點兒回去(他是鄉長嘛),也許是走得太慢,不管什麼理由,他到達山坡的時候已經很晚了。天上有很多黑雲,把天罩得黑沉沉的,只偶然露出淡淡月色。和風中彷彿瀰漫著一些不尋常的東西。終於到達史泰姆司了,他感到很高興。

快半夜了,他突然聽到牛的鈴聲,不是一兩下,而是瘋狂不休的鈴聲。這吵鬧聲裏還有牧牛人的叫喊:「呵呵呵,快走,快走!」驚訝的農民就站住了。那個小夥子在想什麼呢?怎麼這麼晚還趕牲畜到草地去?好的牧人怎麼會這樣呢?一會要好好罵他一頓。

他以為吵鬧的聲音是從新的牧場來的。他生氣地朝那方向跑過去,卻踢著一頭在路上安靜躺著的牛。那頭牛證明牧場上什麼都好。他還是憤怒地跑向小屋。小屋那邊什麼都關了,一點聲音也沒有。鄉長加殿一旦決定了什麼,就不會改變主意。他大聲敲門,害得牧者都醒過來,下來開門。他們得聽罵了,因為鄉長脾氣不好。這算什麼?夜裏不讓牛休息?

One day a farmer from Trimmis received notice that he had to go up to the alp as one of his cows had fallen sick. Perhaps he had been kept back by official business – he was the mayor of the village – or perhaps he had dawdled on the way, but anyway it was very late by the time he reached the mountain slopes. Great masses of dark cloud, pierced every now and then by the thin light of a sickle moon, billowed across the sky. Something uncanny seemed to be afloat in the warm foehn wind, and the man was glad when he finally reached Stams.

It must have been near midnight. Suddenly he heard the sound of cow bells, not just a soft jingling here and there, but a crazy, restless jangling interspersed with the loud call of a cowherd: "Shoo, shoo, gee-up, gee-up!" The farmer stopped in his tracks, astonished. What on earth was the man thinking of, driving the cattle into the pastures at that time of night? A fine herdsman indeed! He'd soon give him a piece of his mind.

The farmer thought the noise was coming from the new chalet. He dashed towards it in a rage … but stumbled on a cow that was lying peacefully in the middle of the grassy path. Although this should have alerted him to the fact that everything was in order, he charged on, shaking with fury. However, at the chalet everything was shut up and there was not a sound to be heard. Now once Mayor Gadient had made up his mind, there was no changing it. He banged and hammered on the door until the men finally came down to open up. Now they would hear something, for the mayor had a fierce temper. What were they thinking of, robbing the cows of their peace at night?

It took some time before he calmed down and started to listen to the herdsman, who explained that they had all gone to bed straight after supper. They certainly had not driven the cows into the pastures at night. All that noise and jangling of bells was not from them. Finally, they managed to convince old Gadient that the commotion had come not from their chalet but from the spot called Old Spring Meadow, which had always been ill-famed. In fact, no animal would ever lie down in that part of the pasture at night, although it was so nice and flat and covered in fine grass.

In former times there had been a chalet on Old Spring Meadow. Things were nice and peaceful until the day a cowherd moved in who was both cruel and corrupt. Since he wanted to make a good impression on the rich farmers, he gave their cows plenty of salt. But the poorer farmers' cows got nothing but blows. Following the death of the evil fellow, there was an end to peace up there. The cattle refused to lie down in the meadow, since they were kept awake by the cowherd's ghost. In dark nights the alpine herdsmen would hear his calls. In the end, the chalet was pulled down and set up again in another place, which they then called New Spring Meadow.

There is a similar tale about the Stutz Alp in the Vereina Valley. The herdsmen there are particularly watchful that each cow get its portion of salt to lick. For they can't help thinking of the little man known as the Fog Manikin or the Salt Manikin who rules there.

Whenever the weather is about to change for the worse, especially before a summer snowfall, the herdsmen see an ancient, grey-bearded little man roaming the mountain pastures. He is fashionably

好一段時間之後，加殿才安靜下來聽牧民解釋：他們吃晚飯後就睡覺，沒有把牛趕到草地去。夜裏聽到的吵鬧和鈴聲，都不是他們發出的。老加殿最後被說服了，他相信聲音不是從他們的牧場傳來，而是從一塊叫「舊溪草場」的地方發出的。那草場的名聲很壞，夜裏沒有一頭牛會躺在那裏的，雖然那裏很平坦而漂亮，且有很多草。

很久以前，舊溪草場那裏也有一間小屋。一切都是美麗和平的。直到一天，一個殘忍卑鄙的牧牛人搬進來。他要給有錢的農民留下好印象，於是給他們的牛很多鹽，但對窮人的牛就不一樣，他只會打牠們。那陰險的牧牛人死了以後，那塊地就變得不安寧了。沒有一隻牲畜想躺在那兒，因為鬼牧人不會讓牠們好好的睡。夜裏，牧場的雇農會聽到他的喊聲。後來小屋被拆下來，在另外的地方重建，當地人就叫那地方「新溪草場」。

維利拿山谷的史土茲牧場也有相近的故事。那邊的牧者都特別小心，會給每一頭牛適當份量的鹽，因為他們總禁不住想起那個叫「霧矮子」或者「鹽矮子」的小矮人。

一旦天氣轉壞，尤其是夏天下雪的時候，牧者就會看到一個灰色鬍鬚、樣子古老的小矮子在高山上散步。他的衣飾很講究，頭戴一頂闊邊帽，腳穿木鞋，白色的毛絨外衣上掛一個鹽袋。晚上，他會在牧民的小屋中出現，但有時大白天他會走到牛隻前面，像牧人喊牠們吃鹽那樣喊牠們。如果一段時間他的叫喊仍不奏效——因為牲畜從來不聽他的——他就會惱怒地消失，但很快又在另外的地方出現。有時可以聽到他歡呼和唱約德爾調，有時又會聽到他呼嘯悲嘆。看到他的時候，通常是灰暗大霧的日子。如果有人特意想偷看他的模樣，卻只會看到一團濃白的雲霧，回到家裏還會頭痛欲裂哩。

那個小矮子從前在史土茲牧場當牧者，而他跟史泰姆司的牧者一樣壞。他沒有把鹽分配給牛隻，所以他要待在這兒當鬼，直到牛隻回應他的喊聲，他有機會補償錯誤時，才可以離開。相信，這還要等很久很久，因為沒有人看過一頭牛回應他，連豎起耳朵也沒有。

所以你看，高山牧場四周無人，什麼不應做的事人們都會做，許多牲畜和農地受到傷害亦沒有人知道。直到沒有良心的牧民死了之後，他們才受到懲罰，被迫在深夜、在同一地方，完成他生前因為懶惰或大意而沒有做好的工作。夜復一夜，一做數百年，直至現在，直至將來……

attired, with a broad-rimmed hat and wooden shoes, and has a leather salt bag slung over his white woollen jacket. He turns up near the mountain chalets in the evening, but sometimes also during the day, and goes up to the cattle calling to them in the way the herdsmen call when they give them salt. After he has called in vain for some time – the animals never listen to him – he disappears, peeved, only to turn up somewhere else. Sometimes he can be heard whooping and yodelling, sometimes wailing and moaning. He is most often to be seen on dull, foggy days, but always without warning. If someone sets out thinking to catch a glimpse of the ghost, all he will see are thick white clouds of fog, and most likely by the time he has reached home he will have a splitting headache.

That particular little man used to be a herdsman on the Stutz Alp. He was corrupt, just like the one on Stams Alp, and did not give each cow its share of salt. That is why he now has to haunt the place until his time has come and the cows answer his call and he is given the chance to make amends for his wrongdoing. It is likely that it will be a very long time before that happens. For no one has ever noticed a cow so much as prick up its ears at his call.

So you see, up on the alps, where there was no one around, people did not always behave as they should. Much damage was caused to animals or property without anyone noticing. It was not until after his death that the unprincipled farmhand or herdsman would be taken to task for his misdeeds, forced to return at dead of night to work at the very place where he had been so negligent or lazy during his lifetime. Night after night! For hundreds of years up to the present day and into the future!

雲霧 Mists and Clouds

In those days, the chalet up on the Cuolm da Vi Alp above Bugnei Forest was inhabited by two herdsmen, together with a dairyman, a cheese-maker and a boy. There was a cowshed next to the chalet, but they only keep sheep in there now. In the days we are talking about, every evening just after vespers, a strange mist, a kind of cloud, would rise up from the landslide debris in Bugnei and from the stream nearby. The herdsmen used to take their cows further downhill after they had been milked, but whenever they saw the cloud, the cattle would panic and start running away. The men were quite flummoxed and did not know what to do, so they asked the dairyman and the cheese-maker for advice.

Now the cheese-maker was a great strong man. He could take on five Italians! In fact he had served as a mercenary in Italy, in Bologna. I knew him well. Down in Italy he drank a lot of wine, and that's where he got his strength from.

So one day he went down to the cows with the herdsmen. As soon as the mysterious cloud came up, he grabbed it with both hands. As he wrestled with the foggy mass, he had to dig his heels into the ground so as not to be carried away. The herdsmen heard his cries and saw his hair stand on end. Finally they saw him shake off the cloud, and it glided off and disappeared into the landslide.

The man returned to the chalet without a word. His hair continued to stand on end for the next few days, but he never told anyone anything about what he had done. From that time on, the cattle remained calm and nothing else happened. The cloud never appeared again.

從前，北尼森林上面卡姆戴維牧場的小屋裏，住著兩個牧牛人、一個奶農、一個做乳酪的人，和一個男孩。小屋旁邊有一個牛棚，但目前那兒只有羊。那時候，每個晚上晚間禮拜之後，便有一陣奇怪的霧，像雲似的從北尼山崩裂的碎礫那兒和旁邊的小河升上來。晚上擠奶之後，牧牛人經常帶牛走下山去。每當牛看見那團雲霧，就會害怕得想掉頭跑。牧牛人疑惑不解，不知道怎麼辦，只好問奶農和做乳酪的人意見。

做乳酪的人高大強壯，敢跟五個義大利人打架。他在義大利博洛尼亞當雇傭兵時，總是喝很多葡萄酒，因此長得很強壯。

一天，做乳酪的人跟牧牛人一起下山。當那團神秘的雲霧升上來的時候，做乳酪的人就雙手抓住了它，跟它搏鬥。他把腳跟陷進泥地裏，免得自己被雲霧拖走。牧牛人聽到做乳酪的人高聲呼叫，看見他的頭髮都豎起了。最後，做乳酪的人擺脫了雲霧，而雲霧就飄往山崩的地方，消失得無影無蹤。

做乳酪的人走進小屋後一言不發。幾天之後，他的頭髮仍舊豎起來，但是對發生過的事沒再說什麼。從那時開始，牲畜就安靜了。以後什麼事都沒再發生，雲霧也沒再升上來了。

瑪德麗沙 Madrisa

The beautiful alpine pastures at the foot of the Madrisa Horn mountain are renowned for their succulent aromatic herbs. The cattle sent up there for summer grazing thrive splendidly. And in former days, when mountain gnomes still lived up there and helped the herdsmen tend their herds, it was the most profitable alp in the whole of the Prätigau district. Even the winter fodder from those pastures worked wonders on the cows.

In those days there was a rich farmer who owned land on Saas Alp, near Madrisa. One winter he had sent his son up to the alp with the cattle, so that they could eat up the remaining store of hay; this is still the custom in many parts of Graubünden to this day. The young man would spend several weeks at a stretch all alone up there, and only went down to the village when his provisions ran out.

One day, after the young man had been away for longer than usual and nothing had been heard from him, his father began to worry that something had happened to him. He was sure, too, that he would soon be running out of fodder. Therefore, in spite of the cold winter weather, he set off for the mountain so as to see for himself if everything was all right.

He did not reach the cowshed until late in the evening, for it had already started to snow heavily, making the climb even more exhausting than usual. His son was just feeding the cattle, and the farmer could not help but notice that, although the cows were not exactly heavyweight, they all looked quite soft and plump. And the haystack had not shrunk by half as much as he had expected: he could see that there was at least a week's supply of hay left. He was even more surprised to see the rich stocks of milk, butter and cheese.

"How come the cows are so fine and sleek, and that they still produce as much milk as in the height

美麗的高山草原在瑪德麗沙的山腳伸延著。它以芬芳美味的香草馳名。夏天在這地方放牧過的牲畜都被養得很健壯。當小精靈還住在這裏幫助牧民的時候，它是柏拉狄高地區收穫最多的牧場。就算到了冬天，它的飼料對牛隻仍是最好的。

那時，有一個富有的農民在瑪德麗沙附近的西沙牧場擁有很多土地。一個冬天，他叫兒子領牛隻上牧場去把剩餘的乾草吃完。到了今天，這種習慣在格勞賓登很多地區還常常可以看到。他一個人住在那兒好幾個禮拜，待牛吃完所有乾草才會回去。有一次，很久沒有年輕牧人的消息，他父親相信小屋的飼料該用盡了，開始擔心兒子，不知他發生了什麼事。冬天的天氣雖然嚴寒，老牧人還是爬上山去，非親眼看看山上的情況不可。

地上蓋著厚厚的雪，老人走得十分辛苦，晚上才到達牛棚。他看到兒子正在餵牛。牛雖不算重，可是很肥美而嬌嫩；而乾草只比預期中消耗了一半，還有一個多禮拜的儲存。看到了豐富的牛奶、黃油和乳酪，老人更驚訝。

「牛隻如此潤澤肥美，下奶量跟夏天

of the summer? And how come the haystack's still so big, after all this time?" he asked his son.

"Look over there Father," the boy answered. "That's Madrisa. She's responsible. She helped me feed the cattle. She collected roots and herbs and mixed them into the cows' salt. That's why they look so well-fed and sleek, that's why the haystack's still so big and why we've got so much dairy produce." And he pointed to his bed which – as is the custom – he had set up in the cowshed where he could benefit from the warmth generated by the cows. His father turned and saw a wild maiden of astounding beauty. There she lay, fast asleep, her long, pale golden hair hanging over the edge of the bed right down to the floor.

The older man gave his son an inquiring look. "But who is she … this Madrisa?"

At that the stranger awoke. She rose slowly from the bed and said to the farmer, "Alas, why did you have to come? It would have been better for you and your herds if you hadn't. I could have helped your son look after them until spring arrived and they could be put out to pasture. No one would have been any the wiser. Oh, how loath I am to leave this cosy chalet and go back out to the forests and crags. But what must be must be. I can stay here no longer. Farewell!"

And so she left. Before reaching the door she turned and cast a last yearning glance at the young man. Then she strode out lightly, more floating than walking across the snow to the mountain peaks that bear her name.

The following summer the young man once again drove his herds up to the magnificent mountain slopes. But, however often he called Madrisa's name, however long he sought in the woods and among the rocks for a sign or a trace of her, it was all in vain. She was never seen again.

時一樣，而過了好些日子，乾草竟沒減少很多，這是怎麼回事？」他問兒子。

「父親，你看，」兒子答道，「她就是瑪德麗沙，多虧她，是她幫我餵養牛群的。她找到樹根和雜草，把它們加了鹽來餵牛，牠們也就這麼肥胖而嬌嫩，而乾草還剩下這麼多，乳品乳酪也有這麼多。」他指著自己的床——按當時習慣，床是設在牛棚內的，這樣人就可以向牛取暖。老人轉過來，見到一個非常美麗的野少女躺在床上睡覺。她金色的長髮從床邊下垂到地上。

父親疑惑地問兒子：「但她……這個瑪德麗沙是誰呢？」

少女這時醒了，慢慢地站起來對老人說：「哎喲，你為什麼要來呢？不來的話對你對牛群都有好處。我原本打算幫你兒子照顧牛群，直到春天才領牠們到草原上。這工作沒人比我做得更好。我多麼不願意離開這舒適的小屋回到森林岩石間啊，但該怎樣便怎樣吧。我不能在這兒待下去了。祝你們好運！」

女孩子離開了。她一再轉頭，很難過地看著少年，然後好比浮在雲彩之上，輕輕地步過雪地，向帶著她名字的山嶺走去。

第二年夏天，少年又到那壯麗的山上牧牛。無論他怎麼叫喊瑪德麗沙的名字，怎麼在森林岩石之間搜尋，卻沒有找到她的一絲聲息。以後，也再沒有人看到她了。

綁架　Kidnapped

卡布司的一個母親因兒子頑皮而罵他，其中一句是：我希望女巫帶你到柏拉地哲山頂上面去。

男孩消失了。

好幾天之後，他們在山頂上找到那個男孩。男孩說一個少女把他帶到柏拉地哲山頂上。原來那天早上，他的母親忘了用聖水祝福他，因此女巫乘機向他施魔法。

In Cumbels a mother once had reason to scold one of her sons for some misdemeanour. Among other things, she said, "I hope the witches take you up to the top of Mount Pala da Tgiern."

The boy disappeared.

It was not until several days later that they found him up on the mountain. He told them a maiden had carried him up to the top of Mount Pala da Tgiern because his mother had forgotten to bless him with holy water that morning. And thus the witches had got power over him.

Three Witches

Once upon a time there was a man and his wife who lived in a village. They had a daughter whose name was Maria. One day, she took herself with her little basket into the woods in search of strawberries. She had already filled her basket when she suddenly saw a red silk ribbon lying on the ground. Delighted, she bent down to pick it up. But as she picked it up she pulled open a trapdoor. Below, she saw a narrow marble staircase. She had only gone down a few steps, when all of a sudden the door snapped shut and she was trapped. What else could she do but continue to go down the stairs? At the bottom she found herself in a fine large room. All alone down there, she started to cry, thinking sadly how her poor mother would worry.

Suddenly she heard women's voices coming from the trapdoor. Then the door opened with a crash, and down came three witches with terribly long teeth. The oldest was called Elizabeth Travers, the second Elizabeth and the third Eliza.

Elizabeth Travers looked the most horrible. She shot poisonous glances at Maria, so that the poor girl trembled all over and did not even dare to raise her eyes.

Now Elizabeth Travers said, "It was your curiosity that led you down here; now you can stay. In the morning you can make the coffee and tidy the rooms. After breakfast you'll do the washing-up; then you'll

從前，一個小村莊裏住著一個男人和一個女人，他們有一個女兒叫瑪利亞。有一天，瑪利亞帶著一個小籃子去森林找草莓。小籃子已經裝滿了草莓，她突然看見地上有一條紅綢帶子。她很高興地彎下身子，準備把帶子撿起來。她撿起它的時候，卻拉開了一道活門，這個門下面是一道狹窄的大理石樓梯。她才下了幾級樓梯，活門就突然關上了。她不能回去，除了繼續走下樓梯，還有別的辦法？她到了一個漂亮的大起居室，孤零零地站在那裏，她不禁哭起來。她十分傷心，尤其想到母親現在肯定惦著她。

忽然，活門外傳來幾個女人的聲音，然後門「啪」的一聲打開了。三個女巫走了進來，她們有非常長的牙齒。最老的一個女巫名叫伊莉莎白塔弗絲，第二個叫伊莉莎白，第三個叫伊麗莎。

伊莉莎白塔弗絲的樣子最可怕。她惡狠狠地看著可憐的瑪利亞。瑪利亞害怕得四肢發抖，不敢抬起頭來。

伊莉莎白塔弗絲說：「你的好奇心帶你到這裏來，那你就留在這兒，早上給我們煮咖啡和打掃房間。早餐以後，你要洗碗，然後餵草棚裏那兩頭牛，還有豬和雞。記著，每天要打掃雞籠。我最不能容忍那些該死的羽毛在草棚裏飛來飛去。你可以和我們一起吃飯，可是我不要看到你穿工作服入座。你可以在凹壁那裏睡覺。早上六點鐘，咖啡便應該煮好放在桌子上。你要按我所說的好好做，否則我們會把你吃掉！」

　　兩天就這樣過去了，瑪利亞按她們的命令做事，可是連一個友善的臉色也沒有。特別是伊莉莎白塔弗絲，她的眼光總是惡狠狠的。她是三個女巫中最醜的，她像一口釘子那麼瘦，有一對綠色的貓眼，她長長的牙齒從嘴裏凸出來。每次看到她，瑪利亞總是感到膽顫心驚。女巫不在起居室的時候，瑪利亞曾多次嘗試打開活門，但都白費氣力。這樣她只好接受她的命運。

　　有一天吃午飯的時候，伊莉莎白塔弗絲說：「今天我們會到六怪姨那裏編織。走之前，我們會從走廊的四個袋子裏取出米，撒在整個房子裏。瑪利亞，我們要你把米撿起來放回袋子裏。你要注意，假如我們四點回來時，只要在任何一個角落找到一顆米粒，又或米粒沒現在的那麼乾淨，我們今天晚上就會吃掉你。明白嗎？」

　　一點鐘，女巫走了。瑪利亞一聽到活門關上，她就開始撿拾米粒。米粒撒得到處都是，桌、床、抽屜裏、櫃子下都有，她拾得很慢。花了很多時間，她只撿了一把米。

feed the two cows, and the pig and chickens in the small shed outside. But be sure to clean out the chickens' cage every day, there's nothing I hate more that having those damned feathers flying around the shed. You may have your meals with us, but I don't want to see you at the table in your working clothes. You can sleep over there in the alcove. The coffee is to be on the table by six o'clock in the morning. Make sure you do everything as I say, otherwise we'll gobble you up!"

Two days passed by and Maria always did everything they said. But they never gave her even a friendly glance. Elizabeth Travers always looked particularly grim. She was the ugliest of the three; she was as thin as a nail and had green eyes like a cat; she had long protruding teeth. Each time Maria looked at her she had to shudder. She had already tried a couple of times to open the trapdoor when the witches happened to be out of the room, but in vain. So she had no option but to accept her fate in God's name.

One day as they were at their midday meal Elizabeth Travers said: "This afternoon we're going to go for a knitting session at Aunt Six Miracles. Before we go, we'll take the rice in the four bags standing in the lobby and scatter it all over the house. We want you, Maria, to pick up the rice and put it back in the bags. But watch out! We'll be returning at four o'clock, and if we find a single grain of rice in a corner, or if the rice is not as clean as it is now, we'll eat you up tonight. Is that clear?"

The witches left at one o'clock. As soon as Maria heard the trapdoor fall shut, she started to pick up the rice. It was very slow work, and a lot of time had passed before she had gathered up even a handful. For the rice had been scattered around everywhere and under the tables and beds and cupboards and chests.

Soon she had to admit that it would be quite

impossible to pick up all the rice by four o'clock. She grew more and more frightened. When she heard the clock chime three, she burst out into loud sobs. Then she heard the trapdoor open. In horror she cried out: "Oh God, they're here!"

She was so frightened she did not notice that there was a handsome young man standing beside her. He had been bewitched, and his name was George.

"What ails you, lovely maiden?" he asked. "Why are you weeping? Is it because the witches ordered you to pick up the rice? I know those evil women well. Weep no more. I have come to help you. Don't be afraid. I may be bewitched, but I shan't harm you."

Maria cheered up when she heard this. She told the young man that the witches had promised to eat her up if she did not pick up every single grain of rice. Thereupon George said, "Give me a kiss and I'll help you immediately."

She gave him a kiss, whereupon he said, "Now go and make me a cup of coffee."

Soon she came back with the coffee and two egg sandwiches on a plate. After George had eaten and drunk, he took a golden wand from his pocket and struck a round table with it three times. Suddenly there was not a grain of rice to be seen in the room, and all the four sacks were standing, filled and tied up, in the lobby outside. Maria was overjoyed and thanked George for having helped her in such a miraculous fashion. But he looked at the clock and saw that it was already a quarter to four. He went up the steps. At his whistle the trapdoor opened. And he was gone.

Now Maria prepared the coffee for the three old women and set a cake on the table to put them in a good mood. She had just finished when the door opened, and the three came down, one after the other, Elizabeth Travers first.

"Have you picked up all the rice?" she asked.

不久，她發覺要在四點前把所有米粒撿起，根本是不可能的。她感到越來越害怕。三點鐘了，她不禁放聲大哭。突然，她聽到活門給打開了，就很驚懼地喊：「我的天，她們回來了！」

她非常害怕，沒留意身旁站著一個年輕英俊的男人。他叫喬治，他中了魔法。

他問：「漂亮的女孩，你幹嗎這樣煩惱？你為什麼哭？是不是女巫命令你把米粒撿起來！我最瞭解這些壞女巫。你別哭，我是來幫助你的。別怕，我雖然中了魔法，但不會傷害你。」

聽到這些話，瑪利亞覺得很高興。她告訴他，如果她沒把每一粒米都撿起來，女巫就要吃她。喬治說：「如果你吻我，我馬上就幫助你。」

她吻了他以後，他說：「你現在就去煮一杯咖啡。」

不一會，她帶著咖啡，還有放在盤子上的兩個雞蛋和小麵包回來。吃喝以後，喬治從口袋裏掏出一根黃金棒子，在圓桌子上敲打三下，這樣，起居室裏便連一顆米都沒有，而那四個袋子裝得滿滿的，繫緊了放在走廊上。瑪利亞開心極了，她感謝喬治給了她那麼神奇的幫忙。他看了看鐘，原來差一刻便四點了。他上了樓梯，吹一聲口哨活門就打開了，然後他走了。

瑪利亞給那三個女巫準備咖啡。為了讓她們開心，她還在桌子上放了蛋糕。她一做完，門就打開，三個女巫回來了。她們一個跟著一個的走下來，最前的是伊莉莎白塔弗絲。

她問：「你把米粒全都撿起來了？」

瑪利亞回答説：「我想你們連一粒也不會找到。」

女巫看了看，果然沒看到任何米粒，就説：「嗯，一定有人幫助你。夠了！我們喝了咖啡以後會走遍全個房子，如果找到一顆米粒，你就倒楣了！」她們一喝完咖啡，就一個跟著一個的走遍整個房子，檢查每一處地方：桌子和櫃子下面、爐子背後、鞋子和拖鞋裏面……，可是她們連一顆米粒都沒找到。

第二天午飯後，伊莉莎白塔弗絲説：「我們今天再去六怪姨那裏。你要把廚房盆子裏的換洗衣物泡在水裏，然後把它們洗乾淨，熨平。我們回來的時候，所有衣物都應該洗熨好，折疊妥當放在櫃子裏。」

瑪利亞哭起來説：「外面下大雨，我怎麼能晾乾和熨平衣服呢？」

「我不管！」伊莉莎白塔弗絲回答，「你要執行這些任務，要不我們就把你吃掉。」

一點鐘，女巫拿著盛編織工具的小籃子出去了。

瑪利亞馬上開始工作。她把最大的鐵盆子放在火上，盛來一桶一桶的雨水，把盆子裝滿。她把乾羊屎、樹皮和木塊放在火裏。水慢慢熱起來，她把衣物放進去泡。接著她洗擦衣物。洗完兩大籃後，她把衣物帶到閣樓曬晾，可是雨已經從屋頂的破瓦片間漏進來了。

她返回廚房，從廚房的門往外看——雨會停嗎？可是天更黑，雷電交加。她

"I don't think you will find any anywhere," replied Maria.

The witch looked around. Not seeing any rice, she said, "Hmm, I daresay someone helped you. Too bad! As soon as we've had our coffee we'll go through the whole house and have a look. Woe betide you if we find a single grain!" And so it was. As soon as they had finished their coffee, they went around the house, one behind the other, peering under tables and cupboards, searching behind the stove and in shoes and slippers. But they did not find a single grain.

The following day, straight after their noonday meal, Elizabeth Travers said, "Today we're going across to Aunt Six Miracles. While we're there I want you to soak all the washing that's in the washtub in the kitchen. Wash and iron it, and by the time we're back I want to see everything laundered and neatly folded in the chest."

At that Maria started to cry, saying, "How can I possibly get everything dried and ironed? It's raining cats and dogs outside."

"That's your problem," said Elizabeth Travers. "Perform your task or you'll be eaten up."

At one o'clock, the witches picked up their knitting baskets and went off to see old Aunt Six Miracles.

Maria set to work immediately. She placed the big tub on the fire, then carried in bucket after bucket of rainwater until the tub was full. She put dried sheep dung, strips of bark and wooden logs into the fire, and soon the water was warm enough for her to put the washing to soak. Afterwards, she started with the rubbing and scrubbing. When she'd finished, she had two full baskets of laundry, which she hung up in the attic to dry. But the rain was already dripping in through the broken roof tiles.

She went back down to the kitchen and looked outside to see if the rain was likely to stop soon. But the sky was blacker than ever, and the thunder and lightning were terrible. Utterly disheartened, she sat down in the kitchen and started to cry. Then she went to the living room to see what time it was. To her horror it was already past three o'clock. At that moment, the trapdoor opened and George came in. He asked her what was the matter.

"Oh, poor, unfortunate girl that I am! I have to soak, wash, dry and iron all the laundry that was in the tub. But look at the weather! It's pouring! If I don't manage to finish everything by four o'clock the witches will eat me up."

George went into the kitchen with Maria and said, "If you give me a kiss, all the laundry will be done in a jiffy."

She kissed him, he took his wand, waved it three times, and at the third wave the washtub had disappeared and the laundry had been dried and ironed and was neatly stored away in the chest.

After Maria had given George a cup of coffee he said, "Now listen carefully. Tomorrow afternoon the old witch will send you to Aunt Six Miracles to fetch the six-miracle casket. Don't be frightened, although her terrible teeth are even longer than those of Elizabeth Travers. She'll be all charming and will offer you an apple. But the moment she leaves you to go down to the cellar to fetch an apple, go into the living room and take the six-miracle casket from the shelves in the right-hand corner. Then run away. If the old woman starts running after you, take this egg and throw it on the ground behind you. Now take care not to forget anything I've told you, or you'll be lost."

Then George left by the trapdoor, and soon the three old witches appeared. Maria had already laid the table, so that they only had to sit down.

That evening, Elizabeth Travers said nothing. But the next day she said to the two other witches, "Today we'll see if we can't get rid of her. I'll send her to see Aunt Six Miracles, and that will be the end of her!"

In the afternoon, she beckoned to Maria saying,

坐下，很氣餒地哭起來。不知過了多久，她站起來到起居室去看時間。噢，三點多了，她很驚慌。這時，活門打開了，喬治走進來，問她有什麼事兒。

「我真是個可憐的女孩，要泡、洗、晾、熨盆裏的全部衣物，但天氣這麼壞，雨下個不停。要是四點鐘還沒把工作完成，女巫就要吃我了。」

喬治陪瑪利亞到廚房去，説：「如果你吻我，衣物一下子就洗熨好了。」

瑪利亞吻了喬治，他就取出魔棒，揮了三次後，洗衣盆消失了，換洗衣物都洗淨熨好，摺疊整齊的放在櫃子裏。瑪利亞給了喬治一杯咖啡後，他説：「你好好聽我的話，明天下午，老女巫要派你去六怪姨那裏取六怪盒兒。你看到她可不要害怕，雖然她的牙齒比伊莉莎白塔弗絲的更長更嚇人。她會待你很好，會請你吃一個蘋果。她去地窖取蘋果的時候，你要打開起居室的門，從右角的架子上把六怪盒兒拿下來，然後很快的逃跑。如果老婦人追你，想抓住你，你就把這個雞蛋扔到你身後的地上。你要好好記著，別忘記任何一件事，若不就沒有希望了。」然後喬治從活門離開了。

不久，三個女巫回來了。瑪利亞已經把桌子擺好，她們就入座。

那天晚上，伊莉莎白塔弗絲一個字都不説。第二天，她對另外兩個女巫説：「今天我們看看能不能除掉她。我派她去六怪姨那兒，這樣她就完蛋了。」

下午，她對瑪利亞説：「你現在去六

怪姨那兒代我們向她問好，請她給我們六怪盒兒。」

瑪利亞出了門。她走之前把喬治給她的雞蛋放在口袋裏。房子不遠處住著屠戶和他的家人及工人，旁邊是麵包店。麵包師的妻子看見瑪利亞走過，就問她到哪兒去。

瑪利亞説：「我要去六怪姨那兒取六怪盒兒。」

「你這可憐的孩子，我們肯定再也看不到你了。」大家都這麼説。

瑪利亞説：「你們別擔心。如果你們看到我遇到危險，願意幫助我，我是會報答你們的。」

瑪利亞到了六怪姨的門前，敲敲門。六怪姨從走廊出來，打開門。她一看見瑪利亞就很友善地説：「哎，親愛的瑪利亞，晚上好。你怎麼樣？　請進起居室來坐一會啊。」

瑪利亞回答説：「不，謝謝你。我很匆忙，馬上得趕回去。」

「我可以為你做什麼呢？我親愛的孩子。」

「我很想要六怪盒兒。」

「唉，如果你只要這個，就稍微等一下，我要下地窖去拿一個蘋果給你。我馬上就會回來。」

她到地窖可不是要拿什麼蘋果，而是要用磨石磨好牙齒。她剛下去，瑪利亞就跑到起居室，把六怪盒兒從角落的架子上拿下來，溜之大吉。

正從地窖上來的六怪姨看到瑪利亞逃跑，就叫：「瑪利亞，你等一下，我這兒有一個很漂亮的蘋果啊。」

可是瑪利亞不在乎，只儘快地跑。不

"Go over to the old aunt and say we send her our best wishes and would like to have the six-miracle casket."

Maria went outside, but before leaving she put the egg that George had given her into her pocket. Not far from her house there was a butcher's shop with a butcher and his family and workers, and next to that there was a bakery. As she passed, the baker's wife asked her where she was going.

"I have to go and see Aunt Six Miracles and fetch the six-miracle casket."

"Poor child! We shan't be seeing you again!" they all cried out.

But Maria said, "Don't worry about me. If you see that I'm in danger, come and help me. I'll repay you for your efforts."

Arriving at the old woman's house, she knocked at the door. The witch opened it immediately, and became very friendly as soon as she saw Maria.

"Good evening, dear Maria," she said. "How are you? Won't you come into the parlour for a while?"

"No thank you," replied Maria. "I'm in a hurry and have to get back home as soon as possible."

"And what can I do for you, my dear child?"

"I'd like to have the six-miracle casket."

"Is that all you want? Well, just wait a minute. I'm going down to the cellar to get you an apple. I'll be back in a moment."

But the reason she was going down to the cellar was not to fetch an apple but to sharpen her teeth on the whetstone. As soon as the witch had gone, Maria dashed into the living room, grabbed the six- miracle casket from the shelves in the corner and fled.

The old woman, coming up the steps, saw her run away and shouted, "Wait, Maria, here's a splendid apple for you."

But Maria paid no attention. She ran on as fast as her legs could carry her. Soon the witch was on her heels, trying to grab her by her dress. Maria flung the egg onto the ground. It broke, releasing a great lake, and the witch fell into the water. Seeing that, the butcher and the baker's wife threw their chopping boards and breadboards after her.

In the meantime, the three witches had gone out onto the balcony expecting to see the old aunt coming to tell them that she had eaten up Maria. However, George was standing beneath the balcony, sawing at the post. He had nearly sawn right through, and the balcony was already beginning to sway. The saw was made of gold and made no sound as the young man sawed. The very moment Aunt Six Miracles started swimming in the lake, the balcony collapsed and the three Elizabeths fell with a great splash into the water. Whenever any one of them raised her head above the water, George and Maria threw stones and whatever else they found at them.

Then there was a thundering crash that shuddered through the whole valley – and the people were freed of the witches. Maria thanked George and also the butcher and the baker's wife with all her heart. But they all said, "May God reward you for having liberated us from the wicked women."

George and Maria went into the house and were very pleased that all the beautiful things now belonged to them. They had a magnificent wedding to which they invited many people, including me.

They gave me as much food and drink as I wanted, and then they gave me a kick in the pants, saying, "Now go off and tell people the story!"

And that's what I've done.

一會兒，六怪姨已經跟上來了，她想抓住瑪利亞的裙子。瑪利亞連忙把雞蛋扔到地上。雞蛋破了，蛋汁變成了大湖，六怪姨掉到湖水裏去。屠戶和麵包師的妻子看到這個情景，立刻把砧板和麵包板扔向她。

同一時間，那三個女巫上了陽臺，看看六怪姨是不是很快便來告訴她們已吃掉瑪利亞。她們不知道喬治正站在陽臺下面，鋸著陽臺的柱子。柱子還沒斷開，陽臺已搖晃起來。那根鋸子是黃金製造的，鋸起來不會發出任何聲音。就當六怪姨在湖水裏游泳的時候，陽台塌下了，三個女巫撲通一聲都掉進水裏。喬治和瑪利亞一見誰從水裏抬起頭，就扔出石頭或任何可以找到的東西。

然後傳來一聲巨響，整個山谷都震動起來——人們從此逃出女巫的魔掌了！瑪利亞衷心感謝喬治，還有屠戶和麵包師的妻子。大家都對喬治和瑪利亞說：「你們從那些壞女巫那裏解救了我們，望上天報答你們。」

喬治和瑪利亞走進房子，現在這些漂亮的東西都屬於他們了，他們感到很愉快。他們舉行了一場盛大的婚禮，邀請了很多人參加，包括我。

他們讓我儘量吃，儘量喝。最後，他們在我屁股上踢了一腳，說：「你現在就走，把這個故事傳開去。」

當然，我照著做了。

野矮人　The Wild Manikin

從前有一個男人，他跟妻子和兩個女兒一起居住，大女兒叫格蕾塔，小女兒叫契爾佳。經歷了一個漫長的冬天以後，那男人發現倉庫的乾草一天一天的少了，但山谷裏還有積雪。幸而，他看到一個山坡已長出美麗新鮮的綠草。

因此他對兩個女兒說：「你們其中一個，明天到山坡那邊放我們那兩頭牛吃草吧，好嗎？」

老大格蕾塔立即說，「親愛的爸爸，請讓我去。」

那男人滿意地說：「好，明天你去吧，後天由契爾佳去。你可別踏上左邊的小路，因為那裏會有野矮人，遇上他你就倒楣了。」

格蕾塔不在意父親的說話，只很高興他讓她去。第二天早上，母親在一個水壺裏放上酒，還用毛巾包起一條香腸和一塊麵包，交給女兒。格蕾塔把她的編織用具放在筐子裏，愉愉快快地跟著牛出發。一到了綠山坡，奶牛就開始吃那些新鮮的草，令人覺得很高興。格蕾塔採了幾朵花後才坐下來編織。過了一會兒，她覺得餓了。看看太陽，原來快十一時了。

格蕾塔就把食物從筐子裏拿出來，把毛巾作為桌布，鋪在地上。她剛吃

Once upon a time there was a man with a wife and two daughters. One of the girls was named Greta, the other Cilgia. After a long cold winter, the farmer noticed that his haystack was getting alarmingly small and yet there was still snow in the valley. Then, to his relief, he saw that there was one slope which was already covered in fresh green.

So he said to his daughters: "What about one of you going over to that slope tomorrow morning to graze our two cows?"

"Oh father, let me go," said Greta, the elder of the girls.

Her father was pleased and said, "All right. You go tomorrow, and the day after tomorrow Cilgia can go. But make sure you don't used the path which goes up on the left side. The wild manikin could turn up … and then poor you!"

Greta did not pay much attention to what he said. She was really happy to be allowed to go. The next morning her mother gave her a flask of wine and a sausage and a piece of bread wrapped up in a towel. Greta put her knitting in the basket and set off gaily with her two cows. As soon as they had reached the green slope the cows began to crop the new-grown grass so that it was a pleasure to watch. Greta picked a few flowers, and then she sat down and started to knit. After a while she got hungry and, judging by the sun, reckoned that it was nearly eleven o'clock.

She took the food out of the basket, and spread the towel on the ground as a tablecloth. She had just taken a bite out of the sausage, when she heard something and then suddenly saw that there was a little man with a pointed hat coming up the hill. She was terribly frightened and tried to flee, but the wild manikin seized her by the arm and said, "Don't you even think of running away. You're coming with me!"

She began to cry, saying, "Oh God, oh God, what shall become of my cows? They can't go home on their own."

"Don't worry," said the manikin. "I'll drive the cows home." And he took out a whistle, gave one blow – and, clippety clop, the cows ran down the hill.

Now the manikin walked on ahead, bidding Greta follow him. They walked and walked and walked, until they reached a door in the rock face. The manikin knocked three times with his stick, and at the third knock the door swung open with a loud creaking. They went into a lobby where several men – tailors, cobblers, butchers and menservants – were waiting. As soon as they saw the manikin they all cried out in unison: "Good morning, good morning, Gian Pitschen of the pointed hat – which is more pointed today than it's ever been before."

After the little old man had greeted his domestics, he bade Greta step into the living room. There he took a pretty little sewing-basket out of a bureau, and from the basket he took a box which contained, wrapped up in cotton wool, a pin with a big golden head. He showed the pin to Greta, and said, "This pin is a gift from me to you. You may wear it every day. But be careful to keep it clean and shiny. Otherwise things will be bad for you."

Then he took poor Greta around the house to show her the rooms. They were all magnificently furnished. But in front of one of the doors – the key was in the lock – he stopped. "Make sure you never go into this room," he said, "or ill will befall you."

After that they went into the kitchen, where he

了一小口香腸，就聽到了一個聲音。她看見一個戴尖帽的小矮人往山頂走。她感到非常吃驚，想逃跑的時候卻給那個野矮人抓住她的胳膊。野矮人說：「別想逃，你跟我走。」

她哭起來，說：「哎呀，哎呀！我的奶牛怎麼辦？他們不能獨自回家啊。」

「沒事，」野矮人回答說，「我會把牛趕回家。」他掏出哨子，吹了一下，牛就叮叮噹噹的跑下山。

野矮人走在前邊，命格蕾塔跟著他。他們走了又走，來到一個通往岩洞的門。野矮人用棒子在門上敲了三下，門就咯吱一聲打開了。他們走到一個大廳，那裏有幾個人，都是野矮人的雇工，他們是：裁縫、鞋匠、屠夫，還有僕人。他們一看見野矮人就大聲喊道：「早安，早安，戴尖帽的加恩皮辰，您的尖帽從來沒像今天那麼尖。」

野矮人給他的雇工打了招呼後，便讓格蕾塔走進客廳。他把一個很漂亮的小針線籃從一個寫字桌的抽屜裏拿出來，再從小針線籃裏掏出一個小盒，裏面有一根包在棉花裏的別針，針頭很大，是黃金做的。他把別針交給格蕾塔，說：「這隻別針送給你。你可以每天戴上，不過要把它弄得乾乾淨淨，亮閃閃的，要不然你就倒楣了。」

然後他帶著可憐的格蕾塔走遍整個房子，給她看佈置得很漂亮的房間。走到一扇門鎖上插著鑰匙的門前，他停下來說：「要注意，你決不要進這個房間，否則你就倒楣了。」之後他們走到廚房去。他說：「你就留在我這兒。別擔心，你的工作不辛苦。你早上七點給我煮咖啡。白天我總是在森林裏，那時你必須給我家裏的傭人做飯。晚上我回家的時候，你得再給我煮咖啡。」

格蕾塔哭了起來。

「哎，我可憐的爸爸媽媽怎麼樣？我不要留在這裏，我想回家。」

這時野矮人生氣了，他舉起棒子說：「別吵！安靜！我不要聽人呻吟嘆息！你得到黃金別針就應該滿足，只要保持針頭乾淨就可以了。這裏的工作不會要了你的命。」

時間一天一天的過去。每天晚上，野矮人回家的時候，格蕾塔要給他看她戴著的黃金別針，讓他知道針頭仍然像第一天那麼閃亮。

大概十四天以後，格蕾塔在房子裏走來走去，看著一個擺滿寶物的房間。她心裏想：「如果這一切都屬於我和我的家人，我們就不會那麼辛酸貧困了。」

她發現快四點了，到了煮咖啡的時間。她連忙下樓到廚房去，經過那扇她不准內進的門，她想：「為什麼老頭不許我

proclaimed: "Now you will have to stay with me. But don't worry, you won't have to do any hard work. All you have to do is make me coffee at seven o'clock every morning. During the day I'll be in the woods and you'll have to cook the meals for my domestics. When I come home in the evening you'll have to make me coffee again."

But Greta began to cry.

"Alas, what about my poor father and mother? I'm not staying here any longer. I want to go home."

The little old man was furious at this. Raising his stick he said: "Quiet! Silence! Stop moaning and groaning! Be glad you have your gold pin, just make sure to keep the head clean. Your work won't kill you."

Time passed. Every evening when the wild manikin came home Greta had to show him the gold pin, which she always carried on her. The head still shone as brightly as on her first day.

One day, about a fortnight later, Greta was wandering around the house looking at all the treasure-filled rooms. "If only all this belonged to me and my family," she reflected, "we'd never be needy again."

Suddenly she saw that it was almost four o'clock, time to go to the kitchen and make the coffee. But as she passed the forbidden door she thought, "Why on earth won't the old fellow allow me to go in? What's he hiding? Whatever! I'm going in. How would he know if I've opened the door or not?"

She turned the key in the lock. Instantly the door opened. Greta peeked inside ... and froze in terror at what she saw. The floor was covered in blood. Bodies of dead women lay all around. In her horror Greta dropped her gold pin on the floor. Picking it up instantly, she discovered to her dismay that it was stained with blood. She rushed out of the room, slamming the door behind her, and ran downstairs to wash the pin. But no matter how much she rubbed and scrubbed, she could not get rid of the stain. So she took the pin, wrapped it up in cotton and put it back in its box. Sobbing with fear and horror she went into the kitchen to prepare the coffee.

The little old man came in and, seeing that Greta was in tears, asked her, "Why are you crying, my dear? Let me have a look at the pin. Have you by any chance been curious?"

Greta had to show him the pin.

As soon as he saw the bloodstains he seized the girl by the arm, dragged her upstairs and, opening the door to the chamber of horrors, said, "Now you can go into the place that you were so curious to see." He pushed her inside and shut the door. She heard the key turn in the lock.

All this time Greta's parents were extremely worried about their vanished daughter. The villagers all helped them look for her, yet no one dared to take the left-hand path up to the mountain pasture.

Cilgia, the younger daughter, also went out day after day in search of her sister. One evening, as she was almost in despair at still not having found any sign of her sister, she met an old man.

"What's the matter? What's all this wailing and lamenting about?" he asked.

"I've given up all hope of ever finding my sister," she replied. And then she told him how Greta had disappeared.

The old man immediately remarked: "That's Gian Pitschen of the pointed hat! That's one of his pranks. If you want to find your sister, go to him. But be astute. When you meet him, bow, and greet him politely saying, 'Good morning, good morning Gian Pitschen of the pointed hat – which is more pointed today than it's ever been before.' Then everything will turn out all right."

Cilgia thanked the old man and returned home.

"Tomorrow I'm taking the cows up the left-hand path. I'll see if I can't find Greta," she told her

進去？這裏面藏著什麼？我不理！我就是要進去，老人怎麼知道我打開過門呢！」

她轉動鑰匙，門就打開了。她偷望進去，卻被地上到處是血和死去的女人嚇呆了。她驚恐得很，連黃金別針都掉了下來。她立即把別針撿起，發覺它染滿了血污，她很沮喪，連忙衝出房間，使勁的關上門，跑到樓下把別針擦乾淨。不過怎洗擦也沒有用，污漬去不掉了。她便用棉花包起別針，放在盒子裏。她很恐懼，很害怕，一邊哭一邊到廚房煮咖啡。

野矮人進門看見格蕾塔在哭，馬上問：「你怎麼哭了？讓我看看黃金別針！你不會因為好奇而……」

格蕾塔只好遞上別針。

他一看見別針上的污漬，就抓住格蕾塔的胳膊，把她硬拉上樓，打開那可怖的房間的門，說：「你那麼好奇要進去，現在就進去吧！」他把她推進去後即關上門。她聽見鑰匙轉動的聲音。

女兒不見了蹤影，格蕾塔的父母非常擔心。村子裏的人都來幫助找她，但是誰也不敢走上左邊的小路。

契爾佳每天都去找姐姐。一天晚上，她因為還沒找到姐姐而感到非常失望。這時，她碰到一個老人。他問她：「你為什麼哭得這麼傷心？」

她回答：「我已不敢奢望找到姐姐了。」她告訴那個老人格蕾塔失了蹤。

老人就說：「這是戴尖帽的加恩皮辰搞的鬼。如果你想找你的姐姐，就去他那裏。不過你要機靈點，碰到他就向他鞠躬，很友好地給他打招呼——早安，早安，戴尖帽的加恩皮辰，您的尖帽從來沒像今天那麼尖——這樣，一切便會順利得多。」

契爾佳謝了那個老人後回到家。

「明天我和奶牛上左邊的小路。我想看一下能不能找到姐姐。」她對父母説。

無論父母如何懇切請求契爾佳不要冒這個險都不管用。第二天，契爾佳上了左邊的小路。她覺得餓的時候，就把食物從筐子裏拿出來吃。突然，她聽到腳步聲，看見野矮人往山頂走。她一看到就站起來，向他走了幾步，深深的鞠躬説：「早安，早安，戴尖帽的加恩皮辰，您的尖帽從來沒像今天那麼尖。你想不想和我一起吃午餐？」

「算了吧，你現在就跟我一起走。」

「我願意和你一起走，」她説，「可是我擔心我的奶牛找不到回家的路。」

野矮人把他的哨子掏出來，一聲哨響，牛就叮叮噹噹的向山下跑。

契爾佳和野矮人挎著胳臂，順著小路直到岩洞門。同樣，野矮人用棒子在門上敲了三下，門就打開了。走廊上的男人又大聲叫：「早安，早安，戴尖帽的加恩皮辰，您的尖帽從來沒像今天那麼尖。」

契爾佳聽到這個問好，就想：我已控制了局面！

老人也給契爾佳看房間，也給她一隻黃金別針，也給她講了一遍以往曾跟格蕾塔説的話。

契爾佳盡力給野矮人做飯。她還打掃起居室和房間，給他擦鞋，一切都弄得乾

parents.

They pleaded with her, begging her not to put herself in danger, but in vain. The next day Cilgia took the left-hand path up the slope. When she felt hungry she took her provisions from her basket and started eating. Suddenly she heard footsteps and saw the wild manikin coming up the hill. She immediately stood up and went towards him. She bowed deeply, and said, "Good morning, good morning Gian Pitschen of the pointed hat – which is more pointed today than it's ever been before. Wouldn't you like to come and share my meal?"

"Enough of that! You're coming with me now."

"I'd love to go with you," she replied. "But I fear my cows won't find their way home without me."

The little old man took out his whistle, gave one blow – and, clippety clop, the cows ran down the hill.

Cilgia and the wild manikin walked arm in arm along the path until they reached the door in the rock. At the third blow of the manikin's stick the door opened, and the men who were assembled inside all shouted out, "Good morning, good morning, Gian Pitschen of the pointed hat – which is more pointed today than it's ever been before."

Now I've got him, thought Cilgia, when she heard the greeting.

The manikin showed her the rooms and gave her a gold pin, using exactly the same words as he had with Greta.

Cilgia made great efforts to cook well for the little old man. She swept the living room and the bedrooms and cleaned his shoes, and everything was so neat and tidy that he always left the house in the best of spirits. She was also very good to the other men; she even sometimes cooked them rice pudding with chestnuts! And whenever they wanted to thank her she'd say, "Don't mention it. Just be sure to help me when I'm in need!"

On the very first day, while the wild manikin was away in the wood, Cilgia went upstairs to open the forbidden door. But she left her gold-headed pin downstairs in its box. Standing in front of the door, she heard soft sounds of moaning and crying. On opening the door, she nearly collapsed with horror. But when she saw that her sister was still alive among all the dead, she flew towards her and they fell weeping into each other's arms.

Then Cilgia said, " Don't cry anymore. Your days of woe are nearly over. I'll soon find a way to put the old scoundrel out of action. I'll do whatever is necessary to set you free. But for the time being, I'll bring you as much food and drink as you want every day. And while the rascal is out of the house I'll come up and keep you company."

Of course Greta was delighted to have her sister at her side, and she plucked up her courage, for she knew that Cilgia's head was not filled with straw.

A week passed. Then, one Saturday evening, when Cilgia heard the old man coming, she suddenly started to cry, pretending to be in despair. When the little old man saw that, he grew angry. "What's wrong with you?" he asked. "Why are you crying? Show me the gold pin. Have you let your curiosity get the better of you?"

Cilgia took the pin out of its box and showed it to him. Seeing that the head of the pin was still shining like new, he asked, "What's wrong with you?"

She began to weep again saying, "I can't stop thinking of my father and mother. They're sure to starve, now that both their daughters have gone. Neither of them can earn their living. They're old and weak. They can't work anymore."

"If that's the only problem," said the old man, "well, you can fill a bag with cheese, sausages, butter and bread, and also add a couple of bottles of wine. But don't put in too much for me to carry: I don't want to get tired out. Tomorrow morning, I'll take the

乾淨淨。他離家時心境特別愉快。她也好好對待野矮人家裏的傭人,甚至有時候給他們做有栗子的米布丁。他們想感謝她的時候,她就説:「不用謝,只要記著,當我有需要時你們要幫助我!」

來到野矮人家的第一天,契爾佳就趁他去了森林的時候,上樓打開禁止她內進的門,只是她把黃金別針留在樓下的盒子裏。到了那道門前,契爾佳聽到微弱的呻吟和哭泣聲。她打開門的時候差點兒跌倒在地上。可是當她看到姐姐在那堆屍體中還活著時,即飛奔過去投入她的懷抱,和她抱頭痛哭。

契爾佳給格蕾塔説:「別再哭了,你這些不開心的日子快過去了。我會看看有什麼辦法制服那個老惡棍。為了解救你,必須做的我都會做。每天你要多少食物和飲料,我都會帶給你。老人不在的時候我會上樓來陪伴你。」

格蕾塔因為妹妹在她的身邊,心境當然愉快。她得到了新的勇氣,因她知道妹妹是聰明的人。

一星期就這樣過去。一個星期六的晚上,當契爾佳聽到野矮人快要進來時,便立刻哭起來,臉上顯得很絕望似的。野矮人一看她的樣子,就很生氣地説:「你怎麼啦?你怎麼哭著呢?你給我看看黃金別針!你有沒有因為好奇而……」

契爾佳從盒子中取出別針來給野矮人看。他看見針頭像新的那麼亮,就問:「你有什麼困難?」

契爾佳又哭起來説:「我總是想念父母。他們的兩個女兒都不在,一定餓壞了。他們年老衰弱不能工作啊，誰還會掙錢呢？」

野矮人說：「這個容易辦。你今天晚上把乳酪、香腸、牛油和麵包放在一個袋子裏，再加幾瓶酒。你不要裝得太多，要不我便拿不動。明天早上我會把袋子帶到你父母家前。你現在快一點兒讓我喝咖啡。我今天晚上覺得很累，很想休息。」

老人很早便睡覺了。契爾佳下樓去地窖把沙司茲香腸、風乾牛肉、火腿和香草乳酪裝滿一大袋。第二天她很早就上樓去看姐姐，說：「親愛的格蕾塔，如果你現在按我所說的做，你今天就可以回家。我在樓下大堂準備了一個裝有食物的袋子，那老頭會把它帶給我們的父母。你要躲在那個袋子裏。每次老人想休息的時候，你就小聲叫：我看見你！」

格蕾塔一進袋子，契爾佳就把袋口綁得緊緊，還在袋子上剪了幾個小洞，好讓空氣流通。然後她去叫野矮人。

野矮人把袋子放在肩膀上。他說：「該死，這袋子太重了！」

「不重啊，」契爾佳回答，「只是你還很睏，才覺得重。你該知道，你不可以休息。我會從陽臺上好好監視你。如果看見你想休息，我就會大叫：我看見你！如果你把袋子放下，我就馬上跳進水裏淹斃自己。不騙你的！」

說這番話之前，契爾佳把自己紅色的裙子拴在一條圓木上。

那野矮人——那個老笨蛋——只好帶著袋子上路。他還沒走幾步，就大汗淋

bag and put it down in front of your parents' house. Now hurry up, I want my coffee. I feel tired today and want to rest."

Soon the old man went to bed. Cilgia went down to the cellar and filled a big bag with Salsiz sausages, air-dried beef, ham and Ziger cheese. Very early the following morning she went up to her sister's room and said, "Now, dear Greta, if you do everything I say, you'll be at home before the end of the day. I've got a big bag of provisions ready down in the entrance hall. Old Wrinkly is taking it to our parents. Hide yourself in the bag, and each time he wants to take a rest, call out softly: 'I can see you.'"

After Greta had got into the bag, Cilgia bound it up tightly and then cut some air holes in it. Then she went and called the old man. He came immediately, but hoisting the bag onto his shoulder, he said, "What the devil! It's much too heavy for me."

"Not at all," protested Cilgia. "It only seems so heavy because you're still half asleep. And you'd better know: you're not allowed to take a rest. I'm going out onto the balcony and if I see you slacking, I'll call out: 'I can see you!' And if you set the bag down, I'll drown myself in the lake, that's for sure!"

Before that, she had tied her red weekday dress around a big wooden log.

Now the old man – the silly old muttonhead – set off with his bag. But he'd hardly gone a few steps when the sweat began running down his face and he rested for a moment. Immediately he heard a voice calling: "I can see you."

"To hell with you!" thought the old man, picking up his bag again. But his strength failed him, and the bag fell to the ground. At that very moment he heard a splash and saw Cilgia's red dress in the water. He ran up to grab it, but slipped and fell into the water himself. Upon this Cilgia, who had been hiding behind a big pine tree, ran up to the bank of the lake, picked up a big stone and hurled it after the manikin. Then she called out for help, and all the men from the house rushed up to help her. The butcher threw bones at him, the tailor his red-hot smoothing iron, the cobbler his lapstone – they all threw whatever came to hand. All of a sudden, a terrible crashing sound was heard, and it became clear to all that the crafty scoundrel, who was responsible for so much human misfortune, had finally met his end. As they ran to rescue Greta from the bag, their cheers resounded through the valleys.

Then, full of joy at having been released from their long years of captivity, they returned to the house and rushed down into the cellar to unchain a poor old man who had been kept imprisoned there for years and years.

They led the old man into the living room.

"You are the only one who's ever tried using trickery to free us from the evil wild manikin," he said, addressing Cilgia. "You've been successful, and for that you shall be rewarded. In the drawer of that table over there there's a document no one knows about but me. It states that whoever manages to kill Gian Pitschen of the pointed hat can keep the house and everything inside it."

They opened the drawer and found the document just as the old man had said, and also a purse full of gold coins. Cilgia took the coins and shared them out among all the people there.

The same day, the two sisters packed a basket with Salsiz sausages, meat and a bottle of wine, locked up the house, and made their way back home. Late that evening they arrived at their house in the village.

The house had low windows, so, although the shutters were already shut, they could hear their mother wailing to their father, "My God, my God, what can have happened to our daughters? I fear we may never see them again."

Cilgia could not contain herself any longer. She

涔的。他想休息一會兒，就聽到一個聲音説：「我看見你！」

「她看見我，我應該走下去。」可是他的膝蓋禁不住發抖。他又想休息，而那個聲音又馬上響起：「我看見你！」

「你給我滾開，」野矮人想。他又扛起袋子。不過，他再支撐不住了，袋子跌落到地上。這時，他聽到撲通一聲，然後看見湖水裏契爾佳的紅裙子。他忙跑過去想抓住它，自己卻摔倒掉到水裏。躲在一棵大松樹後的契爾佳連忙跑到湖邊，向野矮人扔出一塊大石頭，然後高聲叫人來幫忙。野矮人家裏的男人都跑過來幫忙：屠戶用骨頭，裁縫用灼熱的熨斗，鞋匠用鞋板，大家都用身邊的東西扔向野矮人。突然響起砰然巨響，誰都知道那個狠毒狡猾，使很多人遭受不幸的壞人死了。他們跑過去從袋子裏救出格蕾塔，大家發出的歡呼聲在山谷中產生回響。

經過長期的煎熬，他們終於得救了。他們愉快地回到那個房子，下地窖放出一個已經被俘虜了許多年的可憐老男人。

他們領著那個老人走進客廳。

「你是唯一一個人嘗試用計謀使我們擺脱那個邪惡的野矮人，」他對契爾佳説，「你成功了！我們應該給你報酬。除了我，沒有人知道那邊桌子的抽屜裏有一份文件，上面寫著誰殺死戴尖帽的野矮人，就會得到這座房子和裏面的一切。」

他們打開抽屜，果然找到了老人所説的文件，還有一兜金幣。契爾佳把金幣分給每個人。

之後，姐妹倆把房子鎖好，拿了沙司茲香腸，一點肉與一瓶酒趕回家。那天深夜，她們回到村子的家。

　　窗戶很低，窗板葉雖然關了，但她們仍然聽到母親哭著對父親說：「我的天，我的天，我們的女兒怎麼啦？我怕再也見不到她們了。」

　　契爾佳再不能克制自己了，她出力的搖動門環子，父親來開門。他一看到兩個女兒就熱烈地擁抱她們。三人隨即走到起居室，女兒緊緊的擁著母親。他們心中感到無限快樂。

　　第二天，姊妹倆和父母一起去了加恩皮辰的家。她們得到那些財富，父母既驚奇又高興。他們舉行了盛大的慶祝活動，邀請了所有朋友來跳舞。他們狂歡高歌，真不知自己身在何方。

　　天亮了，是大家說「各位早安」的時候了。

ran to the door, seized the knocker and banged it so violently that her father came out immediately. He had hardly had time to open the door before both girls were hanging at his neck. As they joined their mother in the parlour, their hearts were overflowing with joy.

The next day the girls took their parents to Gian Pitschen's house. How astonished and delighted they were at all the riches it contained! That very evening, they invited all their friends to a grand party with lots of dancing. They all had such fun that, before they knew where they were, it was time to say, "Good morning, ladies and gentlemen!"

The Monsters in Graubünden

格勞賓登州之怪獸

Every day, while the dairymen were making cheese on Luvis Alp, a man carrying an axe under his arm would come into the chalet. He would stand there for a time without saying a word. Then he'd go away, no one knew where.

The alpine herdsmen found all this very strange, but for a long time none of them dared to speak to the stranger. Finally, one of them plucked up his courage and asked him who he was.

"I'm a most unfortunate man," he answered. "But you can relieve me from my misery – if you have the courage. All that is required is for a herdsman or a dairyman to go up to that little lake over there just before midnight. He'll see two massive oxen, one red and the other black, come out of the deepest part of the lake and start battling for their lives. The red one will gradually lose ground. If the man manages to strike the stronger of the oxen with my axe, I'll be saved. If he cannot, he should throw the axe into the water."

The herdsman agreed to help him. He took the unhappy stranger's axe and, at the appointed time, went up to the sinister lake. He had not waited long before he heard a tremendously loud bellowing, and the two monsters came to the surface. The black ox was obviously at an advantage from the start. He drove his red opponent out of the water and then

當奶農每天在魯維司的高山牧地上做乳酪的時候，總有一個腋下夾著長柄斧子的陌生人走進小屋子來。他總是站著，好長一段時間也沒說一個詞，然後就走了。別人都不知道他會到哪裏去。

高山的牧民都覺得有點不對勁，只是沒人敢先開口跟那陌生人說話。有一天，終於有人鼓起勇氣問他是誰。

「我是一個最不幸的人，」他回答，「如果你們夠勇敢，就可以解救我。只要牧人或奶農在午夜前到那邊的小湖，就會見到兩頭巨牛，一頭紅色的，一頭黑色的。牠們會從湖水最深處出來進行生死決鬥。紅色的那頭會漸漸敗退。如果能用我的斧子擊倒正佔上風的黑牛，我就得救了。若不成功，斧子就要丟進湖水裏。」

牧人答應幫忙。他從這個不幸的陌生人手上接過斧子，在預定的時間去到那個陰森森的湖邊。不久，兩頭巨獸隨著恐怖的吼聲躍出湖面。黑牛一開始便佔上風，牠把紅色的仇敵驅出水面，然後瘋狂地追趕牠。牠們走到草原上。

　　雖然牧人極願意幫助那個可憐的人，但任務要比想像的難得多。黑牛靈敏地把紅牛驅趕到牧人站的地方；如果他這時舉起斧子砍下去，很容易會錯砍那頭紅牛；而且，他這個這場惡鬥的唯一目擊者，越來越害怕自己的生命有危險，因為兩頭巨獸隨時會把他推倒在地上，然後把他踩死。於是，牧人忘了原來的意圖，忘了要幫助那個可憐的陌生人逃脫悲慘的命運，他只想快點結束這場惡夢，於是絕望地把斧子扔到湖裏。他一這樣做，兩頭巨獸大吼一聲便跳進水裏，消失於湖的深處。

　　往後，牧人沒再見過那個中了魔法的人拿著斧子出現。可是有人說從那時開始，湖面不時會被某些神秘的力量翻動，令湖水洶湧澎湃，而湖底就清楚傳來怪物搏鬥的吼叫聲。

chased him wildly around on the firm ground of the meadow.

　　Much as the herdsman wanted to help the unfortunate man, the task was much more difficult than he had imagined. The black ox adroitly drove the red one towards the herdsman; if he had used his axe, he would have struck the wrong animal. Again and again the sole spectator of the ghastly battle had to fear for his own life. He was in great danger of being thrown to the ground and trampled on by the wrestling monsters. So, in desperation, and forgetting his resolution to rescue the unfortunate visitor from his sad fate, he threw the axe into the lake – thus putting an end to the nightmare apparitions. With a roar, the two monsters flung themselves into the water and disappeared into the depths.

　　Never again did the herdsmen see the bewitched man with the axe. But it is said that from time to time the small lake gets stirred up by mysterious powers and throws great waves onto the shore. At such times, the loud bellowing of the battling monsters can be heard quite distinctly coming up from the depths.

仙族無蹤　The Vanished Fairy Folk

In Guarda, there once lived a man who was on bad terms with his wedded wife. So when the time came for him to transport the hay from his alp down to his barn, he had no one to help him load it onto the cart. For after all their bickering and quarrelling, his wife had preferred to stay at home and have a rest from her husband.

But then, a wild woman – the kind of fairy known in the region as a 'Diale' – turned up in the meadow and kindly offered to help him load his cart. All the time they were working together, the man thought she was an ordinary woman, until she climbed up on top of the hay, and he noticed that her feet were shaped like the hooves of a goat.

Now, in the depths of his black heart, he named her 'devil incarnate' and contrived a vicious plan to destroy her. So, when she asked him his name, he answered cunningly "Jeu mez". In the Graubünden dialect that means 'I myself'.

As soon as his cart was loaded, the evil man thrust his iron pitchfork through the wild woman's body. Then, pleased with himself for having so easily

從前，瓜爾達有一個農民，他和老婆相處得不好，所以當他想把乾草裝上車，從牧場運到草棚去的時候，總沒有人幫忙。爭吵之後，他老婆寧願留在屋子裏休息。

那時侯，草地上出現了一個野女子，她屬於一個族群，當地人稱他們為「帝艾樂」的仙人。野女子好意地幫忙他把乾草裝上車。男人一直以為來幫忙的只是一個普通的女人，直到她站在草堆上，他才看到了她的羊足。

這時，他黑暗的心讓他叫她「魔鬼化身」，陰險地打算毀滅她。所以當她問他的名字時，他狡猾地回答「祖馬茲」，那是格勞賓登話的「我自己」的意思。

車子一裝滿，那邪惡的人便把鐵製的乾草叉刺穿野女子的身體。他好高興這麼容易便殺了一個女魔鬼，得意洋洋地繼續拉車上路。

　　那野女子就是帝艾樂仙人。她痛苦地大聲呻吟，驚動了僻遠山洞裏的野仙人。他們急忙湧下山來。他們非常生氣地問：「是誰刺傷了你？」垂死的女人痛得只可以低聲地說：「祖馬茲。」野仙人聽到後，除了說「自作自受」外，還有什麼別的辦法呢？於是他們回到他們偏僻的藏匿處。狡詐的瓜爾達農民沒有受到野仙人的大報復。

　　從那時開始，帝艾樂仙人再沒和人類有什麼關係了，亦再沒有人看到他們在森林裏或草地上出沒，更沒有仙人願意和人類住在一起，或和人類分享他們的知識了。

destroyed a she-devil, he went on his way with his load of hay.

The Diale let out terrible cries of agony, alerting the wild folk up in the distant mountain caves, who all came rushing down. "Who did this to you?" they asked angrily. The dying woman could only whisper: "Jeu mez." What could the others do but say, "As you sow, so shall you reap"? And they all retreated back to their lonely hiding places, and the crafty haymaker was spared the terrible revenge of the wild folk of the mountains.

However, since that day the Diale folk will have nothing more to do with human beings, and they have never been seen again in the woods or in the fields. And as for having close relationships with mortals, letting them partake of their special knowledge, or even living with them, that has never ever occurred again.

天氣冷杉　The Story of the 'Wettertanne'

In Switzerland, fir trees standing alone, exposed to all weathers in fields or among the cliffs, are known as 'Wettertannen' or 'weather firs'.

Once upon a time, on Oberbüz Alp above Weesen, there was a ghost who lived inside a fir tree. Whenever bad weather was imminent, a great rumbling, banging and whooping could be heard coming from this tree.

One day, the tree was chopped down to make a roof beam. But if anyone had hoped that would be the end of the tree ghost's commotion, he was soon to be disappointed. For the ghost remained inside the wooden beam and continued to make a frightful din whenever he felt like it. In fact, he made such a terrible noise, and so often, that finally the inhabitants of the chalet felt compelled to take out the beam and replace it with a more harmless piece of wood.

To this day, according to the mountain farmers, the restless ghost continues to make a nuisance of himself up on Oberbüz Alp, disturbing them with his usual din every time the weather is about to change for the worse. Sometimes he even goes after the pigs, driving them into such a fury that they all charge out of the sty. He also enjoys shaking the cow bells, setting them all clanging at the same time.

Whenever that happens, the farmers have to keep calm. If anyone tries to stop the monster, or even to see him, he can be sure to wake up the following morning with a splitting headache.

在瑞士，孤零零在田中或崖邊生長的冷杉樹，暴露於各種天氣之下，受盡風吹雨打，故又名「天氣冷杉」。

多年以前，維森的奧伯畢茲高山牧場有一棵冷杉樹，裏面藏著了一個魔鬼。每次天氣轉壞，樹便發出隆隆的、嘭嘭的、呼呼的巨大聲響。

為了建造一座小屋，這棵冷杉終於被砍伐了，它被用作屋頂的樑木。誰以為樹鬼不再吵鬧？那就完全錯了！樹鬼仍然留在冷杉樑裏，它隨時隨地狂吼喧嚷。他實在吵得太厲害，也太頻密了，居民終於把那根支撐樑換上普通的木。

山上的農夫說，直到今天，那永不安靜的樹鬼還在奧伯畢茲高山牧場裏胡作非為。它仍然在天氣不好的時候大吵大鬧，煩擾房舍裏的人。有時它更弄得豬隻瘋狂起來，衝出豬圈。它也愛搖動牛鈴，讓它們同時大聲地響。

農夫沒辦法，只好保持冷靜。如果有人想制止樹鬼，或只是一睹樹鬼的面貌，他第二天起床時肯定會頭痛欲裂。

The Three Tests

智裏是奧伯沙撒山的一個牧羊人。他是個
聰明勇敢的孩子。他從不怕什麼，縱使黑
暗的夜裏，他還有勇氣在漆黑的峽谷裏走
一回，就好像在大白天一樣。要他躍過激
流，或者照顧最惡的公牛，他都不當一
回事。從小他就熟悉洶湧的山澗，也可以
跟每個動物結成朋友。若見到一隻在穀倉
或城堡遺址裏睡覺的貓頭鷹，他就不會騷
擾牠。冬天，他會在雪上撒麵包渣兒，餵
飽飢餓的寒鴉。他特別喜歡的是螞蟻和蜜
蜂，他會花數小時觀察螞蟻在冷杉針葉堆
上亂跑，看牠們辛苦地搬運沉重的東西；
他會看蜜蜂忙碌地鑽進花鈴去。他決不會
胡亂攪動蟻穴，或打擾蜜蜂工作。若田鼠
給捕鼠器逮著，他會放了牠。他只怕蝙蝠
和狗。

　　他的父親對兒子特別感到驕傲。他的
父親習慣説：「孩子，你應該幹別的活，
不應該叉乾草和糞肥。」有一天，一位巡
迴工作的鑄鐘師傅來到這裏，他受雇為舊
的教堂尖塔鑄一些新鐘。父親趁機請鑄鐘
師傅收智裏為徒，教他那尊貴的工藝。師
傅同意了。

　　智裏的手那麼靈巧，工作做得那麼
好，師傅禁不住稱讚他。師傅答應如果智
裏繼續這樣的幹，不久就會教他鑄鐘這種
精巧的手藝。

　　但是師傅要智裏先通過三個測驗，這

Järi – let's call him Jerry – was a young shepherd
from the Obersaxen mountains. He was a very bright,
plucky boy. Nothing ever scared him. He'd go through
the darkest of gullies in the blackest of nights just as
if it were broad daylight. If he had to jump across a
raging torrent, or if he was given the fiercest of the
bulls to guard, he didn't mind at all. After all, he had
grown up beside the rushing mountain streams, and
was friends with all the animals. If he found an owl
sleeping in the barn or in the ruins of the castle, he
left it in peace. In winter he scattered breadcrumbs
in the snow for the starving alpine daws. He was
particularly fond of ants and bees. He could spend
hours observing the ants running hither and thither
on the heaps of pine needles, struggling to carry their
heavy loads; or the bees as they slipped busily into the
bells of the alpine flowers. Never did he poke around
in the ant heaps or disturb the bees at their work.
If he saw a field-mouse caught in a trap, he would
release it. The only animals he avoided were bats and
dogs.

Jerry's father was proud of his son and used to
say, "Son, some day we must find you a better job
than pitchforking hay and manure!" And then one day
an itinerant bellfounder, who had been summoned to
make some new bells for the old church tower, arrived
at the farm. The father seized the opportunity to ask
if he would employ Jerry as an apprentice and teach
him his noble craft. The master craftsman agreed.

The lad turned out to be so good that his master
praised him, promising that if he persevered he might
soon be initiated into the sublime art of bellfounding.

However, he would first have to pass the three difficult tests that the fire spirits set every apprentice. For, as strict guardians of the noble craft, they took great care that no one unworthy was ever initiated into the highest secrets of bellfounding. That did not worry Jerry. Why should he be scared? He had never done anyone any harm. So he continued cheerfully with his work, and time passed in a flash.

The day set for the master craftsman test finally arrived. That evening, as Jerry came up to the fireplace, a little man in a red jerkin and with a bright red leather cap on his head leapt out, chanting:

> *The spirits of fire*
> *Thy master inspire.*
> *If thou dost succeed*
> *He'll be happy indeed.*
> *But if thou dost fail*
> *He must go down to Hell*
> *With reptiles and snakes*
> *For ever to dwell.*

Then he disappeared back into the fireplace. At the same moment, the bellfounder came into the room and bade Jerry follow him. He led him down into a deep, dark cellar. It was here he had to perform the first task. All Jerry could see was a big pile of sand. His master told him his task was to pick out all the little grains of ore needed for the alloy. He had to have finished by the morning. Then his master went back upstairs, bolting the door from the outside.

Jerry sat down on the heap of sand and waited calmly to see what would happen next. He soon saw that it was quite impossible for him to perform the task himself. However he remained optimistic. He was sure he would manage somehow. But the fire spirits did what they could to make him give up. Their keen-

是火神給每個學徒所設定的。火神嚴格保護這尊貴的工藝，不容許不配的人知悉鑄鐘的最高秘密。智裏可不擔心，也不怕，他從沒有傷害別人，於是他很快樂地幹活。光陰似箭，時間很快地過去了。

滿師了，測驗那天到了。那天晚上，智裏走近火爐時，一個穿紅衣戴火紅皮帽的小人跳了出來說：

> 火神，火神
> 啓發你師傅
> 你通過測驗
> 他開心大笑
> 你不過測驗
> 他得下地獄
> 跟爬蟲和蛇
> 永遠在一起

然後他便溜到火爐裏去。這時鑄鐘師傅走過來，招手讓智裏跟著他走。他領智裏走到一個深長的、昏黑的地下室。智裏要在那裏接受第一個測驗。智裏在黑暗中只看到一大堆沙。師傅給他解釋：他要在第二天早晨前把鑄鐘用的礦石從沙丘中揀出來。師傅說完後，便走上樓梯，從外面鎖上了門。

智裏在沙丘上坐下來，安靜地等待著，看看什麼事情會發生。他很快就明白這是他一個人做不來的，但是他仍然樂

觀，心想應該有某種方法的。然而，火神
用盡方法要智裏放棄——火神尖耳朵的傭
人蝙蝠從牆邊的小窗飛進地下室來，橫七
豎八緊挨著智裏的頭飛舞，想看他在幹什
麼，又擦過他的頭髮逗弄他。突然，一隻
長卷毛狗從地下室一角跳出來，雙眼火紅
的瞪著他，向他齜著牙。智裏就是不怕。
他向長卷毛狗伸出手，吹口哨喚狗説，
「來吧，讓我數數你漂亮的牙齒。」那隻
狗可不敢過來咬他。

　　一夜這樣過去，快到破曉時分了，連
一撮沙子的礦石他也還沒揀出來。小助手
終於到了——一隊螞蟻從牆的裂縫裏爬出
來，牠們每個的頭上都戴了一盞小燈，因
此全個地下室都亮起來。這隊勤快的小生
物開始在小沙丘裏搜查，牠們找到礦石，
便把它放在一堆。至於蟻后和牠的僕役，
牠們向長卷毛狗的眼睛噴了些腐蝕液，免
得牠看見發生什麼事情。終於，長卷毛狗
嗥嗥地溜到地下室的角落裏去。

　　第一線陽光透進小窗的時候，礦石同
沙子已經仔仔細細的分開了。螞蟻在蟻后
後面黑壓壓的一大團聚集起來，好像想表
示：「如果你需要我們的幫助，是可以指
望我們的。」然後就爬走了。

　　不久門就開了。鑄鐘師傅進來看到那
一堆礦石，感到很驚訝，也很滿意。

　　第一項任務完成了。師傅告訴智裏第
二個測驗：他得找一根被奧伯沙撒女巫藏
在一條危險山澗裏的魔索。智裏要用這根
索子吊起他的第一個鐘，這個鐘會決定他
成為師傅的資格。

eared servants, the bats, who had flown in through the cellar window, swirled around just above his head to see what he was doing, and whisked through his hair to tease him. Suddenly a poodle with flaming eyes leaped towards him from a corner of the cellar, baring its teeth. But Jerry was fearless. He stretched out his hand to the dog, whistling to it to approach. "Come here," he said. "Let me count your beautiful teeth!" But the dog did not dare to bite him.

Night passed. Dawn was already breaking, and still not a handful of the sand had been sorted. And then, at last, Jerry's little helpers arrived – an army of ants that suddenly came scrambling out of the joints between the flagstones. Each one had a little lamp on its head, so that the whole of the cellar was lit up. The diligent creatures immediately started sorting through the sand, placing all the pieces of ore they found onto a separate heap. Simultaneously their queen and her maidservants squirted their venom into the dog's eyes so that he could not see what was going on. Howling, he retreated to where he had come from.

By the time the first rays of the sun came poking through the cellar window, the ore had all been separated from the sand, and the ants had all crept away again. But not before they had massed themselves in a dense black clump behind their queen as if to say, "We'll always be around to help you in case of need."

Soon the door opened, and the bellfounder came in. He was surprised and delighted to see the fine pile of ore.

The first task had been completed. Now his master disclosed Jerry's second task: he had to find the magic rope which the witches of Obersaxen had hidden in a dangerous gully. This rope was to be used to raise Jerry's first bell, the one that would qualify him as a master craftsman.

Lost in thought, the lad went up the steps which led from the farm where the bellfounder had installed his workshop towards the ravine through which St Peter's Brook flows. Where on earth could the rope be hidden? He leaned over the rail of the bridge and looked down into the water below. Suddenly, an old owl landed on his shoulder. He knew the owl well, for he had once defended her from some thieving ravens while she was sitting on her eggs.

"Look in the Devil's Ditch," she whispered in his ear.

Straightaway Jerry made for the Devil's Ditch, a hidden ravine not far from Schwarzenstein Castle. He was the only person to know of it. Looking down into its depths was really frightening – nothing but smooth wet rocks receding towards the bottom, making it quite impossible for the best climber – or even the goats Jerry used to mind near there – to clamber down. Jerry sat down on the edge of the ravine, dangling his legs.

"I'll just wait," he thought. "The ants promised to help."

Again the pestering bats flitted around, trying to frighten him. But the owl returned and scared them away. As for the dog, it did not dare put in an appearance again, after its experience in the cellar.

"Help is on its way," whispered the owl.

This time it was the mice who wanted to thank Jerry. Arriving in droves, they climbed down into the depths of the abyss, so far that Jerry could not make them out any more. But the owl told him that there was a black snake there guarding the magic rope.

"The mice won't find it easy to get the better of her," whispered the owl. "But don't worry, the spiders are on their way too."

You see, Jerry had never ever destroyed a spider's nest, and had always been careful not to tear any spider's webs.

"Down in the ravine," continued the owl, "near where the snake is curled up on the rope, there are big spiders climbing up the cliff so that they can drip their poison down onto that hideous reptile. That'll make it sleepy. Oh yes, now it's fallen off the rope, it's fallen down to the bottom of the ravine. The mice are holding on to the rope with their teeth."

智裏一面走到農莊內鑄鐘師傅的工場，一面沉思著。他步上梯階，那梯階通往聖彼得溪流過的山澗。他便朝那裏走過去。女巫的索子藏在哪裏？他靠在橋的欄杆上，看著溪流。這時一隻老貓頭鷹飛到他肩膀上停下來。智裏很熟悉牠，因為這隻貓頭鷹在樹林裏孵蛋的時候，他曾幫牠趕跑一隻想偷蛋的烏鴉。

貓頭鷹悄悄地跟他說：「在魔鬼溝那邊！」

他徑直走到那裏去。魔鬼溝是黑石城堡附近一個隱蔽的峽谷，就光他一個人熟悉那個地方。往下看誰不害怕？那裏全是濕滑的崖石！沒有人會爬下去的，連智裏在附近放牧山羊的時候也不會。他在山崖的邊沿坐下來，雙腿向下掛著。

「我就等一會兒，」他靜靜地想著，「螞蟻答應來幫忙的。」

討厭的蝙蝠又飛過來，想嚇怕他。貓頭鷹立刻趕來驅趕牠們。狗這次不敢來，牠在地下室受夠了。

貓頭鷹低聲告訴智裏：「你的助手快來了！」

這次是老鼠想感謝他。牠們成群的到來，沿著深谷的峭壁爬下去，直到智裏看不清牠們的蹤影。貓頭鷹告訴智裏，魔索是由黑蛇看守著的。

「老鼠要打敗黑蛇並不容易。」貓頭鷹低聲告訴他，「可是你放心，蜘蛛也開拔了！」

就是因為智裏從來沒有毀壞蜘蛛的窩，亦總是當心不扯斷牠們的網。

「在峽谷下面，」貓頭鷹繼續説，「蛇蜷曲在索子上躺著，但是很大的蜘蛛正沿著岩石向上爬，要把牠們的毒素滴落可惡的爬蟲身上，那會使牠昏昏欲睡。現在，啊，牠剛從索子上掉下來，落到深谷下面去了。索子被老鼠的牙齒抓住了。」

然後智裏看到友善的小老鼠把魔索拉到峽谷邊。他把手伸進褲袋取出一根小繩子——小夥子褲袋裏總是有小繩子的，然後把它往下垂。老鼠伶俐地把小繩子繫在那根魔索上，那麼智裏就可以把魔索拉上來了。

這樣，第二項任務完成了。

可是，火神私下煩惱了，因為智裏那麼容易便通過了第一個和第二個測驗。他們討論了許久，才定下最後最難的一個測驗。第三天，師傅告訴智裏第三個測驗：鐘已經用從沙裏找到的礦石鑄好了。智裏現在得把這口鐘的聲音，調得跟另外所有的鐘不一樣。

找一個全新的、沒聽過的調！這真是個為難的事情。有那麼多口鐘：大的、小的、舊的、新的等等，每一口都有自己的聲調、自己的音色。智裏沒辦法了，他只好暗自希望動物朋友快來幫忙。貓頭鷹試唱了點什麼，但，哎呀，真沒個好聲音！老鼠吹起口哨，也不起什麼作用啊。

這口鐘已經在鐘架上吊著，晚上得調出新的音調。智裏試了許多次，可是每次結果都一樣，響起的都是個熟悉的聲調。

And then Jerry saw the good little mice drag the rope to the side of the ravine. He groped in his trouser pocket for a piece of string – boys always have string in their pockets – which he then hung down over the edge. The mice tied it adroitly to the rope, and then all Jerry had to do was pull it up.

That was that: now he had solved the second problem.

The fire spirits were secretly rather annoyed that Jerry had solved the first two problems so easily, and they deliberated for a long time before they decided on the last and most difficult test. Finally, on the third day, the master said that, now that the bell was cast with the ore found in the sand, Jerry would have to tune it so that it had a sound unlike that of any other bell.

Now, finding a new sound is an extremely difficult task. There are so many bells, big ones and small ones, old ones and new ones, and each has its own particular sound, its own timbre. Jerry really did not know what to do, but he secretly hoped that his friends, the animals, would again come to his aid. Well, the owl did try to sing something, but alas, it really did not sound nice. And the squeaking mice were not of much use either.

The bell had already been hung up in its frame, and by the evening it had to be finely tuned to the new sound. But however often Jerry tried, he kept getting a sound which was already known.

He was beginning to lose confidence. "Can a new sound really still be found?" he asked himself as he paced the meadow next to the workshop.

Then he suddenly heard a loud humming, and a huge swarm of bees was flying around his head. They settled on the nearby garden fence. Calling their queen, they started to sing, very softly, delicately – a wonderful sound! That was what the queen bee had ordered them to do, at the request of the queen of the ants who had gone to see her in her hive.

Jerry, who had never in his life annoyed a bee with hasty gestures or prodding, now listened carefully.

"That's exactly the tone I've been trying to find!" he called out. "There's never been a bell that sounded like that."

Soon his first bell rang out in chorus with the bees. The fire spirits accepted the new tone. So Jerry had passed all the tests. He became the most famous master bellfounder in the region. But he never forgot the kind animals who had helped him. Thus it was that the most nectar-rich flowers for bees were to be found in his garden; the official mouser was not allowed to place his traps in his meadows; and Jerry still frequently conversed with spiders and ants. As for the old owl, she could often be seen sitting at night at the bellfounder's window.

他開始失去信心了。「真的可以找到一種新的音調麼？」他一面在工場旁邊一個草地上走來走去，一面問自己。

然後一大群蜜蜂飛過來。成千上萬的蜜蜂圍著智裏的頭嗡嗡低鳴，然後牠們在一個圍圍的籬笆上停下來。牠們一邊呼喚蜂后，一邊嗡嗡地歌唱：柔和的、細緻的、極美的。牠們是奉蜂后之命這樣做的，因為蟻后到蜂巢來請求蜂后幫忙。

智裏從來不會用急躁的動作觸怒蜜蜂，或戳牠們的巢。現在他留心細聽……

「這正是我要找的新音調！」他呼叫著，「從沒有一個鐘會發出這樣的聲音來。」

不久，他的第一口鐘跟蜜蜂合唱了。火神接受了這個新音調。對智裏來說，他通過了所有測驗，成了這周圍一帶最有名的鑄鐘師傅。可是智裏從來不會忘記曾經幫助他的善良動物。蜜蜂在他的園圍裏找到的花是最香甜的，市政府的捕鼠員不可以在他的草地裏設陷阱。智裏亦常常跟蜘蛛和螞蟻談話。至於老貓頭鷹，牠時常夜裏在鑄鐘師傅的窗臺前坐上好一會兒。

耶爾格到庫爾去　Jörg in Chur

來自柏拉登的耶爾格是個高大強壯的漢子。一天，他得到庫爾城去，因為市長傳他出庭為非法伐樹答辯。到法庭的路上，他連根拔起一株松樹來作拐杖。

他一到庫爾市政廳前，便用力把拐杖靠在牆邊，教松樹上的松果直飛進窗戶，落到了市長的桌子上。

然後他走進市長的房間，問道：「找我有什麼事？」

One day a great brawny fellow from Praden, whose name was Jörg, was summoned by the stern mayor of the worthy city of Chur to account for having illegally chopped down trees. On his way to the courts, the man pulled up a pine tree by the roots and used it as his walking-staff.

When he got to Chur town hall, he leaned his staff against the wall in such a way that its pine cones went flying straight through the window onto the councillors' table.

Then he stepped into the room and asked," What do you want of me?"

"Nothing, Jörg," the mayor answered meekly. "Please just go back home."

The Herdsman

拯
救
國
家
的
牧
人

who Saved his Country

Once upon a time a herdsman from Graubünden, who bore the not uncommon name of Hans, was accosted by the commander of a heavily armed troop of soldiers from across the Austrian border. The arrogant officer ordered him to show them the way to the villages, which he knew to be rich and unprotected. He promised him a large sum of money for his services. But the fellow refused his generous offer, for he had no wish to be a traitor.

"You wretch!" snorted the bloodthirsty warmonger. "Either you do our bidding or we'll cut you to pieces forthwith."

"Oh dear," replied Hans, rather good-naturedly. "But then I'd have to put up a fight."

"Indeed? And what would you fight with?" scoffed the soldiers, who could not make out even the simplest of weapons anywhere near the mountain man.

"With this," retorted the herdsman in a fury, tearing up a pine tree from the ground. And he swung it around, sweeping to the ground all those who could not run fast enough to get out of his way.

Only a couple of those soldiers of the great Austrian Empire managed to escape with their lives. They told others what had happened, striking awe and fear into the hearts of all who heard them. And thus, thanks to the strong fellow Hans, the country was left in peace, and for many years there were no more hostile incursions or other disagreeable incidents.

從前有一個格勞賓登的牧人，他有一個尋常的名字叫漢斯。一天他遇到一隊全副武裝的士兵從奧地利的邊界過來。傲慢的軍官命令漢斯指出到村子的路，因他知道村子很富有但沒有防護。他答應給漢斯許多錢作回報，但漢斯拒絕了，他不想作叛徒。

「蠢材！」嗜殺成性的軍官氣得直呼叱，「如果你不立刻服從，我們就馬上把你切成肉塊！」

「老天，」漢斯好脾氣地說，「那樣我不得不自衛了！」

「怎自衛呀！」士兵嘲笑著，因為這阿爾卑斯山人身上連最簡陋的武器也沒有。

「用這個呢！」牧人氣憤地回答，隨即拔起一棵松樹，向走避不及的敵人橫掃過去，把他們全部擊倒在地上。

結果，這偉大的奧地利帝國軍隊只有幾個士兵能夠逃出生天。他們把這件事講給別人聽，聽到的人無不感到敬畏和害怕。有賴強壯的漢斯，他的國家很長時間沒有敵軍入侵，也沒有其他不愉快的事情發生。

Sir Jeuch

Rescues Klosters

有一個星期天,漢斯祖楚爵士站到窗戶前,往斯拉平的方向遠眺的時候,他看見一大隊兵士從麥塔方的奧地利山谷攀下山坡來。

他很快便穿好了皮革甲冑。騎上滿身戰跡的白馬前,他給馬飲了一木桶葡萄酒來鼓勵牠,增加牠戰鬥的勇氣(一木桶可以盛兩至三加侖的酒)。

然後他騎到克羅斯特教堂前,因為人人都來望彌撒。他們一聽見武士號召作戰,都急忙回家拿武器。漢斯祖楚沒有等他們,就獨個兒向麥塔方人那裏跑去,只大聲對卡魯斯提司的男人說:「我會把敵人全部擊倒,你們就一個也不讓他們再站起來。」

One Sunday, Sir Jeuch was standing at the window and looking out towards Schlapin, when he suddenly saw a troop of soldiers from the Austrian valley of Montafon coming down the slopes of the mountain.

He immediately put on his leather armour. But before mounting his battle-scarred steed, he gave it a 'Gelte' of wine to drink to give it courage for the battle. (A 'Gelte' is a wooden vessel that can hold two or three gallons.)

Then he rode up to Klosters church, for all the other men were at mass. As soon as they heard the knight's battle-cry, they rushed home to fetch their arms. Hans Jeuch did not wait for them, but raced up towards the Montafon troops, just taking the time to cry to his own men, "I'll mow them all down, you lot just make sure they can't get up again."

Then he shot like a bolt of lightning into the midst of the enemy, striking down whole rows of soldiers with his sharp sword, while others were mown down by the hooves of his drunken steed. When the men from Klosters arrived, all they had to do was "ted the hay," that is finish off the wounded men lying in the grass. The few surviving soldiers, bloody-headed, fled back up the slope towards home. For three days the Schlapin brook ran red, so murderous had the encounter been.

On their way back to Klosters, the victorious men took a rest in a meadow. There Sir Hans Jeuch removed his leather suit of armour. Lo and behold! Hundreds of pellets of enemy musket shot rolled out onto the ground. Obviously, the knight was a man who fed on more than bread alone: he had mastered the craft of making himself bullet-proof.

他閃電似的衝到敵陣中，用銳利的劍砍倒了一列敵兵，其餘的就給他醉馬的蹄絆跌，倒地不起。當克羅斯特的人趕到時，他們只需「割禾草」，這就是説，殺掉倒在地上的傷兵。剩餘的幾個敵人頭沾滿血，爬上山坡往家裏逃。整整三天，斯拉平的溪水是紅色的，可見戰事是多麼的凶殘。

在回家的路上，勝利的克羅斯特人在村子裏的一個草坪上歇息。漢斯祖楚爵士把他的皮革甲冑脱下。瞧，幾百顆敵人步槍的子彈滾落到地上來了。武士顯然不是光吃麵包的人，他把自己練成刀鎗不入，子彈不穿哩。

格勞賓登人怎麼戰勝黑死病

How the People of Graubünden Vanquished the Plague

以前，在格勞賓登山谷一帶，鼠疫很厲害，人們都叫那個地方「黑色死亡」。很多人死了，農舍丟荒了，基地裏也找不到地方來埋數不清的屍體。

山谷的人發現野人民族中沒有一個被黑死病傳染。

「藏在高山裏的矮人和他們的妻子一定有黑死病的解藥。」山谷的人一致地說。

只是，怎麼說服那些神秘的男女小矮人披露他們的祖傳秘方呢？這是不可能的事啊，因為他們善於保衛知識和技能。一個聰明的格勞賓登人有了個很好的主意。

山上有一塊孤零零的岩石，岩石裏有一個洞，那裏住著一個野人。他給人照顧牛隻，因此人們在他的洞裏放一些食物來酬謝他。那個聰明的山谷人把這個習慣改變了一些，沒給他吃的，而放了點酒。

The Plague, also known as the Black Death, was raging in the valleys of Graubünden. The population had been decimated, farms abandoned, and in many a village there was no space left in the graveyard to bury the dead.

Then it suddenly occurred to the people in the valleys that not a single one of the wild folk had succumbed to the terrible disease.

"To be sure, the manikins and their wives up there in their mountain hiding places know of some marvellous remedy …," they all agreed.

But how could the mysterious little men and women be persuaded to reveal the secrets of their science? It seemed an impossible task, for they had always jealously guarded their ancient lore. However, in the end, one of the men thought of a clever trick.

Up on the mountain there was an isolated rock which had a hole in it. Here people used to pour food to reward one of the wild manikins who helped them with their cattle. Now this resourceful fellow just modified the old custom slightly by pouring strong wine into the cavity instead of food.

After some time, when he was sure that the wild manikin would have had his meal, the crafty fellow stepped out from his hiding place. He soon came upon the manikin, who was well and truly drunk on the unfamiliar beverage.

"What's a good cure for the Plague?" the man asked.

"I know the answer to that," answered the manikin, smiling impishly. "Carline thistle and burnet-saxifrage are what you need, but I'll never tell you!"

Delighted, the man hurried back home to tell his neighbours about the remedy. After that, there were no further deaths from the Plague.

However, some people were still not satisfied.

"Just imagine," the insatiable fellows would say, "just imagine what a lot of useful secrets the manikin would have revealed if the man who had outwitted him had stayed to ask him some more questions, instead of running away so stupidly after the first reply. What a pity! A chance like that is hardly likely to come our way again!"

當聰明人肯定野矮人吃過了飯，他便從藏匿的地方走出來。野矮人不習慣喝酒，現在已經醉醺醺了。

聰明人問：「你知道黑死病的解藥是什麼？」

野矮人頑皮地笑起來，回答說：「我當然知道，你需要卡蓮薊和虎耳草來治這種病，但是我永遠不會告訴你！」

聰明人高高興興地回到村子，告訴他的鄰居鼠疫的解藥該怎麼做。從此，格勞賓登山谷裏再沒有人得過鼠疫。

這故事的結局聽來很理想，可是還有人不滿意。

「想想看，」不知足的人會說，「如果他向小矮人多提一點問題，不是這麼笨問完第一個問題便跑，小矮人還會洩露更多要緊的秘密哩。他放過這麼好的機會，真遺憾！」

很多個世紀前，住在蘇茨夫魯山的牧人，和奧地利境內麥塔方山谷的牧人經常吵架。這些矛盾一開始並不嚴重，甚至可以說有點像開玩笑而已。可是事情一發不可收拾，越來越暴烈。

有一天，一個牧牛人在柏寧牧場放牛時，想出了一個向麥塔方人報復的狠辣計畫。他獨自行動。他知道如果他的朋友得知他的計畫，便會阻止他，於是他保密了。

在晴朗的某天，他出發了。他走過分隔兩幫牧人的格魯賓峽道，到達敵手廣闊漂亮的麥塔方山坡。他來到了一個農舍。那裏的人雖然知道他們之間的矛盾，仍很熱情地歡迎這個牧牛人，很客氣地請他吃飯，喝東西。那個牧人起先很感動，幾乎令他放棄那惡意的計畫，不過很快他根深蒂固的仇恨又露頭了。

夜裏的時候，這無賴子起床，偷偷的潛入牛棚，牽走了兩隻最漂亮和寶貴的牛。他覺得自己很聰明，他的驕傲掩蓋了他的良心。

For centuries skirmishing between the alpine herdsmen on Mount Sulzfluh and the men from Montafon Valley on the Austrian side had been more or less good-natured. But in time the clashes got out of hand and became more and more vicious.

One day, while minding his cows on Partnun Alp, a cowherd devised a reckless plan to wreak vengeance on the Montafon fellows, alone, without using anyone else's help. He did not tell any of his friends of his plan, for fear they might try to talk him out of it.

One fine day he set off, and, after crossing the Gruben Pass which divided the rival camps, set foot on the splendid, broad alpine slopes of Montafon. There he stopped at a chalet to rest. The inhabitants, who still regarded hospitality as their sacred duty, never mind the disputes, made the cowherd welcome and gave him such a good meal that he almost forgot all about his mischievous plan and nearly gave it up. But then old feelings of hatred gained the upper hand.

In the middle of the night, the scoundrel slipped out of his bed, crept into the cowshed, and led away the two handsomest cows. Pride at his own cleverness helped silence the voice of his conscience.

He drove his booty across the mountain pass down to his alp. Proud as a peacock, he joyfully greeted the farmhand who had been looking after his cattle while he was away.

"My God, what have you done?" was the man's instant rejoinder. "Those fellows are sure to want to get their own back. It'll cost us all our possessions!

We'll all be made to suffer for what you've done now, you fool!"

That very afternoon his grim premonition turned out to be right. A gang of Montafon men carrying thick sticks came charging down from the pass, in their midst the furious owner of the two brown cows. Not only were they determined to regain their possessions, they had also decided to lead away the rest of the cattle that were grazing on Partnun Alp. In just retribution! The only animal they left behind was a bull who happened to be lame and would therefore not have been able to cross the mountains safely or quickly enough.

As to the cowherd who had abused their hospitality, they gave him the choice between the two forms of capital punishment in use among the alpine folk at the time. Either he could leap to his death into a cauldron of boiling milk; or he could blow on an alphorn for as long as it took for his lungs to burst.

He chose the second punishment, climbed up onto the chalet roof, and started blowing, so loudly that the sound echoed throughout the mountains and valleys: "Oh! Oh! Oh! ... They've taken the brown cow and all the others too ..."

Although everyone down in the valley heard the strangely lingering, trembling strains from the cowherd's horn, no one managed to interpret his plaint. Except for the girl who was at that moment drawing water from the well: she understood his cry for help and explained it to the men.

Now at last the farmers down in the valley realised that their goods and chattels were in danger.

他帶著那兩隻珍貴的牛爬過山道,回到自己的牧場。他碰到自己不在時照顧他牛群的雇農,便得意洋洋地把一切告訴他。

「天呀!你瘋了!」雇農大吃一驚,「麥塔方人一定要找我們算帳!我們傾家蕩產也不夠賠償,全村子都要為你的所作所為受罪,蠢材!」

下午還沒到,雇農的預感就應驗了:一幫麥塔方人拿著大棒子,穿過山道跑下來,他們中間包括怒髮衝冠的牛主人。他們不僅想取回自己的財物,還打算偷走所有在柏寧牧場吃草的牛,這算是公平的報復!他們輕手輕腳地幹,只留下一隻公牛,因為那牛腳不好,不能安全而快速地翻過山脈。

至於那個牧牛人,他濫用別人熱情好客之道,麥塔方人讓他選擇死刑的方式。當時阿爾卑斯山中人比較常用的死刑有兩種:一種是跳進沸燙的牛奶裏去,另一種是吹阿爾卑斯山長號直到不能呼吸。

蘇茨夫魯山的牧人選擇了第二種。他站在農舍的屋頂，用很大的力氣吹阿爾卑斯山號角。號聲很響，哪裏都可以盪起回音，傳到每一個人的耳裏：「喔喔喔！他們把我們的棕色牛和所有的牛都拿走……」

在蘇茨夫魯的山谷裏，大家都可以聽到這奇怪的、緩慢又震慄的號角聲，不過大家都弄不清楚號角傳來的信息，只有一個正從井裏打水的女孩子明白。那是求救信號。她便告訴周圍的人。

山谷的牧人終於明白他們的財物有危險了，於是匆匆趕到山上的牧場去。可惜他們來晚了。用盡氣力想警告朋友和親人的牧牛人，已經在茅舍的屋頂上死了。他們的牛全部不見了，都被麥塔方人偷走了，而他們已經跑得很遠。

事到如今，他們都無能為力了。他們知道無法再尋回失牛了，除非他們用高價從敵人手上買牠們回來。

他們沮喪地回到山谷的家裏。牧場的雇農因為牛沒有了，沒事兒幹了，也沒理由留在山上，便跟著他們下山。美麗的牧場現在空無一物。幾個鐘頭前牛還在這裏平靜地吃草，牛鈴愉快地叮咚響著，現在四周是死寂一片。

They stormed up to the alps. Too late! The cowherd, who had summoned every last drop of his energy to alert friends and relatives, lay dead on the chalet roof. As for the cows and the Montafon fellows, they were already over the mountain and far away. There was no chance of catching up with them now.

So that was that! There was nothing to be done. The valley folk knew that they would never see their cattle again – unless they bought them back from their rivals, at a high price.

Downcast, they set off back to their homes in the valley, accompanied by the farmhands who had no reason to stay up on the alp, now that the cows had gone. Bleak silence descended on the magnificent, now deserted, pastures which, only a few hours earlier, had resounded to the merry jingling of the peacefully grazing herds.

The Dwarf Named Beardy

A Fairytale from the Mountains of Glarus (excerpt)
Lorly Jenny (1900-1982)

High up above the valley, at the foot of a mighty cliff, there's a broad green platform with a dark forest on one side and on the other a little mound with a few short saplings. If you looked through their crowns you'd see a tiny door as brown as bark. One fine day in early spring the door opened and a dwarf, Beardy, stepped out. He was wearing a brown jerkin and had brown twinkling eyes and a long, long grey beard which almost reached down to his shoes.

"Hooray," he whooped, hopping around the pine trees, "spring has come and chased away the snow!"

Beardy sat down on a stone and surveyed the beautiful world around him. The sky was dark blue, the few patches of snow left in the hollows were dull grey. There was a small brook bubbling through the meadow, white and purple crocuses were all around, convolvulus peeped out among the leaves, and the flowers of the saxifrage shone out like stars just fallen

在山谷上方，高峻的懸崖腳下，有一塊廣闊的綠色平地。平地一邊是一個幽暗的森林，另一邊是長著幾棵嫩樹的小丘。從樹頂望過去，你會看見一道門，樹皮一樣棕色的小門。突然，門打開了，小矮人巴廸踏出門來。他穿著一件棕色的短身皮衣，眼睛明亮，長長的灰色鬍子差不多掉到鞋子上面。

「啊嗨！」他一邊環繞松樹跳躍，一邊歡呼道：「春天把冰雪趕跑了！」

巴廸在一塊石子上坐下來，審視著周圍美麗的世界。天空是深藍色，低窪地方上幾片積雪是暗淡的灰。一道小溪潺潺穿過草原，周圍是白色和紫色的番紅花，攀緣植物從葉間探出頭來，虎耳草的花朵則像天上掉下來的星星一般閃耀。一陣狂風颯颯吹過松樹，刮下幾顆松子，有一顆直掉到巴迪的鼻子上來。

「喂！風啊，小心點！」他叫道，「不用叫醒我了。我全醒啦！」他趕快跑到草原，雪融的土地在他腳下吱吱作響。青蔥的溪畔間金盞草發出閃耀的亮光，清澈的溪水汩汩流過晶亮的卵石。一隻布穀鳥飛過樹頂，「布穀，布穀。」鳥兒叫道，巴迪向牠招手，一邊大喊，「唷呵！唷呵！」他抬頭看著天卻沒有注意要走的路，一把踏著自己的長鬍子，絆倒在前面隆起的地上，整個人一頭栽進一堆積雪裏。

「老天爺，巴迪啊！」兔子媽媽從一堆松枝下走出來嚷道，「你想捉鼹鼠麼？」

小矮人站起來，有點迷糊，擦擦眼睛說：「別取笑我啊，兔子媽媽。鬍子在我冬眠時長得很長哩。現在我跑到那裏都給它絆著。你可否用你的尖牙齒把它咬短些？」

「辦不到啊，巴迪。它會令我鼻子癢哩。而且，我趕時間，我要去照顧我的孩子。」不待巴迪說什麼牠已經在一塊石子背後消失了。

於是巴迪把鬍子掛在左臂，沿著茂密的溪邊走到上游。他找到厚厚的一小團葉子，滿足地坐下來直至夜幕降臨，晚星在群山的上空閃爍不定。

突然一把聲音嚷起來：「吐域吐胡！是你麼？」

from the sky. The foehn wind blustered through the pine trees, shaking down the cones, One of them fell right onto Beardy's nose.

"Hey, foehn, watch out," he cried. "There's no need to wake me. I'm already awake!" He quickly ran down to the meadow, the snow-soaked earth squelching under his shoes. The marsh marigolds gleamed brightly in the verdant banks of the stream, the clear water washed gurgling over the shiny pebbles. A cuckoo flew over the treetops. "Cuckoo, cuckoo," he cried, and Beardy waved to him shouting, "Yoo-hoo, yoo-hoo!" He looked up at the sky instead of looking where he was going, stepped on his long beard, tripped over a bump in the ground and fell full-length into a patch of snow.

"Goodness me, Beardy!" exclaimed Mother Hare, coming out from under a pile of pine branches. "Are you trying to catch moles?"

The little dwarf got up, quite dazed, rubbing his eyes. "Don't make fun of me, Mother Hare. My beard seems to have grown extraordinarily long during my winter sleep. Now it gets in the way whenever I walk about. Couldn't you bite off a bit with your sharp teeth?"

"Quite out of the question, Beardy. It would tickle my nose. Anyway, I'm in a hurry, I've got to go and see to my children." And in the blink of an eye, she'd disappeared behind a rock.

So, hanging his beard over his left arm, Beardy walked upstream along the leafy banks. He found a nice little cushion of leaves and sat there contentedly until darkness fell and the evening star could be seen twinkling above the mountain.

Suddenly a cry rang out: "Towit-towoo! Is it you?"

"Oh, hello, Night Owl, yes it's me. Please come here and help me. My beard's much too long. Please chop off the end; your beak's so nice and sharp!"

The owl glided silently down from the treetop.

Beardy spread out his beard on a flat stone so that the owl could hack off the bottom bit.

"Is that enough?"

"Oh yes, thanks ever so much. Now I'll be able to walk better. Let me know, Owl, if ever you need me."

The answer came floating up from the depths of the dark forest: "Towit-towoo!"

By the time Beardy had bolted his tiny door and was lying on the pallet in his little room, the sky had filled itself with stars. How tired he was after his first spring day!

The next morning Beardy goes to see an old herb lady named Tildy. On the way there he tears a hole in his trousers. She patches them for him, and he promises to bring her some alpine herbs as thanks.

Now that the winter is over, Beardy spends each fine day wandering around in the beautiful alpine countryside in search of herbs. He sees from afar the immense rock known as Dwarf's Castle. It's the abode of the King of the Dwarves who's said to be a very remarkable person. Beardy would dearly like to meet him and visit his castle.

One day, as he's digging up fern roots to eat, a squirrel leaps down from a tree above him and says its front paw is terribly painful. Beardy removes a pine needle which he finds stuck in the skin between the squirrel's claws. In return the squirrel shows Beardy how to eat pine kernels.

Then it's the height of the summer, and the cattle come up from the valley.

In groups they came, the cows, the heifers and the calves, to the accompaniment of jangling bells and yodelling herdsmen. The animals were tired after their long climb, but as soon as they smelled the lush grass they started grazing. Only after a while did they go and lie down in the shade. Beardy watched them, and from that day on started minding them. And when

「噢，你好，貓頭鷹，是我啊。請你過來幫幫忙好嗎？我的鬍子太長了。請把它弄短一點，你的喙又尖又有力！」

貓頭鷹悄悄地從樹頂滑下來。巴迪把鬍子在一塊平滑的石塊上鋪開，讓貓頭鷹把末端啄去。

「夠了麼？」

「夠了，真是謝謝你。現在我可以走得好一點了。貓頭鷹，你將來若需要我的幫忙，儘管告訴我。」

從黑森林的深處飄來一聲回答：「吐域吐胡！」

待巴迪把他的小門鎖好，躺到他小房間的草牀上時，星星已佈滿夜空了。春日第一天過後，他是多麼的疲倦啊！

第二天清早，巴迪去見一位名叫窕娣的香草婆婆。路上他把褲子撕破了一個洞。窕娣把褲子補好了，巴迪便答應給她捎來一些高山香草作為答謝。

冬天過去了，巴迪每天都在美麗的阿爾卑斯山野找尋香草。他從遠處看到那名叫小矮人城堡的巨石。那是小矮人國王的居所，據説他是很特別的一個人。巴迪真的很希望見見國王，並探訪一下城堡。

一天，當他正掘羊齒草根充飢的時候，一隻松鼠從他頭上的樹跳下來，説他的前掌痛得厲害。巴迪把刺在松鼠爪子皮上的一根松針拔出來。松鼠便教巴迪吃松果作為回報。

然後盛夏來了，牛從山谷結隊上來。

牠們一群一群的前來，母牛、公牛、小牛，伴著鈴聲及牧人的約德爾歌聲。牛群走了那麼久的山路，都累了，但嗅到茂盛的青草氣味又立刻吃起來，好一會才躲到樹蔭下休息。巴迪看著牠們，從那一天起，便開始照顧牠們。當牠們跑到紅山的草原上放牧時，他手拿樹枝跟著去。

一天下午，在牧鈴的叮噹聲之外，巴迪——他有一雙靈敏的耳朵——突然聽到高山某處傳來一隻小牛可憐的叫聲。他朝山上走了一會，果然發現那隻小牛孤單的給卡在一道斜坡的碎石堆上，前進後退都不成。牠看到巴迪時害怕地往後縮了一步。巴迪抓了一把草伸到牠鼻子下面。小牛踏前一步，巴迪卻同時後退一步，小牛想吃草便再走近些……突然牠已經踏在青草地上，巴迪可以領牠下山回到牛群裏去了。

第二天清晨，巴迪首先跑到西伯蘭的小湖上摘覆盆子醬果。摘滿一籃子之後，他坐在樹枝上休息。天氣已經非常炎熱，他得用手帕揩額上的汗。他一邊休息一邊看著木螞蟻忙碌地跑來跑去，要把松針拉到蟻穴去。然後他聽到有人談話，又看見一個小女孩和一個小男孩從松樹的枝枒下冒出來。

「噢，安德烈，看！很多醬果啊！」女孩子嚷道。之後他們便在矮叢中蹲下來開始採摘。巴迪看著這兩個可愛的孩子，很想跟他們談話。奇怪得很，人類是看不見小矮人的。他無法跟他們說話。只有雀鳥和動物可以明白他的語言。他帶著點點憂傷看著孩子遠去，慢慢消失在叢林中。

they went up to their pastures on the Rotberg (Red Mountain) he followed them, stick in hand.

One afternoon, above the jingle jangle of the bells, Beardy – who had very good ears – suddenly heard the piteous bleating of a calf coming from somewhere higher up the hill. And sure enough, after a short climb, he found the little creature standing all alone in the middle of a scree, unable to go backwards or forwards on the steep gravelly slope. On seeing Beardy, it cringed in fear. But then Beardy tore up a handful of grass and stretched it out under the calf's nose. The calf took a step forward and at the same time Beardy moved back, the calf wanted to grab the grass and came nearer … Suddenly it was standing on grassy ground again and Beardy could take it down to join the rest of the cattle.

The next morning, first thing, Beardy went up to the little lake on Seblen to pick bilberries. When he had filled his basket, he sat down on a log for a rest. It was already so hot that he had to wipe his forehead with his hanky. As he rested he watched the wood ants running around busily dragging pine needles to their ant-hill. Then he suddenly heard voices and saw a little girl and a little boy emerge from beneath the pine branches.

"Oh Andres, look! A sea of berries!" exclaimed the girl. Whereupon they both squatted down in the low bushes and started picking. Beardy watched the two good little children and would have liked to talk to them. But strange as it seems, dwarves are invisible to human beings. There was probably no way he could speak to them. Only birds and beasts could understand his language. With a tinge of sadness he gazed after them as they disappeared into the wood.

Then he helped a little mouse whose tail had got stuck between two stones. He reached home at nightfall. There was a thunderstorm which cooled the air. He decided to go and see Tildy the following day.

Very early in the morning, he set out for the dark forest. When he got there, he filled his rucksack with lady's mantle, and on the way back he picked a handkerchief-full of watercress. Then, with his rucksack on his back and his basket of bilberries over his arm, he mounted the steep path to Tildy's house.

He knocked gently at the door. But no one answered. He knocked again a little louder, then once more, still louder. But no one replied. So he pushed open the door and stepped inside. The first thing he saw was the little old herb lady, lying sick in bed. She was so hoarse she could hardly croak. She also had a fever.

"Oh Tildy, what can I do for you?" asked Beardy, alarmed. "Look, I've brought you some bilberries. I'm sure they'll be good for you."

At first, Tildy refused to eat any. But when Beardy fed her the cool blue berries with a spoon she swallowed them gratefully saying, "Ooh, that's really soothed my throat!"

Afterwards, Beardy fetched water from the stream and brewed a cough potion out of Iceland moss. But Tildy started complaining again: "Oh dear, oh dear, what on earth can I do? How can I get up in my condition? But I really ought to go down to the village shop with a load of lady's mantle and other herbs. They need them to make their Ziger cheese. And it's the only way I can earn the pennies I need to buy coffee and sugar. Oh dear me, what bad luck!"

Listening to her complaints, Beardy felt heavy-hearted beneath his little brown jerkin. Then it occurred to him how he could help her. Taking a deep breath he said, "Don't worry Tildy, I'll go to the shop for you."

He'd soon packed up all the things that Tildy had got ready. He listened carefully as she explained the way. Then, as soon as darkness started falling, he walked out through the wood and down to the village. Not that he liked going there. For a start,

然後他幫助了一隻尾巴夾在兩塊石子中間的老鼠。回到家裏時已是黑夜了。先前一場風暴令空氣清冷了不少。他決定第二天去見窕娣。

第二天清早他便向黑森林出發。到達後他把羽衣草塞滿背囊。回程時又拾了一手帕的水芥子。他把背囊背好，把一籃覆盆子掛在臂彎，便爬上陡斜的小徑到窕娣家去。

他輕輕拍門，但沒人答應。他大力一點拍，再大力一點，但仍然沒人應門。他便推開門走進去。他第一眼看到的是那瘦小的香草婆婆病了躺在床上。她聲音很沙啞，差點不能說話，也有一點發燒。

「噢，窕娣，我可以為你做點什麼嗎？」巴迪吃驚地說，「看，我給你帶來了覆盆子哩，相信對你有益的。」

窕娣起初不肯吃，但當巴迪把清涼的藍莓盛在茶匙裏餵她時，她又感激地吞下去，一邊說，「噢，真令喉嚨舒服多了！」

巴迪到溪邊打水，用冰島青苔煎了一服咳藥給窕娣喝。然後窕娣嘆起氣來：「天啊，天啊，我該怎麼辦啊？我這樣子怎麼起床？但我真的要把羽衣草和其他香草拿到村子的店裏，他們要拿來做昔加乳酪哩。這是我唯一可以賺點零錢買咖啡糖的方法啊。噢，可憐我，真倒運！」

巴迪聽著她訴苦，短皮衣下的心感到有點不安。他突然想到可以怎樣幫忙她了。他深呼吸一口氣說，「別愁，窕娣。我代你去一趟。」

他不久便把窕娣要帶的東西收拾好。他仔細聽她說路怎麼走。天一開始黑，他便步出森林下山到村子去。他並不是喜歡到村子去的。首先是那裏有狗。牠們鼻子靈敏，什麼也嗅得出來，比人類厲害多了。他很害怕，他要帶的東西越來越重，但他繼續走。他首先經過一所茅舍，然後是些大一點的房子。在燈籠微弱的光線下，他拐一個彎，店子就在前面了。他試圖按門鈴，但他太矮小了，碰不到鈴子。他把背囊除下，跟裏在手帕裏，用來做昔加乳酪的香料一起放到門前，然後重重地踢了門一下，使整間房子震盪起來，再趕緊躲在木堆後面。門開了，店員跑出來。當他看見地上的東西便拾起來，並高聲說，「嗯，嗯，真奇怪，窕娣還沒等及我給她咖啡和糖便跑了。不要緊吧，我把東西放在門前便行。」

門一關上，巴迪便悄悄地走出來，把盛著咖啡和糖的袋子曳在背上，把手帕放在口袋裏。

他愉快而疲乏地回去，柯士托山坡在月色下已全是銀白色。他平穩地走著，到窕娣家時已經午夜了。他把咖啡和糖交給她，然後慢慢踏步回家，他很疲倦，但短皮衣下他感到愉快而溫暖。

there were the dogs. They had such good noses and smelled everything, much better than humans. He felt frightened. His load seemed to be getting heavier and heavier. But he walked on. First he passed a shed, then bigger houses. In the dim light of a lantern he turned a corner. There was the shop.

He tried to ring at the door, but he was too small to reach the bell. So he took off his rucksack and set it down in front of the door, together with the handkerchief containing the herbs for the Ziger cheese. Then he took such a hefty kick at the door that the whole house shuddered. He quickly ducked behind the woodpile. The door opened, and the shopkeeper came out. When he saw the things lying on the ground, he picked them up and said in a very loud voice, "Well, well, I wonder why Tildy left before I could give her her coffee and sugar. Never mind, I'll just put the things down by the door."

As soon as he'd shut the door, Beardy crept up, hoisted the bag with the coffee and sugar onto his back and put his handkerchief back into his pocket.

The slopes of Mount Ortstock were already all silvery in the moonlight as he trudged happily homewards. He marched steadily, and in the middle of the night he reached Tildy's house. He gave her the coffee and sugar and then plodded slowly home, very tired – but with a lovely warm feeling under his jerkin.

About a month later the cowherds drove their cattle back down to the valley. Beardy went higher up the mountain and enjoyed himself watching the marmots and chatting with them. As it grew colder he prepared for his winter sleep by collecting mountain hay for his bed. Arriving back at his little house, he found a dwarf named Balz waiting for him, a messenger from the Dwarf King come to invite him to a feast at his castle, together with all the other dwarves and the flower maidens. Balz added:

"But there's something else I must tell you, so listen carefully. The feast will be held the night of the full moon prior to the shortest day. But before the moon sets, every single one of the guests must be back home, otherwise ill will befall him. Those are the King's orders. Just come to the castle entrance when you hear the owl hoot three times. That's all. Farewell."

Beardy was delighted and rushed off to tell old Tildy of his good luck. She gave him a white handkerchief to use at the feast.

After what seemed like an eternity the shortest day finally came. On that cold morning Beardy got up early and went straight to the leafy stream. First of all he thought he'd wash only his face … and perhaps his neck. But then he remembered that he'd be seeing the King, and that he really ought to be particularly clean for such a feast. So he took off all his clothes and stepped into the icy water. He rubbed and scrubbed himself until he was red all over. But he was still shivering with cold as he jumped back into his old brown clothes. Then he took a good look at his dirty shoes – they were all scuffed, and there were holes in the toes He cleaned them with moss and water and polished them with spit, but they still didn't look very good.

"Too bad! They'll just have to do. I haven't got any others."

一個月後，牧人把牛群帶回山谷。巴迪跑到高山上看土撥鼠，又跟牠們談話，自得其樂。天氣漸涼了，他開始收集高山稻草做床準備冬眠。回到自己的小屋時，他看到一個名叫包爾茲的小矮人正等著他，他是小矮人國王的信差，特來邀請他和其他小矮人及花朵姑娘到國王的城堡參加宴會。包爾茲補充說：

「還有一些事情我要告訴你，仔細聽啊。宴會將在最短一日的前一個月圓夜舉行。月落前每個客人都要回到家裏，不然便會生病。這是國王的命令。聽到貓頭鷹叫三聲，你來到城堡入口便成了。就是這樣，再見。」

巴迪很高興，他趕快到窕娣家，告訴她他多麼幸運。她送給他一條白手帕，讓他在宴會上用。

經過一段差不多是永恆的日子後，最短的一日終於到了。那是一個清冷的早晨，巴迪很早便起床，直來到青綠的溪畔。他最先只想洗洗臉，或者還洗洗脖子，但之後他記起要謁見國王，真的應該特別清潔去參加宴會哩，於是他脫下所有衣服，踏進冰冷的水裏。他擦呀擦的，直至通身紅透了。他穿回棕色的舊衣時仍是抖個不止。他仔細察看自己那雙髒鞋子，它們磨損得實在厲害，腳趾那裏還有洞哩。他用青苔和水把它們洗乾淨，又用唾液擦亮，但它們仍然不大好看。

「糟糕！但也算吧，我沒有其他的了。」

然後他用樹枝梳好鬍子，又把窕娣送給他的新手帕放進口袋裏。

天一開始黑，巴廸便站到門前。他聽到自己的心「卜冬蔔冬」的跳。他聽著……圓圓的大月亮已經升起了，它淡藍色的亮光覆蓋了整個阿爾卑斯山。然後遠處傳來貓頭鷹的叫聲：

「吐域吐胡！吐域吐胡！吐域吐胡！」

巴廸把門硼然關上，像一隻小伶鼬般趕快從溪畔跑到草原，再沿著小徑走向奧巴士達菲。高聳的松樹幽黑的罩在兩旁。巴廸朝堡壘的方向望去，看見懸崖旁一座巍峨的城堡在星空下矗立著。然後他聽見腳步聲，小矮人從四方八面向同一個方向走去。他們像他一樣都有一把灰色的長鬍子。他們靜靜地步上小徑，一個跟著一個，到了彎角一塊通往一個黑洞的黑石那裏。他們走進洞內，下一級石階，沿著一條狹長漆黑的甬道往前走。巴廸走到最後。山內面多麼陰森詭秘啊！只有從上面射下來偶然的幾線光刺破黑暗。

突然他們再回到光裏。巴廸發現自己和一群小矮人一起站在一個洞室內，他們全部沉默如鼠，詫異地觀察著四周。巴廸認出包爾茲，便跑上前打招呼。

「當全部人都到齊了，便帶你們去謁見國王。」包爾茲說，「這以前誰也不能發聲。看，巴廸，小小的花朵姑娘來了。」

她們都走進來了：藍鈴花和雛菊、龍膽花、高山玫瑰、金山車和番紅花、牽牛花和毛地黃、春龍膽、無忘我、白頭翁和金盞草、仙履蘭和火百合、蘭花、火

Then he combed his beard with a twig and put Tildy's new handkerchief into his pocket.

As soon as it started getting dark, Beardy came out in front of the house. He could hear his heart thumping. He listened … the big round moon was already there, shedding its pale blue light all over the alp. A sound rang out from afar:

"Towit-towoo! Towit-towoo! Towit-towoo!"

Beardy slammed the door shut. Like a little weasel he scurried down the bank to the meadow. From there he followed the path up towards Oberstafel. High pine trees crowded in darkly on either side, but Beardy looked up towards the castle, a mighty cliff fortress standing out against the starry sky. Then he heard footsteps and saw dwarves converging from all around. They all had long grey beards like his own. Silently they marched up the path, one behind the other, as far as a bend where there was a black rock slab leading into a dark hole. In they went, first down a step, then along a long dark passage. Beardy followed last. How eerie it was inside the mountain! The darkness was only broken by a few rare glints of light coming from above.

Suddenly, they came out into the light. Beardy found himself in a great grotto amid a crowd of dwarves, all of them as quiet as mice, staring around in amazement. Beardy suddenly recognised Balz and went over to greet him.

"When everyone's arrived, you'll be presented to the King," said Balz. "Until then, no one is allowed to make a noise. Look, Beardy, here come the little flower maidens."

And in they came: harebells and daisies, gentians, alpine roses, arnica and crocuses, convolvulus and foxgloves, spring gentians, forget-me-nots, anemones and marsh marigolds, lady's slippers and fire lilies, orchids, edelweiss, silver thistles … and all the rest – all those tiny faces beneath their lovely flower caps gathered together into a living posy!

Balz clapped his hands, and immediately each of the dwarves was joined by one of the little flower girls. And then the big doors opened and they saw the great hall, dazzlingly bright in the light of a hundred little lanterns. The floor was covered with a carpet of moss, and mountain crystals and mica sparkled on the walls.

Along one wall there was a black rocky ledge. And there, on a white limestone throne sat the King! He was wearing a dark red robe with a chain of quartz hanging down in front. A crown of gleaming gold sat on his snowy white hair. His white beard reached down to his knees. His stern eyes surveyed the turmoil in the hall.

Balz clapped his hands again and signalled to the dwarves. Each of them took his flower girl by the hand, and they formed a long procession around the hall. One after the other, the couples went up to the King, paused briefly, and then made a deep bow.

Beardy felt quite faint and couldn't stop looking at the King. It took a moment for him to realise that he had to join the procession too, and that his harebell maiden was waiting for him. He took her hand, and together they followed the procession around the room … and now they had to stop, they were in front of the King. Beardy bowed so deeply that his beard touched the ground. Suddenly there was a loud giggling sound behind him: "Hi hi hi."

Deathly silence!

絨草、銀薊花……及其他許多許多種類的花，她們小小的臉孔在可愛的花帽子下結成一個活生生的花束！

包爾茲拍手，每個小矮人身旁立刻有一位花朵小姑娘作伴。然後大門開了，他們看見宏偉的禮堂，給一百個小燈籠照得光亮耀眼。地上蓋著青苔的地氈，牆上閃著山裏來的水晶和雲母。牆的一邊有一塊黑色的石平臺，上面白色的大理石寶座裏，便坐著國王！他穿了一件深紅色的長袍，前面有一串石英鏈子。他雪白的頭髮上是一頂金光閃閃的王冠。他白色的鬍子垂落到膝蓋上，雙眸炯炯，觀察著整個鬧哄哄的禮堂。

包爾茲再拍拍手向小矮人示意。他們每人牽著花朵姑娘的手，繞著禮堂排成一條長長的隊伍。他們一對跟一對的走到國王面前，停下來，再深深的鞠躬。

巴迪感到有點暈眩，卻又不能自制地盯著國王。好一會才醒覺，他也要加入行列，而他的藍鈴花姑娘正等著他哩。他牽著她的手，一起跟著隊伍進入禮堂……現在他們要停下來，站在國王跟前了。巴迪很深很深的鞠了一個躬，鬍子都拖到地上了。突然他背後傳來一陣咭咭的笑聲，音量很大，「嘻嘻嘻……」

死寂一片！

「笑的是誰？」國王高高的在他的寶座上問，看來很不高興。

包爾茲走上前答：「陛下，是銀薊花小姐。」

「銀薊花，」國王輕輕責備道，「你不知道列隊進入禮堂是莊嚴的儀式麼？有什麼可以笑的地方？」

銀薊花在巴迪和藍鈴花背後答道，「陛下，巴迪鞠躬時我禁不住笑，因為他褲子上打了補釘，很像一扇小窗子哩。」

聽罷，巴迪立刻像公火雞那樣滿臉通紅。他的補釘吸引了每個人的注意，他感到很難過。

「巴迪，」國王說，「你參加我的宴會為什麼不穿好一點的衣服？」

心情激動，熱淚湧上巴迪的眼眶，他感到咽喉有一大塊東西哽著，結結巴巴地低聲說：「陛下，我……我……我沒有別的了。」兩顆大大的淚珠滾下他的鬍子。

國王仁慈地看著他，然後向包爾茲招招手。包爾茲跑過來把巴迪帶到外面。他們一起走進一個小房間，裏面一根長棒子上掛著許多小矮人的衣服，什麼顏色的也有，像彩虹一樣。

「你可以挑一套衣服。」包爾茲說。

「給自己？」巴迪問。他差點不能相信，亦不曉得選哪一套才好。

「快點，我們要回到宴會去啊。」

巴迪指著一套深綠色的衣服，包爾茲便把它拿下來。巴迪立刻脫掉舊衣服，披上新衣。綠褲子，釘金鈕的綠色短皮衣，腰間繫著一條棕色腰帶，再加上一頂尖帽。還有一雙簇新的鞋子！他站在鏡子前面，差點不相信眼前的人是自己，巴迪！

"Who was that laughing?" asked the King from high up on his throne, looking most displeased.

Balz went up to him and answered, "Your Majesty, it was Miss Silver Thistle."

"Silver Thistle," admonished the King, "don't you know perfectly well that the procession through the hall is a solemn ceremony? What's there to laugh about?"

Silver Thistle, from just behind Beardy and Harebell, answered, "Your Majesty, when Beardy bowed down I couldn't help laughing because there's a patch on his trousers that looks like a little window."

At this poor Beardy turned as red as a turkey-cock, he felt so upset that he'd attracted everyone's attention because of his patch.

"Beardy," said the King, "why didn't you put on better clothes for my feast?"

Hot tears welled up in Beardy's eyes, and he felt a great lump in his throat as he stuttered faintly, "Your Majesty, I, I, I haven't g-got any others." And two big tears rolled down into his beard.

But then the King looked at him kindly and waved to Balz. Balz came up and took Beardy outside. Together they went into a small room where, hanging from a long pole, there were lots and lots of dwarf's suits in all the colours of the rainbow.

"You may choose a suit," said Balz.

"For myself?" asked Beardy. He could hardly believe it and didn't know which one to choose.

"Hurry up," said Balz, "we have to get back to the party."

Beardy pointed to a dark green suit and Balz took it down. In next to no time Beardy had slipped out of his old clothes and into his new suit. Green trousers, a green jerkin with golden buttons, a brown belt around his waist and, to top it all, a pointed cap. And brand new shoes! He stood in front of the mirror and could hardly believe that the person he saw there was him, Beardy!

Balz gave him a shove: "Hurry up, go on out. I'll put your old clothes in a box so you can take them home after the party."

Beardy strutted into the hall, his head held high, his new shoes creaking wonderfully, his golden buttons gleaming. He went straight up to the King, bowed again and, beaming all over his face, said, "A thousand thanks, Your Majesty."

The King nodded. "That's all right Beardy," he said, chuckling into his beard. "Now go and enjoy yourself."

Then he clapped his hands, the musicians started playing, and everyone started dancing. Now the hall, which had been so quiet, was filled with the sound of music, with chattering and loud laughter.

Miss Harebell came up to Beardy and said, "Oh what fine clothes! You do look nice!"

They danced around the hall together. And all the dwarves and flower maidens felt very glad that things had turned out so well for Beardy.

Then the musicians had a rest, and everyone went back into the grotto where tables had been set up. There they sat down to a meal of bilberry wine, redcurrant cider or raspberry syrup with black bread and fresh mountain cheese. Beardy was among the jolliest of the guests; he even started yodelling. Everyone was having a marvellous time!

All of a sudden the King stood up, walked through the company and left the room. Now everybody knew

包爾茲推他一下，「趕快點，出去吧。我會把你的舊衣服放在一隻箱子裏，讓你宴會後帶回家。」

巴迪高視闊步的走進禮堂，頭抬得很高，他的鞋子愉快地吱吱作響，他的金鈕子閃閃生光。他直走到國王跟前，再鞠一個躬，臉上神采飛揚，說：「一千個謝謝。陛下。」

國王點點頭。

「別客氣，巴迪，」他說，一面在鬍子後微笑。「現在去吧，玩得開心點。」

他拍拍手，樂師便開始奏樂，每個人都開始跳舞。本來寂靜一片的禮堂，現在充滿音樂聲、談話聲和歡樂的笑聲。

藍鈴花小姐跑到巴迪跟前說：「噢，衣服很漂亮啊！真的，你很好看！」

他們跳遍禮堂每個角落。每個小矮人和花朵姑娘都因為巴迪得到這麼好的待遇，感到十分高興哩。

然後樂師稍作休息，他們也回到石室裏，桌子都已經擺好了。他們坐下來飲覆盤子酒、紅葡萄汁，或野莓糖醬，吃黑麵包和新鮮的山乳酪。巴迪是最開心的客人之一，他甚至開始唱約德爾歌。每個人都玩得很開心！

突然國王站起來，穿過眾人離開房間。大家都知道宴會要結束了，他們開始回家去。

月亮仍然照耀，令托迪山的雪閃爍發亮，亦照明了阿爾卑斯山。藍鈴花姑娘和巴迪挽著臂步下小徑到草原去。她告訴他一定要在月落之前回到家裏，不然她會把巴迪的鬍子扯下來高高的掛在松樹上。這令巴迪笑得頭也幾乎掉下來。

「那我就不知道怎麼辦了！……噢，天啊，」他突然記得，「我把舊衣服遺在堡壘啊。」

「快點啊，巴迪，跑啊。我在這兒等著，但趕快啊！」

他毫不遲疑地飛奔上山。堡壘已經漆黑一片。他敲門高聲叫道，「包爾茲，包爾茲。開門啊……我忘記拿衣服啊。」

他不用等多久，門便開了，包爾茲探出頭來。

「是誰？」

「是我，巴迪啊。我很趕，請你，請你……我的衣服。」

「老天，巴迪！箱子在這裏，拿著。你沒多少時間了！」

巴迪飛奔下山到藍鈴花姑娘等他的地方。他們一起跑過草原。

「快跑，巴迪，我到家了。」

他到達高辛貝爾。他的小屋子就在前面。他衝進門裏……就在那時，月亮落到山的背後。

「嘩！剛趕得及！真危險啊！」他把新衣服脫下，整齊地疊好，愛惜地把弄著亮閃閃的鈕子。

「今晚真好玩啊！現在，大家晚安。」

that the party was over, and so they all set off back home.

The moon was still shining, making the snow on Mount Tödi gleam and lighting up the alp. Arm-in-arm, Harebell and Beardy went down the path to the meadow. She told him he must be sure to be back home before the moon went down. Otherwise, she would have to pull out his beard and hang it high up in a pine tree. That made Beardy laugh his head off.

"That would put me in a fine pickle! ... Oh my goodness," he suddenly remembered, "I've left my old clothes back in the castle."

"Hurry up, Beardy, run. I'll wait here, but do hurry!"

Without a moment's hesitation, he shot back up the hill. But the castle already lay in darkness. He knocked at the door and shouted, "Balz, Balz. Open up ... I forgot my clothes."

He didn't have to wait long. A shutter opened and Balz poked out his head.

"Who's there?"

"It's me, Beardy. I'm in a hurry, please, please ... my clothes."

"Goodness, Beardy! Here, take your box. You've got no time to lose!"

Beardy bolted down the mountain to where Harebell was waiting. Together they ran on down the meadow.

"Run on, Beardy, I'm home."

It was getting darker and darker, the moon had already reached Mount Ortstock.

"Run, Beardy, run!"

He reached Grotzenbüel. There was his little house. He tore open the door ... and at that moment the moon went down behind the mountain.

"Phew! Just in time! That was a near thing!" He undressed, piled up his new clothes neatly, lovingly stroking the shiny buttons.

"That was great fun! And now, good-night all!"

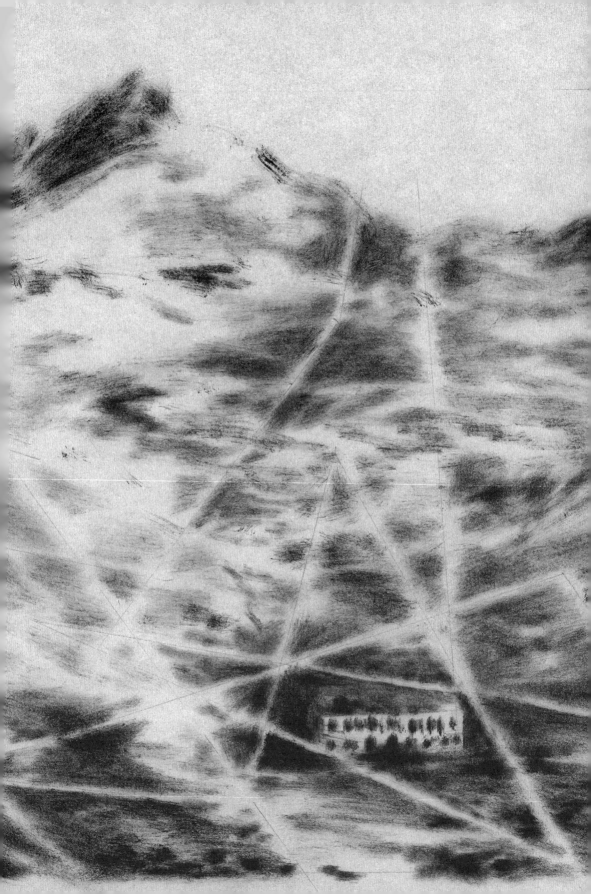

Glossary

Aargau 阿爾高州
Aix-La-Chapelle 亞琛
Aletsch 阿萊奇
Aletsch Glacier 阿萊奇冰川
Alpnach 阿爾卑納赫
Alsace 阿爾薩斯
Andermatt 安德馬特
Austria 奧地利
Basel 巴塞爾
Basel-Land 巴塞爾鄉村州
Bergell* 保格爾谷
Bern 伯爾尼
Bernese Oberland 伯爾尼茲山
Bettlach* 貝特拉和
Bologna 博洛尼亞
Brienz 布裏恩茲
Brig 布裏格
Bülach* 布拉治
Buochs* 布茲城
Chur 庫爾
Cologne 科隆
Einsiedeln 艾因西德倫
Emmental 愛蒙塔爾
Engelberg 英格堡
Etzel* 艾茨爾山
Furka Pass* 夫爾卡山道
Geneva 日內瓦 /日內瓦湖
Glarus 格拉魯斯州
Graubünden 格勞賓登州
Grenchen 格倫興市
Heidelberg 海德堡
Interlaken 因特拉肯
Iseltwald* 艾素華
Jura 汝拉山
Klosters 克羅斯特
Kloten* 克羅登
Leberberg* 肝山

Lenk* 冷克
Liestal 利斯塔爾
Lucerne 琉森, Lake L. 琉森湖
Mittelland 瑞士高原
Montafon* 麥塔方
Neuchâtel 納沙泰爾
Nidwalden 下瓦爾登州
Oberrickenbach* 鹿溪上村
Obwalden 上瓦爾登州
Pilatus 皮拉圖斯
Plateau (Swiss) 高原
Reichenau 興瑙島
Reuss 羅伊斯河
Rhone 羅納河
Rigi 瑞吉山
Selzach* 斜爾雜
Simmental 西門谷
Solothurn 索洛圖恩
Stans 施坦斯
Stanserhorn 施坦斯山
St Gotthard 聖哥達山
Ticino 提契諾州
Thurgau 圖爾高州
Trub* 吐魯比
Unterwalden 翁特瓦爾登州
Uri 烏裏州
Urseren* 烏瑟棱
Valais 瓦萊斯州
Vaud 沃州
Venice 威尼斯
Wolfenschiessen* 狼席森
Zug 楚格
Zurich 蘇黎世

Note: all names marked * could not be traced
in previously published dictionaries or maps,
and are thus our own transcriptions.

Acknowledgments

This selection of Swiss Alpine legends was derived and translated from the following sources:
Golowin, Sergius, 1981. Hausbuch der Schweizer Sagen. Wabern: Büchler.
Hetmann, Frederik (ed.), 1977. Dämonengeschichten aus den Alpen. Frankfurt/M.: Fischer. Jenny, Lorly, 1978. Der Zwäärg Baartli: Es Määrli us de Glarnerbäärg. Glarus: Baeschlin.

The students of the 2004 translation class included:
Jorrit Britschgi
Caspar Chiquet
Gian-Carlo Danuser
Valérie Frey
Barbara Hauser
Marco Hirsbrunner
Thomas Preiswerk
Rosemarie Schindler
My Truong
Sergio Vaccani
Nico Zhang
Doris Milena Zingg
Special (virtual) guest and (real) co-translator: Dr. Clemens Treter, then University of Munich, now Goethe Institute, Beijing

We are much indebted to Swissnex Shanghai, and especially to Flavia Schlegel, who not only secured the financial means for this publication, but also helped us to contact the illustration artist Julia Steiner. Moreover, we would like to express our deep gratitude to Rémy Markowitsch, who kindly discussed the book project with us and was willing to spend much time and energy to improve the project's overall design without ever asking for compensation. Of course, as most often is the case with such purely intellectual/aesthetic pursuits, we would never have been able to offer adequate compensation for such invaluable advice. There are many others who would deserve to be mentioned here; we hope they will accept our collective address of gratitude for everything that had to be done in order to materialize our vision in this present book form.

LEGENDS FROM THE SWISS ALPS 瑞士阿爾卑斯山的傳說

Edited by Leung Ping-kwan and Andrea Riemenschnitter 梁秉鈞、洪安瑞 編

Published by MCCM Creations 2009
www.mccmcreations.com
info@mccmcreations.com

Translation 翻譯/ students from the Institute of East Asian Studies, University of Zurich,
Leung Ping-kwan (Chinese) and Helen Wallimann (English)
蘇黎世大學東亞研究所學生、梁秉鈞 (中文) 及海倫瓦莉曼 (英文)
Illustration 插畫/ Julia Steiner 茱莉亞史泰拿
Cover design 封面設計/ Ho Yee Kuen 何義權
Design & Artwork 內頁設計/ Ho Yee Kuen 何義權, Irene Choy 蔡怡雅

Printing support/

ISBN 978-988-18583-1-3